THE PUBLIC
MANAGEMENT
OF DEFENCE
IN CANADA

THE PUBLIC MANAGEMENT OF DEFENCE IN CANADA

Breakout Educational Network
in association with
the School of Policy Studies, Queen's University

1200 Bay Street, Suite 304

Toronto, ON

M5R 2A5

tel: 416.923.1105

fax: 416.927.9116

info@breakout-ed.net

Publisher: Inta D. Erwin

Cover Design & Layout: Mark Howes

Project Director: Patricia Mitchell

Copy Editors: Richard Johnson, Linda Hyland, Elizabeth LeReverend

Library and Archives Canada Cataloguing in Publication

Public management of defence in Canada / edited by Craig Stone.

ISBN 978-0-9781693-6-7

1. Canada--Military policy.
I. Stone, Craig, 1958- II. Queen's University (Kingston, Ont.). School of
Policy Studies III. Breakout Educational Network
UA600.P83 2009   355'.033571   C2009-901499-8

Printed and bound in Canada

Table of Contents

List of Figures

List of Tables

Foreword

The Canadian Forces and Department of National Defence are undergoing a period of dynamic change that has not been seen in decades. This change is bringing both benefits and challenges to the defence establishment in Canada. During the Cold War, the actions of Canada had a limited impact on Western security. In contrast, the unique circumstances of the post 9-11 environment have provided Canada with the opportunity to play a substantial role in the international community. The Canadian engagement, as part of the international community, has been noteworthy. This decade has seen a significant commitment of personnel and equipment to Afghanistan in support of the government, substantial changes to the command and control of the Canadian Forces, the beginning of an extensive re-equipment program, and steps towards increasing the size of the Canadian Forces. Critical to the effective administration of these various activities within the Canadian Forces and Department of National Defence now shaping both institutions for the upcoming decades is the management of defence in Canada.

This book is a timely and comprehensive contribution towards the growing body of defence management literature in Canada, and reflects the scholarship and interest that is developing in this field. Indeed, the contributors represent the diverse background of defence scholars that are defining a unique Canadian approach to the study of defence management. The authors are Canadians from civilian universities, educational institutions within the departmental Canadian Defence Academy, serving military officers, and defence scientists within the department.

This book is focused on not only the defence community, but also a much broader audience in this country. To be sure, the nature of conflict in the current international security environment demands whole-of-government solutions, integrating military personnel with both diplomats and developmental personnel. This publication endeavours to open the "black box" of defence management to the wider federal public sector, NGOs, and the academic community. The selection of chapter topics achieves this objective by first explaining how various internal processes work, such as how defence strategy is executed within the department, the defence planning and management cycle, as well as budgeting within defence. The chapters then consider selected topics that are key to successful transformation of both institutions. This includes managing change, knowledge management, human resource challenges, as well as the challenges inherent in capital investment.

Acknowledgements

As with any work of a collaborative nature, the finished product would not be possible without the efforts and energy of a large number of people. First, I am indebted to the many colleagues who have directly contributed to this book on defence management. Their contributions represent a collective effort by a relatively small group of individuals with an expertise and interest in defence management and in particular what that means in Canada.

Next, all of us who contributed to the book are indebted to Doug Bland, the Chair of the Defence Management Program at the School of Policy Studies, for providing the facilities and the forum to conduct a workshop at the early stages of the project. This allowed the contributors the opportunity to present the early results of their work to the others involved in the project as well as others with expertise in the field.

Finally, I would be remiss if I did not make special mention of Inta D. Erwin and Patricia Mitchell at Breakout Educational Network. Their assistance, advice and guidance to me as a first-time editor of a collection of scholarly work was invaluable. As well, their support in providing professional editorial and publishing assistance made this project possible. Without that support, the book would not have been as complete or timely.

J. Craig Stone

Introduction

CRAIG STONE

For the first time in decades Canada's politicians have sent members of Canada's Armed Forces into harms way. As the number of dead soldiers associated with the Afghanistan mission approaches 100, those same politicians have extended the mission to Afghanistan to 2011 while at the same time committing to significant purchases of new military equipment. Much has been written in the popular press and debated in the media about both the pros and cons of the Afghanistan mission and about the actual tasks being completed by the Canadian Forces (CF) in Afghanistan. Although often superficial and simplistic the debate is an important part of the democratic process of the Canadian system of government. However, with that process comes responsibility on the part of the people of Canada, elected officials and government. When governments make the decision to send soldiers into harms way they have an obligation to ensure that those same soldiers are properly trained and equipped to do the mission assigned.

Training and equipping military forces in any nation is a very complex and lengthy process. Many of the skill sets required by the "military workforce" are not readily available in the civilian labour market and much of the equipment is unique, both in terms of its use and who manufactures it. As well, training and equipping military forces must be done in ways that meet both the legal requirements of the nation and the rules and regulations established by the Government. In this context, it is important to remember that the CF are part of the Department of National Defence (DND), which is a department of the federal government just like Industry Canada, Foreign Affairs and Transport Canada. This is not to imply the DND is the same as other government departments but rather that DND must still follow the same rules and regulations that all other federal government departments are obliged to follow.[1]

Within the Canadian context there is a Defence Portfolio that includes the DND, the CF and other agencies such as the Communications Security Establishment Canada, Defence Research and Development Canada, the Office of the Judge Advocate General, the national Search and Rescue Secretariate, the Office of the Ombudsman for the Department of National Defence and the Canadian Forces, and the Commissioner Canadian Security Establishment. Consequently, building and maintaining a military force in the Canadian context requires the involvement of more than just the CF. It is a very complicated and multi-faceted process that requires significant effort and consistency over a long time period.

More importantly, regardless of how urgent something may be, significant changes in force composition and available military capabilities take years to implement and must be managed to ensure current capabilities are not sacrificed. The military must also ensure that in protecting current capability, any required changes are made in a timely enough fashion in order that future capabilities are not sacrificed. Achieving the correct balance over time requires consistent and long-term government commitment, a well-defined management system, and effective strategic leadership. The CF and DND can do very little about the need for a consistent government commitment but can control the latter two issues.[2]

This book focuses on one of the issues that are within the control of the CF and DND – the need for a well-defined management system. Management within the CF and DND is conducted within the overall framework of government rules and regulations as laid out in Acts of Parliament, Treasury Board rules and guidance and commonly accepted management practices within the Public Service and government. In order to meet all these competing demands the Defence Planning and Management Framework shown at Figure 1 is used.

Figure 1: Defence Planning and Management Process

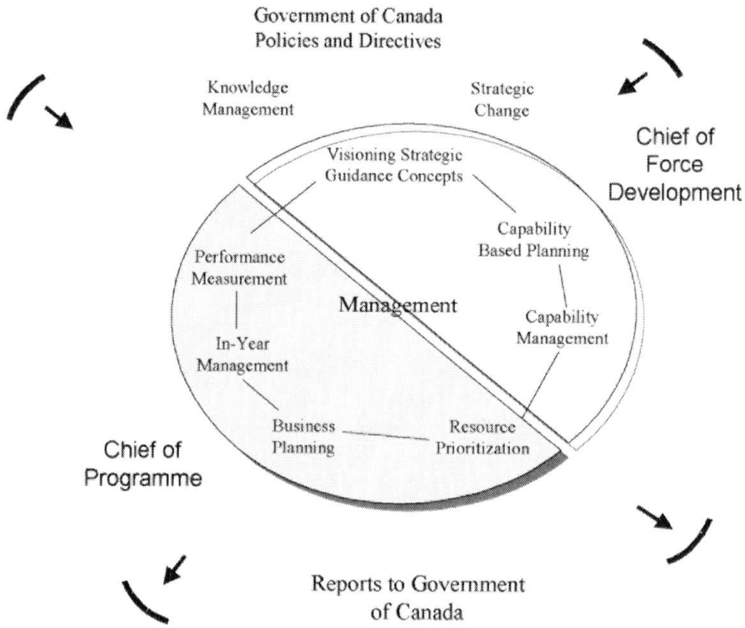

Government of Canada
Policies and Directives

Knowledge
Management

Strategic
Change

Chief of
Force
Development

Visioning Strategic
Guidance Concepts

Capability
Based Planning

Performance
Measurement

Management

Capability
Management

In-Year
Management

Chief of
Programme

Business
Planning

Resource
Prioritization

Reports to Government
of Canada

Source: National Defence, Defence Planning and Management website

This framework is the broad strategic level construct used by DND and the CF to:

a.   Plan its long, mid and short term strategic direction;

b.   Manage the Sustaining and Change Agendas;

c.   Monitor performance and risk management; and,

d.   Report to government through the Report on Plans and Priorities (RPP) and the Departmental Performance Report (DPR).[3]

The DND management framework is implemented within the broader Treasury Board approved Management, Resources and Results Structure (MRRS) for Defence.[4] Based on Treasury Board policy, the Defence MRRS "consists of three elements: a Program Activity Architecture (PAA), clearly defined and measurable strategic outcomes, and a description of the current governance structure that outlines the Department's decision-making mechanisms, responsibilities and accountabilities, ..."[5] In essence, the MRRS is used to underpin all departmental planning, the management of resources, and the monitoring and reporting on whether or not objectives and outcomes are achieved. The 2008 version of the PAA is shown at Appendix 1.

The process shown at Figure 1 and described on the Chief of Programme website within the Vice Chief of the Defence Staff group has been evolving since the early 2000s and is quite different from how the process was described in earlier years. For example, the 1984 edition of *An Introduction to the Defence Services Program and the Defence Management System*, indicates:

> The DPMS is essentially a repetitive process of planning and programming with constant feedback and interaction between all phases. Each step involves the same sequence of activities; a study of available options (consistent with the degree of refinement reached), an identification of available alternatives, an impact analysis resulting in a decision document.[6]

This same document goes on to describe a process that includes the five steps of Policy Planning, Program Initiation, Program Planning and Development, Project Definition and Project Implementation. The 1995 version (edition 10) is not fundamentally different and it is only in the post-2000 time frame that defence planning has really moved from a process that was, for the most part, focused on the procurement process to a process that looks across a much broader spectrum of activities. Comparing Figure 1 above with Figure 5.3 in Chapter 5 shows some of these differences.

In 2008, the Defence Planning and Management System is described as a process that includes "six interdependent components or processes; each with its own set of requirements and steps, and each involving aspects of Risk Management."[7] Table 1 describes these components.

Table 1: Defence Program Management System Components

Strategic Visioning	provides a roadmap (i.e. Strategy 2020), consisting of the overall strategic vision and long term strategic objectives, to steer planning and decision-making to deal with defence challenges that may emerge in the future
Capability-Based Planning	produces the "capability targets and gaps" of the DND/CF consistent with the department's white paper and strategic vision
Resource Prioritization	involves analyzing corporate priorities and establishing resource priorities over multiple planning horizons, including the immediate planning cycle
Business Planning	establishes annual plans and priorities and balances the investment in sustaining ongoing operations and activities with the investment required to modernize the Forces
In-Year Management	involves monitoring the progress against the Defence Plan, managing the impact of significant issues and new requirements and adjusting resources in response to new pressure
Performance Management	outlines the structure and focal areas (i.e. Strategy Map) for measuring performance in the DND/CF through which senior management monitors the achievement of results and reports on performance

Source: National Defence Headquarters, Defence Planning and Management Website

The processes that are described in Table 1 are viewed or examined within three planning horizons that look at the short, medium and long-term issues facing the CF. In actual years, the short-term covers years 1 to 4, the medium-term years 5 to 10 and the long-term years 10 to 30. Viewed within the framework of the earlier reference to current and future capabilities the short term view is focused on maintaining the current capabilities, the medium-term view looks at replacing or enhancing current capabilities and the long term view looks at acquiring new capabilities.

However, regardless of this internal process used by DND and the CF, the defence function for the Government of Canada is only one program, most commonly referred to as *The Defence Services Program*. As indicated in the introductory section of the annual Report on Plans and Priorities,

> It is not a program-based organization as are other federal departments. As such, Defence's PAA encapsulates the three main functions of Defence to deliver on its mission and contribute towards its strategic outcomes. Defence generates multi-purpose forces trained and prepared for the eventuality of an operation; conducts operations when needed; and interacts with domestic and international communities for the prevention of incidents.[8]

The public management of defence in any nation is difficult at the best of times. It becomes much more problematic and complicated when a nation's military is engaged in combat thousands of miles away rather than defending one's own nation. This is the circumstance that Canada and its military find themselves in 2008. This book is designed to provide information and analysis on how the DND and the CF deliver the Defence Services Program to Canadians.

In Chapter 1 Douglas Bland provides an initial broad strategic context for defence in Canada. He notes that Canada's actual defence policy (as opposed to policy declared in white papers, for instance) is the outcome of a continuous stream of decisions, large and small, made by people working in somewhat inflexible, interrelated organizations, processes, and laws and regulations. This structure is itself conditioned by political, budgetary, and public administrative factors subordinate to "the facts of national life." It is within this environment that the administration and management of defence must be conducted and it must be done in a manner that is open and transparent to the Canadian public.

Bland argues that to draw a clear picture of how defence policy is invented, what policies are possible, and what outcomes arise from and can be expected from the defence policy process, students need to understand first, the classic concepts and techniques of public administration. The management of defence requires a broad understanding of how people and organizations can influence the implementation of defence policy everyday, particularly as it relates to the governments allocation of scarce resources to defence.

Chapter 2, written by Colonel Greg Burt and Mr. Shawn McKnight, begins the detailed examination of defence management by discussing how DND and the CF connect the expenditure of public money with actual military capability; a process referred to as Defence Strategy Management. Burt and McKnight indicate that the Defence Strategy Management methodologies used today are those that have evolved over time out of what can be dubbed the "continuum of defence management". They attempt to lift the fog of complexity surrounding defence management issues. This chapter will outline how senior leadership in DND and the CF performs the Defence Management function. The chapter will provide a broad outline of the defence management process within DND in order to set the stage for the subsequent, more detailed and issue specific chapters in the book. The chapter begins with a discussion on how the defence function is governed and controlled in order to meet the demands of the Government of Canada. Next, the chapter will discuss the inputs to the defence management process beginning with defence strategy and how that is articulated within DND and the CF. Finally, the chapter presents how the strategy is operationalized and used to develop military capabilities.

Based on this strategy management framework, the next two chapters address the important issue of money. This is done from the perspective of answering, in Chapter 3, how the government decides how much should go to defence and then examining, in Chapter 4, how DND and the CF allocate the money once the government of the day determines how much will be allocated. In Chapter 3, Lieutenant-Colonel Ross Fetterley provides an overview of the function that the budget performs in the Canadian governmental system. The chapter also provides context for a discussion of defence funding within the federal fiscal framework in the next chapter. Fetterley begins with an overview of the general budget process and an historical review of the manner in which the Canadian federal budget process evolved. Next, he summarizes the Federal Expenditure Management System (EMS), including a review of the federal budget and reporting cycle. Next, the chapter focuses on changes in the expenditure management process within the federal sector and concludes with a discussion of the defence budget within the federal government's fiscal framework.

In Chapter 4, Fetterley notes that resource management in defence is unique and particularly challenging due to the nature of the defence environment. Within this context, management in defence is defined as a complex, high consequence of error, capital-intensive, knowledge-dependent, national security instrument. Categorization of defence in this manner results from the diversity of tasks assigned to the Canadian Forces (CF) and Department of National Defence (DND), the high level of technology employed within both organizations, the aggregate size of the budget, and the significant capital component within that budget. As a consequence, the critical elements necessary to effectively manage defence activities require significant financial resources; therefore, defence funding is a critical enabler in the generation and sustainment of military forces.

The chapter begins with a discussion of defence funding from the end of the Cold War and then considers the three primary budget expenditure categories: Personnel, Capital, and Operations & Maintenance (O&M). Next, the chapter outlines a number of defence resource management tools that are used within DND to manage the budget allocation and then concludes with a discussion of important medium to long-term financial issues regarding the defence budget.

Having discussed how the government decides how much to allocate to defence and how the actual budget is allocated within defence, the next two chapters focus on the issue of capital investment or the purchase of major military weapon systems and how that is connected to the industrial capacity of the nation. Chapter 5 focuses on procurement because, although defence spending is a very small part of overall economic activity in the nation, procurement is an important aspect of our defence policy, especially when major capital equipment is being considered. The intent of the chapter is to explore the procurement challenges facing DND and the CF with specific emphasis on major capital equipment projects.

Craig Stone begins Chapter 5 with some of the basic theory that applies to military procurement and then discusses the Canadian context. Based on this Canadian context, the current procurement process is reviewed, followed by some observations about why future procurement opportunities will need to be conducted in a much more disciplined way than previous years. In other words, Stone argues that there must be a coherent long-term investment plan that will allow for the investment in defence without the huge swings in dollar amounts that are shown at Figure 5.1.

In Chapter 6 Binyam Solomon critically examines the Canadian defence industrial base (CDIB) from an economic perspective. The chapter does not attempt to update statistics on the size and composition of the DIB nor does it provide a finite definition of the DIB since that is dependent on the research question asked and how one wants to operationalize the definition. Instead, using some broad concepts to delineate the boundaries of the CDIB, Solomon conducts economic analysis and critical discussions of the DIB using the following boundaries to define a defence industry. First, a defence industry is an industry in a Canadian industrial sector that is both dependent on military production and relevant to that sector. Second, a defence industry can also be an industry that is to some extent dependent on defence spending and/or defence exports while the nation state is dependent upon it for self-reliance in the production of defence goods. Finally, a defence industry may be an industry that operates in a relatively non-competitive market as a result of economies of scale, technology or government policies.

Next the book turns to the other major input to creating military capability: people. Although the purchase of equipment and weapon systems is perceived to be expensive, the amount spent on people within most militaries is substantially more as a percentage of the overall budget. In the 2000s, it is also one of the biggest challenges facing the CF. Allan Okros highlights this fact in Chapter 7 by addressing the military and civilian aspects of the human resource management processes used within DND and the CF. The chapter provides a broad, conceptual overview of Human Resource (HR) Management as an integral component of ensuring overall organizational effectiveness. It does not, however, provide a practical, step-by-step summary of the actual HR processes used to manage the civilian or military components of Defence.

The first reason for this approach is that, at the time of writing this chapter, the CF HR System was undergoing a number of changes intended to produce an HR/Personnel System that will supports CF Transformation objectives. These latest changes started in April 2006 with the renaming of ADM (HR-Mil) as Chief of Military Personnel (CMP) accompanied with reorganization and/or renaming of some Divisions and Directorates. Among other initiatives currently being developed, it is anticipated that additional changes will be made to the CMP organization structure, that a long range Campaign Plan will be launched and that, for the first time, integrated CF Doctrine for HR will be promulgated. Given the significance of these changes, this chapter has been written to provide a macro, theory-based presentation of HR functions in Defence, rather than a description of the current HR System(s).[9]

The second reason for this approach is that for both the novice and the expert, it is more important to understand why HR decisions are made rather than how to conduct HR activities. Standard HR Management texts provide excellent information on HR processes and techniques, however almost all are focused on applications in the private sector, corporate domain. In particular, none provide the information needed to understand the unique aspects of HR in a military context. Hence, some of the taken-for-granted assumptions underlying the common applications of HR procedures either do not or should not apply when considering HR in the Canadian Forces. Thus, this chapter provides an overview of the key principles, philosophy and objectives to understand why HR could or should be organized, structured and administered so as to fully support the operational requirements of the CF and DND.

The last two chapters of the book deal with two other aspects of managing defence in a modern society – how to manage knowledge within the institution and how to manage change in a complex world. In Chapter 8, John Girard looks at how Defence leaders can achieve knowledge supremacy. The journey begins with a consideration of what exactly is Defence Knowledge and Defence Knowledge Management. With this foundation in place the expedition continues by exploring why leaders would wish to implement knowledge management and more specifically, why now. The last section of the chapter examines how leaders may put knowledge management into action by reviewing tools, techniques, and processes that enable knowledge supremacy. Girard argues that modern Defence leaders are actually well versed on the merits of exploiting knowledge and that for centuries, military commanders have desired to know what was on the other side of the hill. For the first time leaders will not only know what is on the other side of the hill but also whether we (or our allies) have been here before, and what we did to succeed or fail last time. Armed with knowledge leaders will be much better prepared to make decisions or take actions in complex operations.

Finally, the focus of Lieutenant-Colonel Mike Rostek in Chapter 9 is on how DND and the CF changes in an increasingly complex and dynamic security environment. The chapter begins with some very basic, yet fundamental, aspects of managing change. This is followed by issues that are specific to change management in the public sector, and in particular, DND and the CF. Next, a review of the four most prominent change initiatives since 1960 -- Unification, the Management Review Group (MRG), the Management Command and Control Re-engineering Team (MCCRT) and CF Transformation – is examined in an attempt to highlight that instituting change in large organizations portends prospects of both promise and peril.

Endnotes

1. For example, all Federal Government employees are required to obey Acts of Parliament, Employment Equity laws, and the Charter of Rights and Freedoms to name just a few.

2. Consistent government commitment in this sense means elected officials who are knowledgeable about defence and security issues, governments that provide regular policy guidance and consistent funding over time so that effective long term planning can be accomplished. This is seldom the case in Canada.

3. National Defence, Defence Planning and Management website, available at http://www.vcds.forces.gc.ca/dgsp/intro_e.asp; internet; accessed 9 April 2008.

4. National Defence, 2008-2009 *Report on Plans and Priorities* (Ottawa: DND, 2008), 7. The MRRS was approved for Defence on 30 August 2005.

5. 2008-2009 *Report on Plans and Priorities*,7.

6. Department of National Defence, An Introduction to the Defence Services Program and the Defence Management System, 4th edition (Ottawa: DND, 1984), 2-1.

7. Defence Planning and Management Website

8. 2008-2009 *Report on Plans and Priorities*, 7

9. In, particular, it should be read in conjunction with CF HR Doctrine (B-GJ-100/FP-001) and Procedural Doctrine for the Management of the CF HR System (B-GJ-005/FP-010) (when released), Military HR 2020 (and subsequent updates), the CMP Campaign Plan (when published) and the current year Military Personnel Functional Planning Guidance issued in conjunction with annual Defence Planning Guidance.

Chapter 1

THE PUBLIC ADMINISTRATION of DEFENCE POLICY

Douglas Bland

Do strategic studies and their research results matter greatly to the production of and conduct of Canadian defence policy? The evidence, such as it is, suggests that at best since the early 1990s research into the strategic circumstances surrounding Canada's national defence has had little influence on policy despite its high quality and public exposure. If this assertion is even nearly true, then what drives defence policy beyond the rhetoric of occasional white papers? More importantly, what direction is being provided in order for senior officials to administer the Department of National Defence and lead the Canadian Forces?

Defence Minister, Brooke Claxton (1947-56) warned senior officers in 1951 that the strategic plans regarding the North Atlantic Treaty organization (NATO) they offered to government were unrealistic and ignored "the facts of national life" upon which policy must be built. Robert Sutherland, in 1963, advised the then Minister of National Defence, Paul Hellyer, that a wholly Canadian strategic rationale for Canada's defence policy "does not exist and one cannot invent it."[1] When Hellyer, nonetheless, attempted to invent such a strategy as the basis for defence policy in 1964, Prime Minister Pearson dismissed the entire concept.

In the defence white paper, "Defence in the 70s," the Trudeau government declared, "it is not possible simply to state 'defence requirements' and call that the defence budget." Rather, it was argued, defence decisions, including budgetary decisions, ought to be based on a judgement and selection of "defence activities in relation to other government programs."[2] In 1994, the new Liberal government, after having spent months researching defence policy options and encouraging a joint committee of the Senate and the House to conduct a wide-ranging review of defence policy – a review which engaged nearly every leading scholar of strategic studies in Canada – dismissed the committee's detailed report as "inconsistent with the financial parameters within which the Department of National Defence must operate." It is "the facts of national life" that drive defence decisions in Canada and those facts are based in domestic attitudes and domestic needs, not in arguments or concepts drawn from strategic studies, methods or rationale.

Canada's defence policy is founded on the premise that there is no threat and the Americans will save us if there were one. It follows rationally from this foundation that efficient and effective military defence is not the policy goal – "just enough is enough." Consequentially, Canada's national defence will be built not on what strategy demands, but on those resources that are made available for national defence after other policy demands have been addressed. If one accepts these norms as true and constant, then there is little that strategic studies research can contribute to the defence policy process, because, as Claxton proclaimed in 1951, the only rationale is, "the facts of national life." No strategy has yet been offered or invented to overcome the political culture that sustains Claxton's dictum.

Canada's actual defence policy (as opposed to policy declared in white papers, for instance) is the outcome of a continuous stream of decisions, large and small, made by people working in somewhat inflexible, interrelated organizations, processes, and laws and regulations. This structure is itself conditioned by political, budgetary, and public administrative factors subordinate to "the facts of national life." It is within this environment, that the administration and management of defence must be conducted and it must be done in a manner that is open and transparent to the Canadian public.

Understanding and influencing defence policy, therefore, requires a deep aware-ness of how these factors shape and influence the people and structures which manage this defence administration every day. In other words, to draw a clear picture of how defence policy is invented, what policies are possible, and what outcomes arise from and can be expected from the defence policy process, students need to understand first, the classic concepts and techniques of public administration. At the very least, the field of strategic studies must make room for the field of public administration if stra-tegic studies research hopes to inform Canadian defence policy and the government's allocation of scarce resources to defence.

What to Study

The essence of defence policy is to define defence objectives, identify resource require-ments commensurate with these goals, the rules governing the uses of force, and the process by which the civil authority will oversee the armed forces and defence officials. The object of defence administration is to establish, equip, and sustain the Canadian Forces to produce as much useable coercive force as is possible from the resources provided by the government. While strategic analysis, goals setting, resource alloca-tion and public oversight ought to be essential components of defence policy, the key to building defence capability – the bridge between ends and means – is effective and efficient public administration. But the mere recognition of this fact or the inclusion of some topics of defence administration in strategic studies programs will not guarantee that strategic studies-based research will direct decision makers towards an "appropri-ate defence" policy.

Defence policy statements and public discourse in Canada usually concentrate on objectives and the end uses of armed forces. Some 'expert' commentary and pub-lic studies direct attention to budgetary matters, but most often as raw numbers and percentage spending compared with other government programs – guns vs butter – or other states' defence efforts, or supposed international norms. Occasionally, the Office of the Auditor General of Canada decries wasteful defence administrative practices.

Yet, most of these criticisms are abstracted from the whole and are overshadowed by the assumption that if only governments could find the answer to what it is we wish the Canadian Forces to do and provide the funds to do it, then every other matter would fall faultlessly into line.

Public administration ought to change efficient ideas into action and outcomes commensurate with policy intentions. Where public or, in this case, defence administration fails to meet this purpose, then policy has little chance of success and will usually fail, sometimes spectacularly. Moreover, public administration ought to be comprehensive and coherent, blending seamlessly the many facets of administration together and joining them to the intent of policy.

Research into defence administration might address the following themes: what is the purpose of defence administration, where is it practised, who is accountable for successes and failures, and what impediments do governmental methods, rules, and procedures place between defence policy and an appropriate national defence for Canada? More positively, are there other ways of doing business that would yield better outcomes? These are themes and questions that strategic studies cannot answer well, but which are the bread and butter of public administration scholarship.

Purpose, People and Process

Purpose

To declare that "getting more bang for the buck" is the object of defence administration and management does not get one very far, but it is not a wholly inane aphorism. Nations maintain *armed forces* for one purpose, which is to have an instrument to apply coercive and, if necessary, deadly force in the pursuit of the government's objectives. Why otherwise would the force be armed? Certainly, armed forces can serve society and governments in other ways, but these other ways are mostly ancillary to the military's reason for being. Most of these ancillary tasks, moreover, can be performed better and at less cost than by military units that might be assigned to them as secondary duties. The first aim for the management and administration of defence, therefore, is to turn national assets into more bang, more useful, coercive force and to hold that force in high states of readiness and sustain it during military operations.

If the primary goal of armed forces is distracted by other government objectives, then defence administration and management will also become distracted and maybe seriously so. For instance, if defence administrators are directed to produce military capabilities but only so as to benefit home-based industries, then they will expend considerable administrative resources – time, people, money, and managerial skills – in pursuit of this industrial policy when less effort might have been needed to buy the capability directly from the best source. When all or portions of the authority and responsibility for this type of policy falls outside the defence department, as in this case to Industry Canada, among others, then more administrative resources and management effort will be consumed in "coordinating" strategies and fighting "turf-wars."

Additional time will be spent preparing and managing dual-purpose proposals and contracts with industries and the central agencies and defending in public decisions for or against some home-based industrial, regional, or political interest. Even if governments provided resources to cover these additional duties, senior officers and officials responsible for defence procurement are not disembodied or divisible and can become overwhelmed by interests, competitions, and regulations far distant from the straightforward business of procuring the most appropriate capability, efficiently, at the least cost.

Indeed, the evidence plainly stated in many government reports and studies, is that defence administrators and the defence procurement system are overwhelmed by procurement policies and procedures directed at goals far removed from defence policy. These impediments add cost and years to defence decisions and in some cases produce inferior outcomes in all respects. While this example is starkly evident, others of the same nature abound in Canadian defence administration – in personnel, materiel, financial, and reporting policies to suggest only a few. In each case, to some degree, the demands of public administration drag the primary purpose of defence administration from its duty to provide the greatest output of defence capability from the national resources provided for this purpose.

PEOPLE

Skilled combatants are the precious element of defence policy and personify with their weapons and equipment "the sharp end," the coercive force, of defence policy. Yet, they are difficult to recruit, train, motivate and retain in the Canadian Forces, especially in periods of conflict. People are also the most costly element of any defence capability. Poor defence management creates administrative drag, hindering the development of skilled combatants. Administration and management activities, which take members of the Canadian Forces away from primary military combatant functions, robs Canada of national defence capabilities. As the wealthy citizens were asked during the First World War, "Do you have someone digging your garden when they ought to be digging trenches?" Canadians today might ask, "Are there sailors in Ottawa manning desks when they ought to be manning ships?"

The Canadian Forces establishment of some 65,000 full time military people and some 24,000 civilian public servants provide for every duty, function and service for national defence. Defence policy, no matter the size of these separate establishments, ought to aim to create and retain as high a percentage of skilled combatants and essential combat support personnel from this total as possible.[3] Every member of the Canadian Forces who is taken out of combatant status, by administrative requirements, not directly related to operational capabilities, defeats an appropriate defence effort.

Today, numerous programs, military preferences, DND procedures, public policy demands, and other impediments, drain military personnel from operational duties. Although many public servants are critical players in many defence roles, others fill positions and add costs to the defence budget simply to service administrative functions and central agency policies, which are at best, tangential to the production and sustainment of defence capabilities. As the "[Defence] Minister's Advisory Committee on Administrative Efficiency" reported in 2003, a "re-think" of defence administration would "identify activities that not only need not be done in NDHQ, but simply need not be done at all."[4]

No one knows for certain or even approximately what administrative tasks are essential to combat capabilities or how many troops are required to meet them. No one knows which public servant occupies a DND post important to the purposes of national defence and which is a position important only to another department's or central agency's need. What is known, however, is that "an organization that should be focussed on strategic thinking and decision-making has become mired in administrative detail and processes."[5]

On a grander scale, what might result, if defence administration were overhauled to remove policies and procedures that served no direct operational purpose. Surely if the first recruiting, classification and employment priority went to direct operational requirements, then many people could be reallocated to the combatant ranks. Arguably, Canadian Forces combat capabilities would rise, but the cost for military personnel would remain the same. If the public service ranks of DND were scrubbed to remove all who serve non-essential defence purposes and their positions and salaries were allocated to the Canadian Forces, then defence capabilities would increase while total defence cost would remain nearly static. This notion should be a central plank in the government's defence policy.

Process

"Feeding the goat," is a derisive comment Canadian public servants use to describe their duty to provide endless shopping carts of reports, returns, and information to the central agencies, commissioners, and (mostly) the Treasury Board. Hours on end and vast numbers of public servants and military personnel are engaged in producing administrative fodder on issues and policies large and small and often, for no reason related to the production of defence capabilities.

No one has to accept the argument that the sensible notion of public accountability demands a system that must spend great sums to achieve the desired result. In the case of defence policy, what is it that the civil authority really needs to know, if it is to superintend the actions and decisions of senior officers and officials? What demands are not already stipulated in the *National Defence* Act and regulations, in the *Financial Administration* Act and so on? No one knows, because no one has ever asked.

What is the cost to national defence, what resources are diverted from the production and employment of coercive force, by administrative procedures and management processes DND imposes on itself and the Canadian Forces? What is the cost to national defence, what resources are diverted from the production and employment of coercive force, administrative procedures and management processes imposed on DND and the Canadian Forces by other government departments and the central agencies with a hand in DND's pocket? These are important questions for the public management and administration of defence policy. Thus, if the answer is that appropriate national defence is harmed by these demands, then they are questions that need to be addressed by the Minister of National Defence and the federal cabinet immediately.

Ideas in Action

What fundamental ideas ought to guide the construction of a relevant, responsive system of defence administration and management in this new era of global instability? It is, after all, sound ideas, not mindless repeated processes that should form the link between policy and administration directed at producing an appropriate national defence for Canada. Fortunately, the conceptual framework for an efficient and effective system of the management and administration of defence in Canada is neither complex nor so startling as to overthrow the extant machinery of government at the centre.

THE DEFENCE DELIVERABLE

The first idea that must be embedded in the machinery of government is that national defence is not a "deliverable" produced by DND or the Canadian Forces. Rather, Canada's national defence is the responsibility of every Canadian and in governmental terms, a public good, delivered by the government, as a whole.

This notion redirects responsibility from one minister to the Cabinet and from one department and the Canadian Forces to every central agency and department of government. If the notion were promptly interpreted, then the central direction of defence policy would follow and many of the turf wars might be eased. The public management and administration of defence might be simplified, if the central agencies were held to account for the efficiencies and inefficiencies that their processes and procedures impose on attempts to produce an appropriate national defence.

PRODUCING COERCIVE FORCE AND PURPOSE

As argued here and elsewhere, the purpose of the Canadian Forces is to use coercive force at the direction of the government.[6] The purpose of defence administration and management is to produce and sustain military capabilities to this end as efficiently and effectively as possible. Assessments of administrative procedures and management processes, therefore, must be directed solely at measuring operational capabilities produced and sustained and how efficiently (a ratio of resource inputs to capabilities outputs) these aims are achieved.

Melt the Snowball

In his indispensable work, Military Concepts and Philosophy, Admiral (USN) Henry Eccles describes "the logistic Snowball":

> The principle [of the logistic snowball] states that all logistic [and administrative] activities naturally tend to grow to inordinate size, and unless positive control is maintained, this growth continues until, like a ball of wet snow, a huge accumulation of slush obscures the hard core of essential combat support and the mass becomes unmanageable. This snowball effect then permeates the entire structure of military organization and effort.[7]

An essential guiding principle for defence administrators and, therefore, for their supervisors, is that the snowball must be kept small and thrown roughly against the true purpose of the Canadian Forces, every so often, to break off and let melt the administrative slush that will otherwise surely defeat the development and sustainment of core operational capabilities.

A Prejudice for Skilled Combatants

Canada requires, as all other societies have discovered, a group of people under its control who are set aside from society to apply force "in the resolution of social problems." Within the greater group that is the Canadian Forces, these select and unique people are those trained, in and for combat. These are the people who must, in society's interests and because of society's bargain with them, be protected and valued. Moreover, because they are uniquely, irreplaceably at the heart of the purpose of armed forces, and the most expensive component of every military capability, their development, sustainment, and care must be a central object of defence administration. Every military position removed from the group of skill combatants must be challenged and if found redundant to operational output, reallocated to that purpose.

Active Reallocation

As the purpose of armed forces is to apply coercive force at the direction of the government, all resources dedicated to the Canadian Forces and DND must be allocated to this fundamental need. Parts of the Canadian Forces required to generate coercive capabilities, to train recruits, for example, are obviously elements of the foundation of the Canadian Forces. Today, the distribution of resources between those who make a direct, measurable contribution to operational capabilities and those who do not seems inappropriately weighted towards the latter group. The reconstruction of the Canadian Forces and the implementation of administrative procedures and management processes must be aimed at redressing this imbalance, not only in people but in all categories of effort and resources. The guiding idea must be the reallocation of people, and resources from the blunt end of the defence spear to the sharp end.

Such efforts will, invariably, be met with stubborn obstinance coupled with predictions of administrative catastrophe from the entrenched special, non-combatant interests inside and outside the defence establishment. These shrill voices must be ignored and administrative backsliders removed from any responsibility for the administration and management of the national defence program. In time, a combat-biased reallocation policy would take effect and sustain, by its own momentum, the fundamental principle of purpose. But senior leaders must be ever mindful of Eccles' reality – the slush on the snowball will always tend to accumulate.

The Uniqueness of Defence Administration

The business of defence administration and management, the building and sustaining of combatant capabilities, separates the DND and elements of the Canadian Forces from the business of other departments and central agencies. Defence policy is based, inescapably, on the premise that the government is willing to spend lives to achieve its policy ends. Members of the Canadian Forces understand and accept this fact, if only in the abstract most of the time. For their part, however, members of the Canadian Forces expect that they will not be put at risk unnecessarily or in circumstances beyond their capabilities. Keeping faith with this unspoken contract and not tidy administrative procedures and management processes, is the real basis for the public administration of defence.

The demands of this contract, the nature of military operations in 2005, the complexity of administrating a policy with wide-ranging influence on other federal policies and programs, in the dynamic of domestic and international affairs, places enormous burdens on senior officers and officials. Public administration ought to be the servant to these individuals, not their master.

These factors and others are not only unique to the Canadian Forces and DND, but they are also not entirely amenable to rules, regulations, and operating norms applicable to other departments of government. Getting defence administration right is not a matter of how best to follow the rules flowing from the machinery of government, but rather how to protect Canada and Canadians at home and abroad most effectively in the circumstances of the moment, according to military definitions of efficiency.

The question for today, therefore, is what administrative concepts, norms, and procedures can best deliver an appropriate national defence? Moreover, what structure of persons with authority, what organization, and decision making procedures will best provide and sustain defence capabilities effectively and economically in peace and war (without changing fundamentally, as circumstances change), while allowing for adequate parliamentary oversight of complex decisions? It is not obvious, at all, that the extant federal structure and the centrally dictated procedures for the administration and management of policy provide the answer to these questions. Some might argue that they are the antitheses to what is needed in the circumstance, a heavy weight thoughtlessly thrown on the backs of dedicated people to the detriment of the nation.

Parliament ought to examine these questions with intent to find and remove administrative impediments to national defence. The overseer has a responsibly, not only to monitor his workers, but also to monitor and discipline those who impose themselves on their work and might even, if unintentionally, hinder their chances for success.

Establishing Administration and Management as Relevant to Strategic Studies

Advancing the study of defence public administration and management is not a challenge to strategic studies in Canada, as such. Rather, it is a plea for leaders in the field to recognize the essential link between policy objectives advanced by strategic studies norms and policy outcomes. That link is public administration and management in all its aspects. As strategic studies research takes scholars closer to government advocate, advisor, or critic of defence policy, then the greater the demand for such research to include a strong emphasis towards the public discussion and analysis of the administrative procedures and management processes offered or advanced. To do less, may simply render the research irrelevant or even dangerous to the nation's defences.

Strategic studies research need not include, at every turn, great administrative detail about how conclusions and recommendations or predictions, drawn from that research, will play out. Rather, research should pay attention to the longer term consequences of such research and how extant public administration will or might influence, advance, or retard strategic conclusions. In many cases, strategic studies research might concentrate on defence management and administration entirely to show, for instance, how changes in procedures and processes will change strategic outcomes. Research close to policy must take note, at least, of the macro elements of defence administration – people, organizations, procedures, and budgets – to test the feasibility of strategic studies conclusions and to hint at how such conclusions can be advanced.

Reaching these goals would require changes to existing programs of study and the creation of new courses and programs in defence administration in Canadian universities. Programs in strategic studies could, for example, require students to study defence economics, organizational decision-making, and the history of the ways and means of implementing defence policy in Canada. New degree programs in defence public administration might be introduced at a few universities, which already house degree programs in public policy and public administration. These efforts would eventually broaden and deepen strategic studies programs and research in Canada. They would also produce in time graduates better trained for employment in defence-related departments and agencies of the federal government. Strategic studies research would be enhanced if more scholars had a deeper understanding of defence administration and the connection of administration to strategy and operations. Finally, policymaking might improve if more scholars trained and experienced in defence administration and management were available to advise governments and parliament in this field.

If strategy is determined by sets of decisions that join ends to means, then we must acknowledge that those decisions invariably are arrived at and implemented by those skilled in the administration and management of defence. Those administrators and managers use techniques and practises taken from concepts which define public administration and management as intellectual fields of study. No matter the brilliance of strategic studies research, it cannot be carried into effect if it is administratively obtuse or impractical. If strategic studies is to mature and to remain relevant to governments, then it must acknowledge the central part public administration plays in strategic analysis and begin the long process of bringing public administration into the strategic studies fold.

Endnotes

1.   Department of National Defence, Report of the Ad Hoc Committee on Defence Policy (Ottawa:DND, 1963), 7.

2.   Department of National Defence, "Defence in the 70s," in *Canada's National Defence, Volume 1*, Defence Policy, ed. Douglas Bland (Kingston: Queen's University, School of Policy Studies, 1997), 171. All the major defence policy statements between 1947 and 1994 are contained in this volume.

3.   Department of National Defence, *Department of National Defence Report on Plans and Priorities 2007-2008* (Ottawa: DND, (2007), 6. The numbers of 65,000 and 24,000 are provided as planned numbers in the report. These number do not include some 24,000 Primary Reserve (or part time) military members that are active participants on CF operations abroad and at home.

4.   Department of National Defence Department of National Defence, *Report to the Minister of National Defence by the Advisory Committee on Administrative Efficiency* (Ottawa, August 21, 2003), 12.

5.   Minister's Efficiency Study, 11.

6.   See, for instance, Bland, Douglas and Maloney, Sean, *Campaigns For International Security: Canada's Defence Policy at the Turn of the Century* (Kingston, School of Policy Studies, 2004).

7.   Eccles, Henry E., *Military Concepts and Philosophy* (New Jersey: Rutgers University Press, 1965), 83.

Chapter 2

DEFENCE STRATEGY MANAGEMENT

Colonel Gregory Burt and Mr. Shawn McKnight

> We are resolved to destroy Hitler and every vestige of the Nazi regime. From this, nothing will turn us. Nothing! We will never parley. We will never negotiate with Hitler or any of his gang. We shall fight him by land. We shall fight him by sea. We shall fight him in the air. Until with God's help, we have rid the earth of his shadow.
>
> Winston Churchill

Introduction

Armed with this bold vision, Churchill never failed to confront the most brutal facts. He feared that his towering, charismatic personality might deter bad news from reaching him, in its starkest form. So, early in the war, he created an entirely separate department outside the normal chain of command, called the *Strategic Office*, with the principal function of feeding him – continuously updated and completely unfiltered – the most brutal facts of reality. He relied heavily on this special unit throughout the war, repeatedly asking for facts, just the facts. Likewise today, despite the existence of constant information flow and situational awareness through the normal chain of command, leaders in organizations, at the highest level, still require solid, unfiltered information on how their strategy is actually being executed.

Strategy execution is critical to success and it requires a disciplined process or a logical set of connected activities that enable an organization to make its strategy work. Without a careful, planned approach to execution, strategic goals are extremely difficult to attain. Developing such a logical approach, however, presents a formidable challenge to management. The challenge is in making the plan work. Effective strategy execution requires a culture that is committed to managing change as the organization adapts to new conditions and is dedicated to overcoming problems with traditional functional "silos". The emphasis must be on embracing errors and understanding them throughout the process of executing strategy, not just on conveniently finding a scapegoat to blame or fire.

The Defence Strategy Management methodologies used today are those that have evolved, over time, out of what can be dubbed the "continuum of defence management". They attempt to lift the fog of complexity surrounding defence management issues. This chapter will outline how senior leadership in DND and the CF performs the Defence Management function. The chapter will provide a broad outline of the defence management process within DND in order to set the stage for the subsequent, more detailed and issue specific chapters in the book. The chapter begins with a discussion on how the defence function is governed and controlled in order to meet the demands of the Government of Canada. Next, the chapter will discuss the inputs to the defence management process, beginning with defence strategy and how that is articulated within DND and the CF. Finally, the chapter presents how the strategy is operationalized and used to develop military capabilities.

The Strategic Environment – DND & the Government of Canada

Defence strategy must be executed within the broader Government of Canada (GoC) context, a context that includes operating with emphasis on the governmental priorities of public trust, transparency, accountability, and integrity. Within today's increasingly open and transparent government processes and activities, having the confidence and trust of the public is critical for success. Building public trust is also key to successfully demonstrating proper stewardship. In order to develop this public trust, the elements of transparency, accountability and integrity must be developed.

It is important to inspire a spirit of transparency within the institution to willingly provide the GoC, other stakeholders and ultimately the citizens of Canada, the information needed to make decisions. The GoC exists to ensure that the interests of the citizens of Canada are well served and DND/CF serves those interests by providing expert military advice and executing directed operations. In 2007, transparency is one of the guiding principles for DND/CF Transformation because trust is an essential element to the building and maintenance of strong leader-follower relationships on which the culture of DND/CF is built.[1] More specifically, the Investment Plan framework is a key instrument in the transparency between DND and the Treasury Board Secretariat. [2]

Strong and effective leadership and management are essential to ensure staff are engaged and committed to achieving the goals of the organization. In fact, proper execution of the defence strategy is dependent on elements of accountability, both internally and externally. The overall intent is for a public understanding and belief that DND/CF is a careful steward of the public purse. Accountability also requires that we have the confidence and trust of employees within the organization. The *Federal Accountability Act* in 2006 was introduced by the GoC to help restore Canadians' trust in government. The intent is to create a new culture of accountability that will strengthen and streamline government so it can function more effectively and efficiently. But even transparency and accountability are not enough to establish public trust. In the end, both depend on people of integrity. It is only through the actions and example of the people of Defence in following established ethical and moral guidelines, as identified in *Duty with Honour: Profession of Arms in Canada* for military members and the *Values and Ethics Code for the Public Service* for civilian employees, that we will achieve both the trust and respect of the Canadian public.

Within DND and the GoC the Three-Tier Model of Corporate Transparency provides a framework to improve corporate reporting for the future. The intent of the model is to institute practices that will ensure public trust does not disappear. The three tiers of the model are based on:

a.   A set of truly global generally accepted accounting principles (GAAP);

b.   Standards for measuring and reporting information that are industry specific, consistently applied and developed by the industries themselves; and

c.   Guidelines for organization-specific information such as strategy, plans, risk management practices, compensation policies, corporate governance, and performance measures that are unique to the organization.

The GoC and Canadian citizens will benefit fully from a global set of generally accepted accounting principles only if the organizations communicate the information in an integrated fashion that provides a holistic view of the organization. This includes its operations, its strategies and their implementation, its value drivers, and its financial management structure. Defence, like most government departments, follows generally accepted accounting principles, and the primary guide governing financial management is the *Financial Administration Act* (FAA).

Government-wide standards are needed to compare departments and evaluate the total management landscape. Treasury Board states that:

> Departments should ensure that their information systems, performance measurement strategies, reporting, and governance structures are consistent with and support their organization's MRRS and reflect the manner in which resources are actually managed and allocated in the organization.[3]

The Treasury Board Secretariat (TBS) sponsors two key reporting standards, the *Management Accountability Framework* (MAF) and the *Management Resources and Results Structure* (MRRS). The MAF was introduced by the TBS to translate the vision of modern public service management into a set of standard management practices. The MAF provides deputy ministers with a list of management expectations that focus on results. The MAF also provides TBS the means to work effectively with all departments within an explicit and coherent model for high organizational performance. It is the framework that is used to assess the DND/CF managerial performance.

The MRRS provides a standard basis for reporting to citizens and Parliament on the alignment of resources, programme activities and results. The MRRS supports the development of a common, government-wide approach to the collection, management, and reporting of financial and non-financial performance information. The MRRS reinforces the government's commitment to strengthen public sector management and accountability, consistent with the MAF. The MRRS specifies that each organization will meet the following specific mandated requirements by providing:

a. A clearly defined and measurable set of **Strategic Outcomes** that are linked to GoC priorities, intended results, and horizontal initiatives;

b. A **Program Activity Architecture** (PAA), which is a framework to reflect how a department allocates and manages the resources under its control to achieve intended results. The programs and activities within the architecture should be depicted such that they show the logical relationship both to each other and to the strategic outcome(s) to which they contribute; and

c. A description of the current **Governance Structure**, which outlines the decision-making mechanisms, responsibilities, and accountabilities of the department.[4]

Tier-three assurance on reported information is organization-specific. In DND/CF, it is the Performance Management Framework (PMF) that provides this organization specific information. The PMF focuses on answering questions such as:

a. Did management actually do what it reported?

b. Was the organization's externally reported strategy the same as its internally reported one?

c. Were the risk management practices the organization described actually applied?

d. Was the externally reported performance metric the same one that management used internally?

e. When comparative figures were given over time or across Level 1 organizations, did they constantly and consistently apply the same set of internal standards?

Similar to the private sector, the GoC is committed to increasing accountability and transparency for public reporting and being more responsive to Canadians. The Three-Tier model serves as a framework for improved reporting with the clear aim of maintaining the public's trust in DND/CF. Defence must clearly communicate its strategies and performance goals to the GoC and other stakeholders, both external and internal, whose support is needed to implement the defence strategy. This will ensure that they have critical situational awareness (ground truth) and have a clear understanding of what is being achieved.

STRATEGIC GOVERNANCE IN DND

In the defence department, and more specifically the National Defence Headquarters (NDHQ), "Strategic Governance" refers to the structures and processes used for decision-making at the most senior levels. Specifically, this includes three senior decision makers: the Deputy Minister (DM), the Chief of the Defence Staff (CDS) and the Vice Chief of the Defence Staff (VCDS). Various committees support these decision makers by providing a forum for consultation and advice.

The strategic governance structure discussed below has been in use since February 2008. This structure reflects philosophical and organizational changes introduced by General Hillier, the Chief of Defence Staff of the day, as part of his plan to transform the CF into a more responsive, relevant and effective force for the Government of Canada and Canadians. In addition, there was a desire to make the governance structure more agile, responsive and respectful of the time demands placed on Group Principals (Level 1s) by committee work.[5]

The principles behind the creation of the new strategic governance structure and its committees are to:

a.   Support the decisions makers in making informed, transparent decisions and producing coherent direction both in routine or crisis situations,

b.   Reflect the operational primacy mandate of the CF/DN,

c.   Ensure that authorities and accountabilities for outcomes are explicit, measurable and clearly understood by all,

d.   Provide authorities with the resources, structures and information required to deliver the desired outcomes,

e.   Ensure that the risk associated with pursuing a given alternative is understood and managed,

f.   Comply with statutory obligations and mandated GoC programs,

g.   Be sufficiently flexible and adaptive to handle continuing CF/DND transformation, and

h.   Reflect articulated ethics and values.

THE GOVERNANCE STRUCTURE

Figure 2.1 on the next page shows the new strategic level decision-support bodies. The figure depicts the relative position and key focus areas of the key strategic decision-support bodies. The detailed description for each of these committees and boards is provided at Appendix 2.

Strategy for the Department of National Defence is developed based on several sources. Government direction is, by definition, the primary source of direction for DND but the frequency and clarity or articulation of such direction is not always a given.[6] Although, lately, there has been a more hands-on approach by government to managing the direction and policies of Defence, this is not always the case and it is the vacuum of clear direction (and the subsequent resources to implement it) that present a challenge to managing the defence institution. The Chief of the Defence Staff (CDS) also issues guidance and sets priorities for the Canadian Forces and this guidance is the detailed direction for implementing government policy, whether formally stated in writing or not.

Figue 2.1: Governance Structure

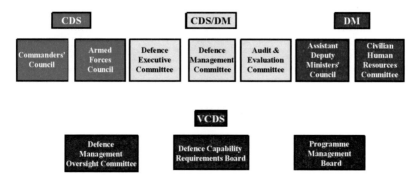

This strategy is then executed:

- with the concurrence of the Deputy Minister (DM) who oversees the civilian Associate Deputy Ministers (ADM) in the department and their functional areas,

- by the VCDS who controls all resource planning and allocations,

- by the Environmental Chiefs of Staff (ECS), largely responsible for force generation and training, as well as planning and initiating procurement for equipment, and

- by Operational Commanders who collectively support and employ forces on assigned missions.[7]

Naturally, there is a fiscal and personnel balance to be struck between achieving force generation/development, which is largely an ECS role, and force readiness and employment, an operational commander responsibility.

Both the Liberal government under Prime Minister Martin and the Conservative government under Prime Minister Harper have provided a more specific government vision and government direction for DND and the CF to use for planning. Based on this government direction, the CDS, General Hillier, has provided both a strategic vision and more specific direction for the transformation of the CF. This additional direction, combined with increased funding commitment to help implement the direction, is important for the alignment of defence strategy, direction, leadership and resources.

This strong direction, increased resources and clear public support to implement the changes and growth for DND and the CF come at a time when increased accountability and transparency on how these resources are spent has become paramount. DND is in an environment of growth. Since this can be considered unfamiliar territory for the department, there is a requirement to show value for the money spent and demonstrate the effective implementation and management of the articulated strategy. The ability to track and prove the judicious use of resources becomes an important function in the management of the defence portfolio. The challenge is to manage the execution of the strategy, provide the proper remits to the government of Canada and its Central

Agency watchdogs (Auditor General, Treasury Board Secretariat) and in doing so, not act as an impediment to the department's operations and operational goals.

Articulating & Communicating DND's Strategy

Depicting and communicating the strategy for a department as large as DND, with over 20 functional authorities and their complex interactions is a necessary, but difficult undertaking. Strategy is the framework of choices that determine the nature and direction of an organization. It establishes boundaries and parameters. Strategy execution is hinged on the organization's ability to describe and manage that articulated strategy. Furthermore, to ensure a culture of strategy execution, the methodologies must become institutionalized.

In order to simplify the strategy into meaningful and manageable objectives, DND uses a Strategy Map that pictorially represents the strategic objectives of the department and allows the casual linkages between the various objectives to be seen and tracked.[8] Figure 2.2 shows DND's Level Zero (ie. CDS/DM level) strategy map – current as of mid 2007 and static for the last several years. The Strategy Map is based on a mission, a vision, five strategic themes, fifteen strategic objectives and three strategic outcomes. The strategic objectives reflect a modified Balanced Scorecard approach to performance management. In so doing, they incorporate from the Balanced Scorecard, the four perspectives of:

- Defence Outputs,
- Internal Processes,
- Programme Resources, and
- Professional, Effective and Sustainable Defence Team.

Figure 2.2: Strategy Map

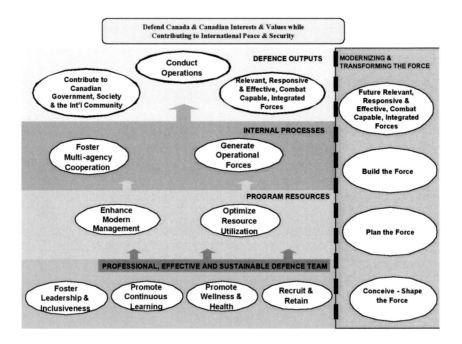

In addition, we have added a fifth perspective called Modernizing and Transforming the CF. In the Strategy Map diagram at Figure 2.2, the large arrow on top connotes a deep strike or overarching plan to ensure a properly equipped, staffed, relevant force, in the future. Recall that the nature of defence management must always incorporate the balance between the present and future requirements. The strategic objectives help drive success in the three main defence outputs that lead to the achievement of defence's strategic outcomes and its mission. The success or progress on these objectives is measured using established performance indicators. To permit effective measurement and to support improved performance management, each of these indicators and/or measures must have clearly established targets and performance thresholds. These provide a framework that enables the organization to determine whether, and how well, it is meeting its mandated obligations in accordance with stated plans and priorities. The economy, efficiency and effectiveness of operational and management practices can then be evaluated. The department can then analyze and discover any deficiencies in sufficient time to take appropriate corrective action. Finally, the department's achievements can be quantified and communicated to government and Canadians in a compelling and meaningful way.

Managing DND Using the Strategy Map

Action Teams

Each of the five perspective areas of the strategy map is managed by an "Action Team" comprised of Level 1's, with one designated as the team leader by the VCDS. The team members meet before a Defence Management Committee meeting to go over the performance information supplied to them by their Working Groups, and to formulate recommendations to the CDS/DM to deal with any performance issues that have arisen. Their key roles and responsibilities are to develop measurement strategies, set & monitor performance targets, ensure corporate initiatives are aligned to the strategy, draw information from across the department to facilitate a discussion of the root causes and required actions, prepare the semi-annual report to the Defence Management Committee, and bring to the attention of senior leadership any concern outside of the normal reporting cycle.

Working Groups

Each Level 1 on the team has a person at the working level (eg. Civilian manager, military officer) representing them on a working group, which is facilitated by a member of Directorate of Defence Strategy Management 4 (the Strategic Performance Management section of Defence Strategy management in the Chief of Programme organization). This working group collects and analyzes the data, proposes changes to policies, indicators, targets and initiatives, all to accomplish the strategic objectives in their perspective. These suggestions are then brought to an Action Team meeting for approval and implementation. The Working Group's key roles and responsibilities are:

a. First, they recommend a measurement structure to support the Key Perspective. They:

    i.   Collect, analyze and synthesize performance data,

    ii. Ensure accuracy and reliability of data,

    iii. Point out anomalies, or unexpected trends,

    iv. Provide explanations of trends and analysis,

    v.   Conduct performance gap analysis, and

    vi. Research, analyze and report on key issues impacting performance of Strategic Objectives

b. Second, they prepare a draft performance report for the Action Team in the following format:

    i.   Situation: List major causes for current performance,

    ii. Implications: Identify what impact the issues have on the performance of the Strategic Objectives,

iii.   Recommendations: Draft recommendations for the Action Team to table at DMCs, and

iv.   Accountability: Recommend which organizations should participate in this effort

Meetings

The Strategy Map is used as an agenda or table of contents for management discussions at the Defence Management Committee (DMC) and the various Level 1's (ADM/LGen/MGen). The meeting can have one of three purposes:

a.   Strategy Meeting: In a strategy meeting the DMC members would determine if the strategic objectives on the strategy map still accurately reflect the department's strategy. There may be discussion on changing the indicators used to measure success against each objective, but in general, performance information is not discussed at this type of meeting.

b.   Performance Review (Entire Map): In this type of meeting, the DMC members would use the map as the agenda and go over the performance results for each objective. Each Action Team lead would brief his/her perspective and the data and recommendations behind each strategic objective.

c.   Performance Review (Focused): In this shorter meeting, the DMC members would only address the Strategic Objectives that had been flagged red as requiring attention.

When a strategic objective (or whole perspective) is discussed, the performance data is usually synthesized into a quick summary slide that shows the objective's placement in the perspective, it's current and past performance as well as a forecast (if available) for the future, and the implications and recommendations that result from the current status of the objective and its indicators. Figure 2.3, below, shows an example of a Defence Output Summary Slide.

Figure 2.3: Defence Output Summary

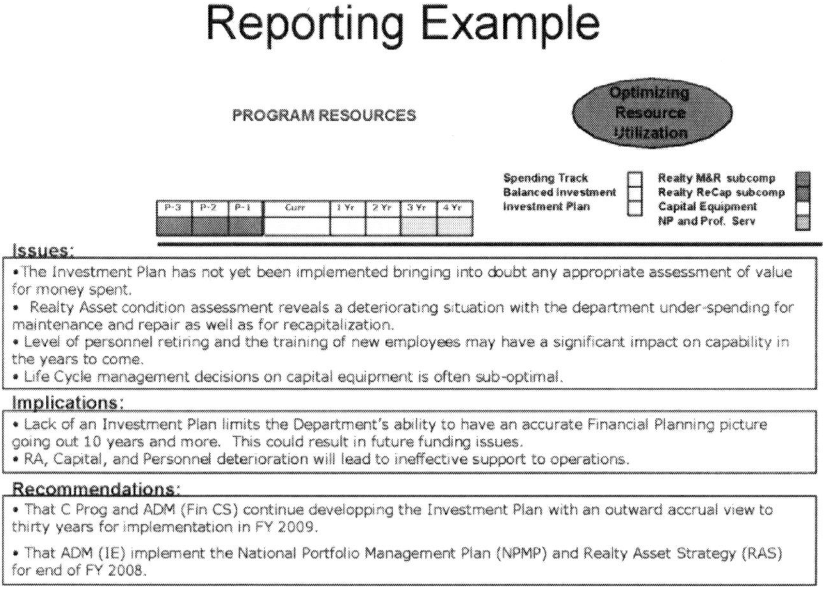

Reporting Example

PROGRAM RESOURCES

Optimizing Resource Utilization

P-3	P-2	P-1	Curr	1 Yr	2 Yr	3 Yr	4 Yr

Spending Track
Balanced Investment
Investment Plan

Realty M&R subcomp
Realty ReCap subcomp
Capital Equipment
NP and Prof. Serv

Issues:
• The Investment Plan has not yet been implemented bringing into doubt any appropriate assessment of value for money spent.
• Realty Asset condition assessment reveals a deteriorating situation with the department under-spending for maintenance and repair as well as for recapitalization.
• Level of personnel retiring and the training of new employees may have a significant impact on capability in the years to come.
• Life Cycle management decisions on capital equipment is often sub-optimal.

Implications:
• Lack of an Investment Plan limits the Department's ability to have an accurate Financial Planning picture going out 10 years and more. This could result in future funding issues.
• RA, Capital, and Personnel deterioration will lead to ineffective support to operations.

Recommendations:
• That C Prog and ADM (Fin CS) continue developing the Investment Plan with an outward accrual view to thirty years for implementation in FY 2009.

• That ADM (IE) implement the National Portfolio Management Plan (NPMP) and Realty Asset Strategy (RAS) for end of FY 2008.

Operationalizing the Strategy and Aligning the Institution

The one concept that all literature in management has in common is that "Change is constant" – for defence this is evident in the evolving security and current operating environment with both asymmetric and symmetric adversaries, in the increased transparency anticipated in the government's regulatory and macroeconomic environment, in technology, international politics, public opinion and demographics. Strategies and their implementation must therefore constantly evolve. An aligned organization, at one time, will soon become unaligned. The second law of thermodynamics teaches us that entropy (disorder) continually increases. New energy must be continually pumped into a system if it is to remain aligned and coherent.[9]

This phenomenon therefore represents an interesting challenge in an organization as large and complex as DND/CF. DND/CF has, through tradition, developed over decades of autonomous operation. These traditions, coupled with add-on corporate functions to satisfy efficiency initiatives, have become silo centric and not aligned. With limited resources, a constantly evolving security environment, an increased requirement for transparency and the reality of shifting political direction, a more holistic and integrated approach is clearly required.

Alignment is not a one-time event and DND is always (and always will be) on a continuum to lift the fog of complexity on defence management. Organizational alignment is defined as the aligning of corporate, business units, support units, external partners, and boards with the strategy. In defence this translates as the alignment of the defence strategy with political policy throughout the threes services, all the support organizations, with the TBS and the GOC.

The transformation activities that DND/CF is presently undertaking is the first step in integrating defence and should, over a period of time, contribute to a more aligned organization. The key components of transformation that should generate alignment are: a single force development process to prioritize the allocation of capital funding, an operationally focused administration to prioritize programme allocation of resources, and a centralized reporting framework to enhance transparency.

It is important to note that the alignment strategy must be complimented with an alignment process. The alignment process, much like budgeting, should be a part of the annual governance cycle. Whatever plans are changed at the enterprise or business unit level, executives likely need to realign the organization with the new direction. In an environment deeply rooted in culture and tradition, this becomes extremely difficult. "Culture will eat change for breakfast everyday"

Just as members of the Vice Chief of the Defence Staff organization coordinate the budgeting process with Associate Deputy Finance Minister members, members of the Vice Chief of the Defence Staff organization should coordinate the alignment process. What is clear is the executing strategy in any large organization requires the alignment of people, processes and technology.

PEOPLE

Enterprises must have active policies to communicate, educate, motivate and align employees with the strategy. They must also align their ongoing management processes – for resource allocation, target setting, initiative management, reporting and reviews – with the strategy. People, the key actors in all organizations, need to align themselves to the central tenets of the strategy.

PROCESS

In addition, well-understood processes provide a roadmap for collaboration and help individuals get engaged. Organizations within DND/CF are able to align themselves much more easily to the strategy if they can understand where and how their work contributes to the larger whole. It is therefore important that the five strategic themes – Strategy Development, Force Development, Capability Production, Force Generation and Force Employment – and four key internal operations processes are aligned as shown in Figure 2.4. Aligning these activities will demonstrate:

a.   who is responsible for what activities within each process;

b.   how the processes themselves interact and influence each other;

c.   what the inputs and outputs are; and

d.   where opportunities exist for process improvement or improved IM/IT support.

Efforts are underway to produce an improved and integrated Defence Planning and Management Framework that will improve coherence of strategy management. This will allow longer-term planning to naturally set the direction needed to guide shorter-term resource decisions, and empowers the Performance Management section to not only monitor progress but also exert a strong guiding influence on financial allocation and implementation schedules as needed.

Figure 2.4: Internal Processes: Strategy Management - Aligning the Institution

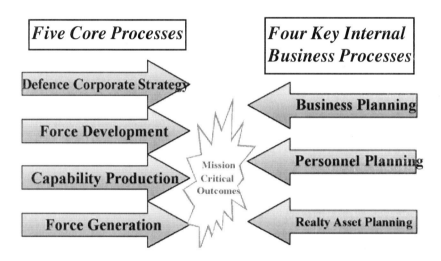

Technology facilitates all aspects of strategy execution, from the automation of key tasks to the analysis of data and the provision of decision support. Information technology is already indispensable to the functioning of the DND/CF. The next step is to ensure that technology is not only a means of automating activities and storing data, but also becomes a means of reinforcing the Defence Strategy across the organization. Important steps have already been taken in this direction. For example, information management rationalization is bringing together all non-operational IM/IT resources across the organization under the management of ADM (IM), providing a rare opportunity to revisit existing IM/IT support. This is essential so that IM/IT facilitates defence strategy management and execution.

Ensuring alignment of the Planning and Executing or the Strategy

For planning and budgeting, the Directorate of Force Planning and Programme Control (DFPPC) and ADM (Fin CS) oversee budgeting and financial allocations to the Level 1 organizations and cross-functional initiatives. These activities are tremendously important and must be done in accordance with the longer-term objectives in mind in order to truly make the budget process a useful means of strategic resource allocation.

The Defence Planning and Management (DP&M) process shown in Figure 2.5 links the processes of policy setting (or describing the strategy), planning, managing (executing strategy), achieving results, performance management, feedback, and reporting. The DP&M process encapsulates the discipline of strategy management. As one might expect in a large organization, the strategy management loop does not churn rapidly. The senior leadership must maintain oversight and cash manage over time in order to satisfy the three key elements of defence strategy over time (institutional credibility, balance of forces to satisfy government requirements and HR sustainment).

All the functional Level 1's make recommendations of one sort or another to improve the state of their particular function. For example, ADM(IM) makes recommendations on investments in databases, infrastructure, and application programmes; and ADM (IE) makes plans for realty asset management (e.g. new construction) and environmental remediation. For a strategy to be effective, these functional plans must be aligned with the overall defence strategy.[10]

Defence Planning & Management Cycle

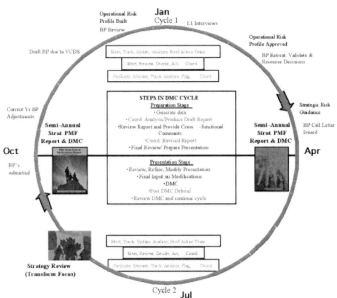

Figure 2.5: Defence Planning and Management Cycle

No strategy can be effective unless those who must carry it out are trained and motivated. Motivation and training are the natural domain of Chief of Military Personnel (CMP) and ADM (HR-Civ), in terms of coordinating annual performance reviews and personal goal setting. They also manage employee incentives, leadership and competency development programs. The goal is to make strategy management everyone's job.[12]

Defence can execute its strategy well only if it aligns the strategies of its business units, support functions, and external partners with its broad enterprise strategy. Alignment creates focus and coordination across even the most complex organizations, making it easier to identify and realize synergies. Ensuring alignment with Defence strategy at all levels of the organization will occur by:

a.   Defining the Corporate Role. It is important to ensure close linkages with all Level 1 organizations.

b.   Corporate Alignment. "Functional silos arise and become a major barrier to strategy implementation, as most organizations have great difficulty communicating and coordinating across these specialty functions."[13] The Level 1 organizations are the building blocks and it is essential that their strategies be aligned around shared goals and objectives.

c.   Aligning External Partners. With an effective strategy management system, an organization can communicate and coordinate its strategic activities with its external partners. The Office of the Auditor General, the Privy Council Office, the Treasury Board Secretariat, and the Department of Finance should therefore clearly understand it. A communications plan will elaborate how this will be achieved.

ANNUAL CYCLE

Strategy management facilitates the execution process so that strategy execution can be accomplished in an integrated fashion. The VCDS ensures the management of strategy, the alignment of processes, and facilitates the execution of the strategy. On behalf of the VCDS, DDSM is responsible for strategy management. It is carried out in accordance with the annual cycle, which is initiated by strategic planning, and includes the establishment of corporate priorities, approval of a corporate risk profile, and initiation of the business planning cycle. This annual cycle is shown at Figure 2.6 below.

Figure 2.6 depicts a typical cycle of planning, analysis, program delivery, monitoring, reporting and feedback. This cycle is cyclical in nature and demonstrates in-year allocation and reporting. It does not however address a holistic picture of the interactions required to administer and align Defence for the future. There are difficulties in working with a long-term horizon when direction and funding are both short term and politically/election focused.

Figure 2.6: Annual Cycle for Strategy Management

The Way Ahead – Alignment Using Strategic Themes

The five strategic themes used within Defence provide a way of demonstrating how consistent and reinforcing cross-functional activities fit together. They are in actual fact the building blocks of strategy. The delivery of the Defence programme occurs through one or more of the five core Defence processes or strategic themes. These five processes were shown at Figure 2.4. Although these processes are parallel and complementary they are not considered to hold the same magnitude of convolution. For example Force Employment and Force Generation, whilst extremely multifaceted in construct are tangible and intrinsic parts of the military culture and therefore tend to be managed much easier than the three intangible Strategic themes of Corporate Strategy, Force Development and Capability Production. In order to ensure and sustain a viable and credible force over time it is important that both the tangible and intangible themes identify where overlaps and synergies can be achieved.

To manage Defence using themes, it is important that a disciplined approach is used to manage these complex processes in order to achieve success in execution.[14] They must be mapped, in order for them to be aligned and comprehensive throughout Defence. Once completed the themes should be used to develop, fund, and monitor the plan and link the planned strategy to operations.

Conclusion

The Strategy Map and Balanced Scorecard are the single most succinct and clear representations of the organization's strategy. They enable the leadership of the organization to understand the strategy and provide the basis for an evaluation of whether the strategy is capable of delivering long-term requirements. In a business context, this is shareholder value at acceptable levels of business, financial and technical risk. In government and defence, it is about providing service to Canadians. Strategy vice quality must be explicitly identified as the focal point of the management system and executing strategy requires the highest level of integration and teamwork among organizational units and processes. A necessary condition for this is sound executive leadership within a strong and disciplined management process.

Endnotes

1. In 2007 the CF was 2 years into a process of transforming how it was organized and structured to deal with the future security environment. For information on this process the reader should see Canada, Department of National Defence, "CDS Vision" (http://cds.mil.ca/cft-tfc/pubs/documents_e.asp). As well, the CDS link on the CF website contains a variety of reports and updates on this process.

2. The Investment Plan is a staff level document that was signed off by the Deputy Minister and sent to TBS in early 2008.

3. Treasury Board Secretariat policy on Management Resources and Results Structure (MRRS) (http://www.tbs-sct.gc.ca/presentations/rma-dpr/poli/page01_e.asp).

4. *Ibid.*

5. Group Principals or Level 1s as they are referred to within the department are the senior level military and civilian managers/leaders. They are generally Lieutenant Generals and Associate Deputy Ministers. The term Level 1 is tied to the Business Planning Process used within the GoC.

6. In 1994, the Government's *White Paper* was a cornerstone of Defence Policy. It is sometimes mistakenly referred to in 2007 as an authoritative guidance document. The International Policy Statement and Defence Policy Statements of the Liberal government in 2005 were also seen as guidance and direction from government, 11 years after the *White Paper.* The latest directives (as of 2007) have been in the form of the Conservative Government's *Canada First* Defence Policy, echoed and included in the DND produced Defence Capital Plan (DCP).

7. Operational Commanders in the new transformed Canadian Forces structure include Canada Command (CANCOM), Canadian Special Operation Forces Command (CANSOFCOM), Canadian SuppoCommand (CANOSCOM)and Canadian Expeditionary Forces Command (CEFCOM).

8. A Strategy Map is a pictorial representation of an organizations strategy and the interaction between strategic goals. It comes from Kaplan & Norton's work on Balance Scorecard Based performance management, and from their book "Strategy Maps". It is important to remember that any diagram, map or statement of Defence Strategy is a snapshot in time that risks being overcome by events or changes in government and priorities as soon as it's published. In spite of that, it is useful to illustrate the concept and usefulness of the strategy map as a communications tool and single page reference. Many of the strategic objectives in this map are intuitive and enduring so time will tell how fleeting this depiction is.

9. http://www.entropysite.com/students_approach.html

10. Kaplan, R. & Norton, D. (2005) The Office of Strategy Management, *Harvard Business Review,* 83(10), 7.

11. Kaplan, R. & Norton, D. (2005) The Office of Strategy Management, *Harvard Business Review,* 83(10), 7.

12. *Ibid.*

13. Kaplan R. & Norton D.(2000) The Strategy Focused Organization: How Balanced Scorecard Companies Thrive in the New Business Environment, Harvard Business School Press: Boston, MA., 11-12.

14. Hrebiniak, L. *Making Strategy Work: Leading Effective Execution and Change*,Wharton School Publishing, 2005, 62.

Chapter 3

BUDGETING FOR DEFENCE

Lieutenant-Colonel Ross Fetterly

The federal government is a multi-billion dollar organization that makes and enforces laws that influence the lives of all Canadians. The government raises revenue through tax revenues, duties and tariffs, which is then spent on a multitude of programs and services that benefit all citizens. In order to manage these revenues and expenses, the government develops and implements a financial plan, commonly referred to as a budget. This financial plan, in effect, consists of two types of annual budgets. The first is a revenue budget, which is a forecast of government income over a twelve-month period. The second type of budget is an expenditure budget, which is a forecast of government expenditures over the same period. Consolidation of these budgets, including the surplus or deficit, is called the fiscal framework, and provides a means of portraying the overall financial position of the government.

This chapter will provide an overview of the function that the budget performs in the Canadian governmental system. This chapter also provides context for a discussion of defence funding within the federal fiscal framework, in the next chapter. The chapter begins with an overview of the general budget process and an historical review of the manner in which the Canadian federal budget process evolved. Next, the chapter will summarize the Federal Expenditure Management System (EMS), including a review of the federal budget and reporting cycle. The chapter will then focus on changes in the expenditure management process within the federal sector. The chapter will conclude with a discussion of the defence budget within the federal government's fiscal framework, as a transition to the next chapter.

Budget Process Overview

The federal budget is a key component of the Canadian democratic system. The budget is an influential signal of national priorities as perceived and acted upon by the government. The budgetary process is not a static activity; it is, in essence, a reflection of the objectives and priorities of the elected government of the day. Indeed, the distinguishing feature of budgetary systems is that they change over time. To a large extent, this change in budgetary process is evolutionary in nature, with each successive reform shaped and influenced by previous reforms. Notwithstanding the evolutionary change that transpires in budgetary processes in Western governments, the fundamentals of resource management remain relatively constant. The fundamental elements in the budget process are outlined in Figure 3.1.

Figure 3.1: The Budget Process

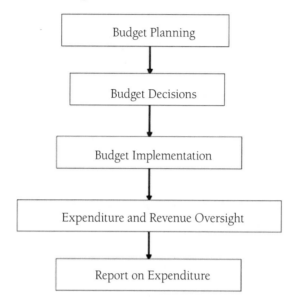

Budget planning is an inclusive process, led by the Prime Minister and the Minister of Finance. Also integral to the planning process are Cabinet members, central agencies (Treasury Board, the Privy Council Office and the Prime Minister's Office), government departments and Parliamentary Committees. This planning process involves setting priorities, determining the affordability of programs and deciding on issues that are political in nature. Budget decisions subsequently require Parliamentary approval, but are largely shaped by the Prime Minister and Minister of Finance, together with Cabinet members and the Treasury Board. Individual government departments implement the budget. Expenditure oversight is provided internally within departments, by central agencies, the Auditor General and Parliamentary Committees. Finally, at the end of the fiscal year, the government departments and agencies report back to Parliament through the Treasury Board on expenditure and policy compliance. These fundamental elements provide for a logical and sequential process that is repeated for each budget cycle. The budget process has to be integrated into the federal program management cycle, which is outlined in Figure 3.2.

Figure 3.2: Progam Management

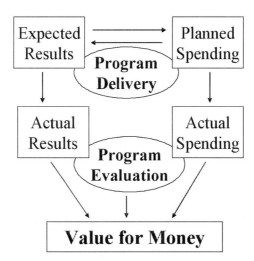

Program management includes an expenditure plan to achieve anticipated results, and occurs through a program delivery mechanism. This, eventually, translates into actual spending and precise results, which is followed by an evaluation and feedback process that both adjusts and improves program delivery, while refining resource requirements.

History of Budget Development in Canada

The traditional budgetary process in Canada, up to the end of the Second World War, was informal and decentralized. The process consisted of the Prime Minister and Cabinet establishing both general government objectives and priorities, with each minister retaining significant independence over policy and budgetary decisions within their departments. This approach, commonly referred to as line item budgeting, resulted in government budgeting from the bottom-up, with the Minister of Finance essentially compiling individual departmental budgets into a consolidated budget. However, the size and breadth of the federal budget began to grow significantly following the Second World War. Canadians demanded more from their national government and the advent of the welfare state brought forth a wide variety of social security programs, including old age pensions, monthly payments to support families with young children, and employment insurance. This resulted in a large expansion in federal government departments required to manage these programs, and necessitated development of an enhanced budgetary process to manage this dramatic change in scale and scope. These changes challenged the government to examine and subsequently adapt the budget process to reflect these new circumstances.

The impact of a very weak economy beginning in 1957, lasting through to the 1960s, combined with increasing demands for social programs put considerable pressure on the federal fiscal framework and led, in part, to the start of a series of budgetary reforms.[1] These reforms began in 1962 when the Royal Commission on Government Organization (the Glassco Commission) recommended a transition from the traditional "line item" budgeting system to a more comprehensive program approach advocated by the Planning, Programming and Budgeting System (PPBS).[2] This movement to adapt financial management processes coincided with a more "rational" approach to governance within Western governments in general. The result was a shift in Canada to an exceptionally centralized, or top-down approach to budget development. Under this system, government departments were categorized into policy groups, and departments within each group submitted budget requests in accordance with established priorities. However, the inability of this system to effectively measure the impact of programs on Canadians lead to further reform in 1980 with the introduction of the Policy and Expenditure Management System (PEMS). This system retained the same broad policy groups, but expenditure limits were established for each group. Despite some initial improvements, the complexity of the Policy and Expenditure Management System was eventually viewed as a significant shortcoming of that system.[3] In 1993, the government undertook an extensive review of the organisation and machinery of government as a prelude to steps required to address a long-standing and growing budgetary deficit. The current Expenditure Management System (EMS) was established in 1995 and has provided a stable institutional planning and decision-making process within the federal government system.[4]

However, in recent years, a number of significant managerial and financial issues have become prominent within both the private and public sectors. This has included for example, increased disclosure, accountability, transparency, and delivery of measurable results to stakeholders.[5] Given these changes, the Expenditure Management System will be updated to incorporate recent changes to managerial and financial practices.[6]

The Expenditure Management System (EMS)

The EMS is at the heart of government operations. The processes and procedures by which the central agencies of government support Cabinet in allocating and managing government spending are key components of the EMS. They are designed to help align resources with priorities, oversee spending, and establish the policies that departments will follow to manage and deliver their programs.[7]

Both political and bureaucratic processes influence the allocation of budgetary resources within any government department. The ultimate objective of this blended process is the translation of government policy into programs and the resulting detailed resource allocations. As indicated, the current mechanism employed by the federal government to allocate resources is the Expenditure Management System. The EMS assists the government in making "responsible spending decisions by delivering the programs and services Canadians need in a way that they can afford and by meeting the required fiscal targets."[8] The Expenditure Management System is based on the four key principles:

a. Establishment of a stable environment;

b. Early strategic planning;

c. Consultation with Canadians and parliamentarians in the budget planning process; and

d. Evaluation of the process

The first principle of the Expenditure Management System is to provide a stable planning environment. This facilitates an atmosphere that is conducive to early planning of modifications to program spending. The second principle is a focus on medium to long-term strategic planning and consists of timely reviews of existing programs and their delivery, as well as the reallocation of expenditures to higher priorities. The third principle includes public input to individual ministers and with the Minister of Finance during budget consultations, as well as, House Standing Committee review and reporting on the Estimates. The fourth principle is achieved through the combined effect of providing incentives to encourage both effective planning and resource allocation, while generating performance information to attain better informed decisions and enhanced accountability. The four principles are linked and form an integrated process. The first three principles, in turn, support establishment of a suitable environment, timely planning and broad consultations, with the fourth principle focussed on improving performance management.

The Expenditure Management System is shown at Figure 3.3. The Estimates process, together with the Federal Budget and the Economic and Fiscal Update, is the foundation of the Expenditure Management System.[9] The Expenditure Management System begins with an internal strategic review process within each individual department. This review forms the basis for the Annual Reference Level Update (ARLU). The Annual Reference Level Update updates the cost of approved departmental programs, which provide the basis for developing the Main Estimates and the budgetary expenditure plan. The Annual Reference Level Update includes such items as approved adjustment to departmental reference levels, revised forecasts for statutory programs, adjustments due to collective bargaining agreements and program reprofiling requests. The next phase is the concurrent tabling of Part I & II of the Estimates in the House of Commons by the President of the Treasury Board, as a joint document.

Figure 3.3: The Budgetary Cycle and The Federal Government Expenditure Management System

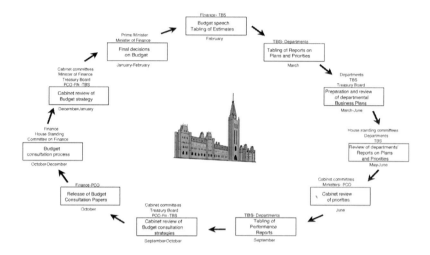

Part I of the Estimates is referred to as "The Government Expense Plan." This document is essentially an overview of planned federal spending for that fiscal year. Both budgetary and non-budgetary spending authorities are presented in the Government Expense Plan, and are generally consistent with the spending plans previously announced in the budget. Whereas Part I of the Estimates provides the overview of planned spending, Part II provides the detail.

Part II is referred to as "The Main Estimates". These Estimates directly support the *Appropriation* Act and categorize spending authorities into subsequent appropriation bills. Appropriation Acts are spending legislation that enables the government to spend money. In particular, "an appropriation act (or supply bill) is a bill to authorize government expenditures, introduced in the House of Commons following the concurrence of the Main or Supplementary Estimates or interim supply."[10] Both budgetary and non-budgetary spending authorities are solicited through Appropriation bills. These authorities are divided into two categories – Voted and Statutory. A vote is a funding limit in an appropriation. Furthermore, a vote provides a framework for the purpose under which the appropriation can be used, including the authority to spend revenue received. It should be noted that the term "vote" is commonly used in the sense of "appropriation". Different types of votes can be used in a particular *Appropriation* Act.[11] The types and descriptions of Votes are described in Table 3.1. Statutory authorities are those that "Parliament has approved through other legislation that sets out both the purpose of the expenditures and the terms and conditions under which they may be made."12

Table 3.1: Type and Description of Votes

Type of Vote	Vote Description
Program Expenditures	In cases where operating expenditures or grants and contributions are under $5M and all program expenditures are charged to one vote.
Operating Expenditures	Used for expenditures when either capital expenditures or grants and contributions in a program equal or exceed $5M.
Capital Expenditures	Used where capital expenditures in a program equal or exceed $5M.
Grants and Contributions	Used where grants or contributions in a program equal or exceed $5M.
Non-Budgetary	Provides the authority for loans, advances or investments to Crown corporations and for specific purpose loans and advances to other governments, international organisations, or private sector corporations.
Special Votes	There are two types of Special Votes. The first is for Crown Corporation Deficits and Separate Legal Entities. The second is for Treasury Board Centrally Financed Votes, which includes funding for government-wide public service initiatives.

Part III of the Estimates are the Departmental Expenditure Plans. These expenditure plans are divided into two parts. The first part is the Report on Plans and Priorities (RPP). This report is tabled before the start of the fiscal year and provides an overview of departmental resource plans. It lays out information on initiatives and planned results, provides more details on forecasted departmental activities and linkages to resource requirements over three years. The second part is the Departmental Performance Report (DPR). This report is tabled after the end of the fiscal year and provides a summary of departmental achievements against planned expectations in the Report on Plans and Priorities.

The Departmental Performance Report completes the Expenditure Management System cycle. Between tabling of the Report on Plans and Priorities before the start of the fiscal year and the Departmental Performance Report following the end of the fiscal year, the Budget speech occurs in the House of Commons and two Supplementary Estimates are subsequently tabled during that fiscal year in September and December respectively. The Budget and Supplementary Estimates are key in-year activities. As shown in Figure 3.3, the Main Estimates are tabled well before the Budget. As such, there are generally a number of initiatives in the budget that are not included in the Main Estimates. This includes, for example, expenditures for initiatives announced in the Budget that need further development, or funding for adjustments in planned expenditures due to economic changes.

The federal government funds departments based on an expected level of activity during a fiscal year. To accomplish assigned tasks and fulfill statutory responsibilities, departments are assigned a baseline funding level.[13] This funding is provided through the annual budgetary process. The budget tabled in Parliament by the government in February or March each year is a spending plan for the upcoming fiscal year. During the fiscal year, circumstances could arise where the government decides to reduce funding if revenues are substantially less than projected. In this event, funding may be reallocated among departments due to shifting priorities, or funding increases may be approved to cover unexpected expenditures. Unplanned expenditures during the fiscal year are submitted to Treasury Board Ministers for approval, and subsequently tabled in Parliament in the form of Supplementary Estimates.[14]

This Appropriation Act provides Parliament with information regarding amendments required in planned departmental spending. The Supplementary Estimates are tabled in Parliament in November and March of each year. Supplementary Estimates are of particular importance to defence because the department is generally one of the main beneficiaries of incremental funding during the fiscal year. This is largely the result of in-year decisions to deploy military contingents on operations and the related additional resource implications associated with the deployment that were not planned for by DND in the initial budget estimate.

The formal decision-making in the budget process by the Prime Minister and Cabinet is firmly supported by three central agencies: the Privy Council Office (PCO), the Department of Finance and the Treasury Board (TB). The role of the PCO is to support the Prime Minister as the head of government and to ensure that ministers and departments are incorporating the Prime Minister's budget priorities into their budget planning. The Minister of Finance, with the support of the Department of Finance, establishes the fiscal framework under which all government departments function.

Change in the Expenditure Management System

The Expenditure Management System of the federal government has been significantly influenced by both domestic and external factors for over four decades, requiring governments to be responsive to both factors. This has resulted in a series of changes to financial management practices and procedures over time. Thus, changes occurring in the present are simply a continuation of changes that began with the Glassco Commission Report in 1962. Consequently, in order for the financial management practices to remain appropriate to current circumstances, the Expenditure Management System:

> is always in a state of flux. Flexibility and the ability to adapt to emerging situations are a prerequisite of a good expenditure management system. The system that works best for the government today will not necessarily be the best one for tomorrow. Consequently, the expenditure management system must be flexible and must respond to the changing environment.[15]

Managing within the government's Expenditure Management System is a complex endeavour and there is a strong requirement for coordination among departments "because of the very nature of the issues now arising in government."[16] The public sector is not immune from issues that are particularly topical and influential in the private sector. In fact, both sectors are confronted with many of the same issues. Prominent issues that transcend the federal sector, which have recently received significant emphasis and attention, include the management framework, financial administration and accountability. These three issues are not unique to this decade and are recurring catalysts for reform, as are the forces of globalization and international competitiveness pressures.

The foundation for ongoing reforms in federal public sector management were derived from the Treasury Board report entitled *Results for Canadians: A Management Framework for the Government of Canada* released in 2000.[17] The focus of that document was to integrate top emerging management practices with identified priorities for change. The report identified a citizen focus, values, achievement of results and responsible spending as priority areas of focus in order to achieve a well-performing public service. This was followed by a number of other reports and studies including the *Management Accountability Framework, Governing Responsibly: A Guide for Ministers and Ministers of State, Strengthening Public Sector Management, and Management in the Government of Canada: A Commitment to Continuous Improvement.*[18]

The foundation of financial management in the federal government is the *Financial Administration* Act (FAA).[19] This Act is the primary source of management authority for the Canadian Public Service. The Act provides for the "financial administration of the Government of Canada, the establishment and maintenance of the accounts of Canada and the control of Crown corporations."[20] In essence, this Act provides the legal framework for the financial management of public service organizations and Crown corporations. Although not all encompassing, the *Financial Administration* Act provides the regulations for governing public management in Canada. Although financial reform started in the late 1990s with the release of the *Report of the Independent Review Panel on Modernization of Comptrollership in the Government of Canada*, reform initiatives began in earnest in the early part of the next decade and focused on modern comptrollership.[21]

The subject of accountability has regularly been an issue in the public sector in recent decades, both for public servants and Ministers.[22] Accountability in *Guidance for Deputy Ministers* is defined as

> linked to the source of an authority, and can be thought of as enforcing or explaining responsibility, and its practice is linked to a judgment about an office holder's action. It involves rendering an account to someone on how responsibilities are fulfilled, on actions taken to correct problems and to ensure they do not recur.[23]

Recently, the document Accountable Government: A Guide for Ministers outlined the core principles concerning Ministerial roles and responsibilities and that was followed by the Federal Accountability Act.[24] This Act that provides for "conflict of interest rules, restrictions on election financing and measures respecting administrative transparency, oversight and accountability."[25]

The focus of this chapter, so far, has been on overall financial management in the federal government. The final section of this chapter will consider Defence within the context of the federal fiscal framework in order to set the stage for the discussion in the next chapter on how Defence allocates its budget once the government decides the level of overall funding.

The Defence Budget within the Federal Fiscal Framework

The 1867 *British North America* Act assigned the division of responsibility for legislative powers in Canada between Federal and Provincial Legislatures. Section 91 of the *British North America* Act assigned exclusive responsibility for defence to the Federal Government in 1867. Budget 2006 estimated expenditures by the Federal Government in Fiscal Year (FY) 2006-07 at $223.6B, with spending on a variety of programs and activities, of which defence was only a small, but significant, component.[26] Certainly, the determination of the "appropriate size of the defence budget can be made only in the context of the Government's national priorities and in the light of its consequent problems."[27]

Figure 3.4 illustrates the trend in federal government expenditures from 1992-93 through 2005-06. The largest growing category is classified as other expenditures. In effect, this is direct program spending, which includes the operating cost of government, payments to Crown Corporations and other transfers and subsidies, such as farm income assistance, transfers to Aboriginal communities and international assistance. Also noteworthy is the decreasing proportional share of public debt charges, which includes the cost of financing the Federal Public Debt. This decrease in proportional debt share is due to balanced or surplus budgets from FY 1997-98 through to the present, and contributions by the government to pay down the debt. Finally, transfers to other levels of government have been increasing as a percentage of overall expenditures during the opening years of this century. Since the early 1990s, Defence spending has maintained a remarkably consistent percentage of overall federal expenditure, with a marginal increase in recent years from 6.6% in 1992-93 to 7.2% in 2005-06, which is reflective of defence budget increases in the current decade.

Figure 3.4: Trend in Share of Federal Government Expenditures

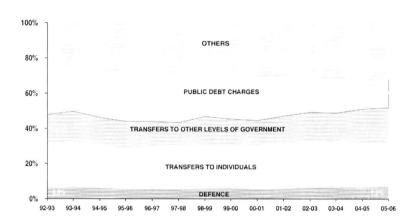

Despite $223.6B in planned spending announced in Budget 2006 for fiscal year 2006-07, the ability of the federal government to make significant changes in the near-term is limited. Total forecasted program expenditures for 2006-07 were $188.8B. This consisted of transfers to persons, at $56.3B, and transfers to other levels of government at $40.1B, leaving only $92.4B for direct federal program expenses. As a result, during a fiscal year, the federal government only has direct control over just under half of overall program expenses. Furthermore, flexibility within direct program expenditures is limited as these include departmental operating expenses, subsidies and other transfers, as well as defence. Indeed, if discretionary expenditures can be categorized as expenditures that can be reduced or delayed by the federal government without significantly impacting on core activities, then short-term options available to the government are limited. This can include such in-year actions as shaving a percentage off departmental operating budgets, implementing a public service hiring freeze, or reductions in transfers to Crown corporations or subsidies. Nevertheless, it is the defence department that provides government with significant flexibility to either reduce expenditures during times of restraint or, alternatively, to spend funds effectively on investment opportunities when other government departments cannot spend their funding allocations. At a budget of $15.25B in 2006-07, Defence accounts for 16.5% of direct program spending and, as will be noted in the next chapter, is the largest spender on machinery and equipment, as well as material and supplies. Note that planned public debt payments were forecasted at a further $34.8B in government expenditure.

Summary

This chapter has provided an overview of the function that the budget performs in the Canadian governmental system. The chapter began with a general overview of the federal budget process and then provided a historical review of the manner in which the Canadian federal budget process has evolved. The main focus of the chapter was a discussion of the current process used by the government - the Expenditure Management System (EMS). This included a brief discussion that highlighted changes that are underway for the financial management system and then the chapter concluded with a very short discussion of how Defence fits into the overall fiscal framework in order to set the state for a more detailed discussion of the defence budget in the next chapter.

End Notes

1.   For a detailed discussion of the economic environment in the early 1960s see Fetterly, Ross, "The Influence of the Environment on the 1964 Defence White Paper" *Canadian Military Journal* 5:4:47-54. (Winter 2004 - 2005) http://www.journal.forces.gc.ca/engraph/vol5/no4/PDF/CMJ-5-4-08_e.pdf accessed 21 February 2007.

2.   The concept of PPBS was taken from the United States where then Secretary of Defence Robert Macnamara was implementing PPBS within the defence department in order to provide better program analysis for decision making. For a detailed discussion of PPBS see Lyden, Freemont J. and Miller, Earnest G., *Planning, Programming, Budgeting, A Systems Approach to Management* (Cambridge: Harvard University Press, 1967), 38. PPB is also discussed in detail at Chapter 5 of Lee, Jr., Robert D. and Johnson, Ronald W., Public Budgeting Systems 3rd ed. (Baltimore: University Park Press, 1983).

3.   For a more detailed discussion of the problems with PEMS see Savoie, Donald, *The Politics of Public Spending in Canada* (Toronto: University of Toronto Press, 1990).

4.   Treasury Board, *The New Expenditure Management System* (Ottawa: Treasury Board, 1995).

5.   Prime Minister's Office, *Accountable Government: A Guide for Ministers* (Ottawa: Prime Minister's Office, 2006). http://www.pm.gc.ca/grfx/docs/guide_e.pdf accessed 21 February 2007.

6.   Department of Finance, *Advantage Canada: Building a Strong Economy for Canadians* (Ottawa: Department of Finance, 2006). http://www.fin.gc.ca/ec2006/pdf/plane.pdf accessed 21 February 2007.

7.   Auditor General, *November 2006 Report Chapter 1 – Expenditure Management Report at the Government Centre* (Ottawa: Auditor General of Canada, 2006) http://www.oag-bvg.gc.ca/domino/reports.nsf/html/20061101ce.html/$file/20061101ce.pdf accessed 20 February 2007.

8. Treasury Board, *The Expenditure Management System of the Government of Canada* (Ottawa: Treasury Board, 1995) http://www.tbs-sct.gc.ca/pubs_pol/opepubs/TB_H/EXMA_e.asp accessed 8 September 2006.

9. Treasury Board, *Backgrounder – The Estimates Process* (Ottawa: Treasury Board Secretariat, 2006) http://publiservice.tbs-sct.gc.ca/media/nr-cp/2005/1027b_e.asp accessed 8 September 2006.

10. Dupuis, Jean, ***Appropriations and the Business of Supply*** (Ottawa: Library of Parliament – Parliamentary Research Branch, 2004), 11. http://www.parl.gc.ca/information/library/PRBpubs/prb0405-e.pdf accessed 22 February 2007.

11. Department of Finance, 2006–2007 Estimates Parts I and II: *The Government Expense Plan and The Main Estimates* (Ottawa: Department of Finance, 2006), 1-24 and 1-25. http://www.tbs-sct.gc.ca/est-pre/20062007/me-bd/docs/ME-001_e.pdf accessed 24 February 2007.

12. *Ibid.*, 1-24.

13. Treasury Board, *Annual Reference Level Update (ARLU) System – User Guide* (Ottawa: Treasury Board Secretariat, 2006). http://www.tbs-sct.gc.ca/emis-sigd/ARLU/guide/ME-001_e.pdf accessed 21 February 2007.

14. The reader should be aware that the actual department in government is called the Treasury Board Secretariate. Treasury Board is a Cabinet committee of Ministers of government. At the time of writing, the Treasury Board consisted of the President of the Treasury Board Secretariate as Chair, the Minister of Finance as Vice-Chair and the Ministers of Foreign Affairs, National Revenue, Industry, and Public Works and Government Services Canada as members.

15. Grady, Patrick and Richard W. Phidd, *Budget Envelopes, Policy Making and Accountability* – Discussion Paper 93-16 (Ottawa: Economic Council of Canada, 1993), 101.

16. Peters, B. Guy, *Managing Horizontal Government: The Politics of Coordination* Research Paper No. 21 (Ottawa: Canadian Centre for Management Development, 1998). http://www.myschool-monecole.gc.ca/Research/publications/pdfs/p78.pdf accessed 21 February 2007.

17. Treasury Board, *Results for Canadians: A Management Framework for the Government of Canada* (Ottawa: Treasury Board Secretariat, 2000). http://www.tbs-sct.gc.ca/report/res_can/rc_e_pdf.pdf accessed 21 February 2007.

18. See Treasury Board, *Management Accountability Framework* (Ottawa: Treasury Board Secretariat, 2003). http://www.tbs-sct.gc.ca/maf-crg/documents/booklet-livret/booklet-livret_e.pdf accessed 21 February 2007; Privy Council Office, *Governing Responsibly: A Guide for Ministers and Ministers of State* (Ottawa: Privy Council Office, 2004). http://www.pco-bcp.gc.ca/docs/Publications/guidemin/guidemin_e.pdf accessed 21 February 2007; Treasury Board, *Strengthening Public Sector Management: An Overview of the Government Action Plan and Key Initiatives* (Ottawa: Treasury Board Secretariat, 2004). http://

www.tbs-sct.gc.ca/spsm-rgsp/spsm-rgsp_e.pdf accessed 21 February 2007;
and Treasury Board, *Management in the Government of Canada: A Commitment
to Continuous Improvement* (Ottawa: Treasury Board Secretariat, 2005). http://
www.tbs-sct.gc.ca/spsm-rgsp/cci-acg/cci-acg_e.pdf accessed 21 February
2007.

19. Department of Justice, *The Financial Administration Act* (Ottawa: Department
    of Justice, 1985). http://laws.justice.gc.ca/en/F-11/ accessed 21 February
    2007.

20. Department of Justice, *The Financial Administration Act* (Ottawa: Department
    of Justice, 2007). http://laws.justice.gc.ca/en/ShowFullDoc/cs/F-11///en ac-
    cessed 19 February 2007.

21. See Treasury Board, *Report of the Independent Review Panel on Modernization
    of Comptrollership in the Government of Canada* (Ottawa: Treasury Board Sec-
    retariat, 1997). http://www.tbs-sct.gc.ca/cmo_mfc/resources2/review_panel/
    report_e.pdf accessed 21 February 2007 and Treasury Board, *Modern Comp-
    trollership: The Foundations of Modern Management* (Ottawa: Treasury Board
    Secretariat, 2003). http://www.tbs-sct.gc.ca/cmo_mfc/resources2/founda-
    tions/MC_e.pdf accessed 21 February 2007.

22. Aucoin, Peter and Savoie, Mark D., *Modernizing Government Accountability:
    A Framework for Reform* (Ottawa: Canada School of Public Service, 2005).
    http://www.myschool-monecole.gc.ca/Research/publications/pdfs/p131_
    e.pdf accessed 22 February 2007.

23. Privy Council Office, *Guidance for Deputy Ministers* (Ottawa: Privy Council
    Office, 2006). http://www.pco-bcp.gc.ca/default.asp?Page=Publications&La
    nguage=E&doc=gdm-gsm/gdm-gsm_doc_e.htm#TOC2_2 accessed 22 Feb-
    ruary 2007.

24. Prime Minister's Office, *Accountable Government: A Guide for Ministers* (Ot-
    tawa: Prime Minister's Office, 2006). http://www.pm.gc.ca/grfx/docs/guide_
    e.pdf accessed 21 February 2007.

25. Library of Parliament, *Legislative Summary – LS-522E – Bill C-2: The Federal
    Accountability Act* (Ottawa: Parliamentary Information and Research Service,
    2006), 1. The Act is available on-line at http://www2.parl.gc.ca/HousePubli-
    cations/Publication.aspx?DocId=2614169&Language=e&Mode=1 accessed
    19 February 2007.

26. Department of Finance, *The Budget Plan 2006: Focusing on Priorities* (Ottawa:
    Department of Finance, 2006) page162. http://www.fin.gc.ca/budget06/pdf/
    bp2006e.pdf accessed 21 February 2007.

27. DND, *Defence in the 70's* (Ottawa, Information Canada, 1971).

Chapter 4

BUDGETING WITHIN DEFENCE - WHO GETS WHAT

Lieutenant-Colonel Ross Fetterly

Resource management in Defence is unique and particularly challenging. This is due to the nature of the Defence environment. Within this context, management in Defence is defined as a complex, high consequence of error, capital-intensive, knowledge-dependent, national security instrument. Categorization of Defence in this manner results from the diversity of tasks assigned to the Canadian Forces (CF) and Department of National Defence (DND), the high level of technology employed within both organizations, the aggregate size of the budget, and the significant capital component within that budget. As a consequence, the critical elements necessary to effectively manage defence activities require significant financial resources; therefore, defence funding is a critical enabler in the generation and sustainment of military forces.

Complicating defence management, however, is that "there are no objective measures of defence output."[1] Thus, the value of output produced by defence is difficult to determine, as is the optimal aggregate funding level. Indeed, in the 1971 Defence White Paper, the government stated, "there is no obvious level for defence expenditures in Canada."[2] The challenge in Defence, therefore, is to achieve the maximum military capability within a defined defence budget. Thus, a thorough understanding of the defence budget is essential for the effective administration and management of defence resources. This chapter will outline how the defence budget in Canada is managed within DND.

The chapter begins with a discussion of defence funding from the end of the Cold War and then considers the three primary budget expenditure categories: Personnel, Capital and Operations & Maintenance (O&M). Next, the chapter will outline a number of defence resource management tools that are used within DND to manage the budget allocation and then the chapter will conclude with a discussion of important medium to long-term financial issues regarding the defence budget.

Defence Funding from the end of the Cold War

The period 1992-93 through 2005-06 was a time of significant transition for the Canadian federal government. Annual revenues increased from $120.3B to an estimated $200.4B, whereas expenditures rose from $159.3B to $196.4B and, as indicated in the previous chapter, were expected to be in the area of $223B in 2006-07. More importantly, the persistent budgetary deficit from the 1980s and early 1990s was eliminated in 1997-98. The elimination of the deficit required significant permanent reductions to government programs and spending.

Figure 4.1 compares changes in terms of real growth to defence and to all other government operating budgets excluding defence from 1993-94 through to 2004-05. As shown in the figure, defence funding was particularly affected with deeper and more significant funding reductions than other government departments. Whereas by 1999-2000 the rest of government had recovered to their effective level of expenditure before the funding reductions, DND had yet to fully recover by 2005-06. Indeed, despite budget increases announced in Budget 2005 and 2006, DND will only return to a 1990-level of real purchasing power in 2008-09. It is noteworthy that DND contributed $10.8B to federal government spending reductions of $38.9B during the period 1994-95 through to 1998-99, which represented 28% of overall Program Review I and II reductions.

Figure 4.1: Federal Government Operating total less Transfers and Public Debt Charges Real Growth Index FY 1993-94 = 100 (Public Account Basis)

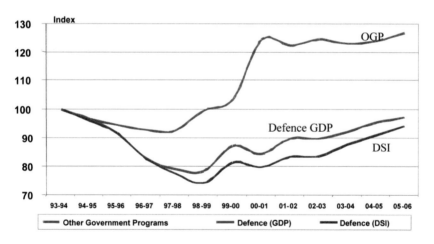

The Financial Challenge: the Legacy of Historical Spending on Defence

The historical legacy of defence funding in Canada, combined with the current international strategic environment, constrains the ability of the department and the government to move forward to address a number of pressing issues in defence. In the mid-1990s, Program Review reductions in defence resulted in a 30% cutback in purchasing power as well as a steep drop in the number of personnel. Concurrently, both the number and intensity of Canadian Forces operations increased. The impact has been that the Canadian Forces has undertaken three times more missions since the end of the Cold War than during the Cold War, while considerable numbers of military personnel have deployed in numerous missions for lengthy periods of time. In addition, Canadian Forces personnel have had to face higher intensity conflicts, the effects of global terrorism and other related changes. Despite this increased operational tempo, funding for investment in new Capital equipment and maintenance of defence infrastructure has declined appreciably. Specifically, the percentage of the defence budget allocated to Capital expenditure dropped from a high point of 29% in 1984-85 to just over 15% two decades later in 2005-06. In addition, DND was not able to achieve expected savings from base closures, previous personnel reductions or procurement reform. Compounding these numerous challenges, the cost and sophistication of new generation military equipment continues to increase, hampering Canadian efforts to maintain technological relevance with close allies. As a consequence of these disparate, but integrated factors, DND is facing a difficult bow-wave of indispensable capital investments over the upcoming decade, as well as growing maintenance costs for existing equipment.

The Composition of the Defence Budget

The defence budget is the end result of a lengthy decision-making process and, in effect, is the operationalization of defence policy. Defence budget allocations can be summarized in the following manner:

> Deciding on budget allocations is the heart of defense policy making. It is in the allocation of defense budgets where force structures and force capabilities are ultimately selected and made feasible. In many ways, then, allocation decisions are as important as deciding on the total level of defense spending itself.[3]

The defence budget is unique within the federal system not only due to its purpose and size, but also most notably due to its composition. As demonstrated by Figure 4.2, DND spending in several influential federal expenditure categories dominates the outlays in a number of central standard objects. In this case, the term standard object identifies the nature of expenditures that are made and provides a consistent format in departmental reports to Parliament. In terms of goods and services procured and personnel employed, DND spends a considerable percentage of overall federal operating and capital funds. This is significant because this category of expenditure is highly visible, generates employment, and to a certain extent is discretionary; accordingly these expenditures are particularly vulnerable to spending cuts during periods of budgetary expenditure retrenchment.

Figure 4.2: Defence Share of Federal Expenditure by Standard Object (2006-07 Estimates)

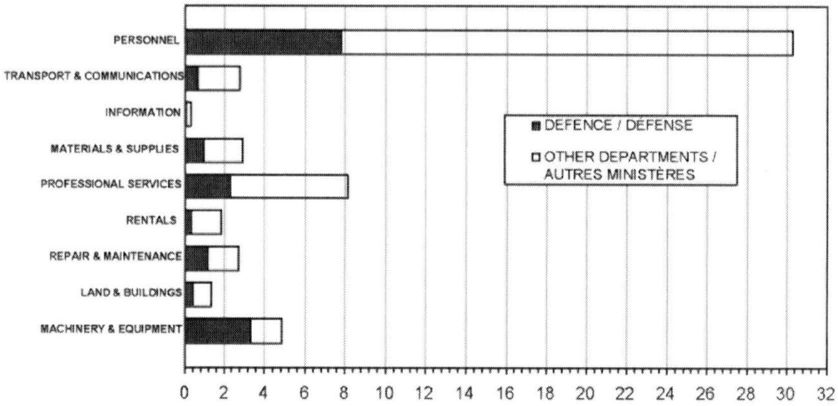

SOURCE: GOVERNMENT OF CANADA ESTIMATES 2007-2008: PART II – MAIN ESTIMATES

The most significant category in terms of total dollar value is personnel. Defence currently accounts for 26% of federal expenditures on personnel, and this percentage is expected to increase in the coming years due to the planned expansion of the Regular Force and the Reserves, together with growth of numbers of public servants in DND to support the military expansion. The other noteworthy expenditure is spending on machinery and equipment by DND which totals 69% of federal expenditure in this category. Also significant is the extensive defence inventory of weapon systems and equipment holdings. Maintaining this DND inventory accounts for 42% of total government spending on repair and maintenance. Within DND, these expenditures are highly correlated to age of the equipment, their activity rate and operating environment.[4] This is now particularly relevant for the Canadian Forces with a commitment of a battle group in Afghanistan through to at least 2011. Defence expenditure on professional services accounts for approximately 28% of federal expenditures on services. This is as a result of the high level of technology employed in defence, the complexity inherent in Western military establishments, and the need for the Canadian Forces to remain current in a diversity of fields in a dynamic international strategic environment.

The Department of National Defence is also one of the largest owners of capital assets in Canada. Table 4.1 lists the major categories of assets held by DND. This capital asset base of $51.0B is distinguished by ownership of maritime vessels valued at $12.7B, aircraft at $12.3B, and military vehicles at $1.3B. In addition, under the category of machinery and equipment, the inventory of arms and weapons amounted to $4.9B, and informatics hardware and software were held at a cost of $4.0B. These assets demonstrate the focus of the Canadian defence establishment. Specifically, the weapon systems they use, and the armaments that support these weapons, together with the information systems that allow the Canadian Forces to communicate and process vast sums of data. Finally, the importance of a strong Capital equipment and infrastructure program is emphasized by the $4.4B in work in progress.

Table 4.1: Department of National Defence Capital Assets March 31, 2007

Asset Category	Value	Value
Land Buildings and Works		$7,331,705,000
Machinery and Equipment		$10,933,379,000
Ships, Aircraft and Vehicles		
Ships and Boats	$12,743,879,000	
Aircraft	$12,296,194,000	
Non-military motor Vehicles	$555,285,000	
Military Vehicles	$1,333,978,000	
Other Vehicles	$160,151,000	
Total Ships, Aircraft and Vehicles		$27,089,487,000
Leasehold Improvements		$14,541,000
Leased Tangible Capital Assets		$1,264,751,000
Work in Progress		$4,373,359,000
Total Capital Assets		$51,007,222,000

Source: DND, Departmental Financial Statements 2006-07 (Ottawa: Department of National Defence, 2007), 16.

Categories of Defence Expenditure

Defence expenditure can be divided into the three main categories of Personnel, Operations and Maintenance (O&M) and Capital. Figure 4.3 illustrates the division of funds between these categories in 2007-08. As shown in the figure, Personnel expenditures account for 39% of defence expenditure and include pay, allowances and benefits. Military forces are first and foremost a people business, and therefore personnel related costs tend to dominate defence budget costs. Nevertheless, as in any employment, the government must compensate military personnel adequately in order to attract and retain top quality personnel.

Figure 4.3: Department of National Defence Estimates Breakdown by Category FY 2006-07 Main Estimates - $14.8 Billion

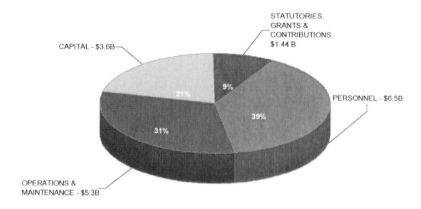

Source. Main Estimates 2007-08 and Director Budget 4

Closely linked to personnel costs are the O&M expenditures, which account for 31% of defence expenditures. This includes the cost of operating and maintaining equipment and facilities, as well as the cost of deployed operations, routine missions and exercises. Operations and Maintenance expenditures are critical to the ongoing day-to-day operations of the Canadian Forces. In this regard, O&M costs are directly correlated with both personnel and Capital. The greater the number of personnel in uniform and the higher the operational tempo, the more O&M expenditures will be incurred. Similarly, the higher the quantity and age of weapon systems, the greater impact they will have on pressures for augmentation of O&M budgets. The final category is Capital, which accounts for 21% of the defence budget.[5] Capital expenditures are a critical element of defence budgets, as this expenditure is used to purchase new equipment for the armed forces, in addition to both replacing old equipment and providing new capabilities.

Personnel Costs

Personnel costs, at 39% of the defence budget are both the most significant and the least flexible expenditure category. Indeed, the number of personnel in uniform drives much of the remaining defence spending. Consequently, the preliminary, and most significant step in the defence decision-making process is the determination of the required number of Canadian military personnel. Forecasted Army, Navy and Air Force personnel levels, to a large extent, guide the force planning process. The requirement for military bases, quantities of military equipment, training facilities, as well as operations and maintenance expenses all flow from decisions regarding personnel strengths. Cost to government for military personnel includes direct pay, environmental and operational allowances, and the employer share of programs such as pensions and Employment Insurance. In 2007-08, the average cost of the salary and benefits of a member of the Regular Force is $98,921.[6]

The ability to adjust the level of personnel in uniform is a fundamental economic, social and strategic tool of the national government. Decreases of significant numbers of military personnel can result in significant long-term budgetary savings, however, short-term costs related to personnel severance packages, as well as reductions in infrastructure and equipment can be considerable. Conversely, increases in personnel strengths have both immediate and long-term consequences. First, although the salary costs of new recruits are relatively minimal, training and accommodation costs are significant and immediate.

From a long-term perspective, spikes or troughs in military manning levels will reverberate through the personnel system and result in subsequent necessary changes to recruitment levels and the level of career training needed as either increased or decreased cohorts move through military careers. In the mid-1990s, the Canadian Forces declined from a high of approximately 83,000 full-time personnel to a steady state 60,000 full-time personnel, as a key component of government efforts to eliminate the persistent budgetary deficit. In the middle of the first decade of the 21st Century the government, in response to demands for military personnel resulting from deployed operations, initially planned and funded growth of full-time military personnel to 65,000, with plans for further growth by 10,000 personnel announced in 2006.[7] Changes in staffing levels since 1994 will have three distinct budgetary impacts for the Canadian Forces over the next decade. The first impact is the follow-on effect of the Forces Reduction Program (FRP) of the mid-1990s.[8] This rapid down-sizing of the Canadian Forces resulted in a significant number of personnel with less than ten years service accepting a buyout package and leaving the military, as well as minimal recruitment through to the end of the decade, resulting in a significant gap in 2008 from the optimal personnel numbers with eight to 16 years experience. The second effect is that recruiting ramped up early in the first decade of the 21st Century in an effort to minimize the future effect of large numbers of personnel entering retirement age. This has now created a surplus of personnel with 1-5 years of service to counter the shortage of military personnel in the later cohort. The cost of funding approximately two thousand personnel in training above the ceiling of 60,000 was absorbed within the defence budget baseline funding during that period. Third, total full-time military personnel passed 65,000 in 2006, and personnel growth in the second of three tranches of 5,000 personnel increases is now underway. Increases in the number of military personnel will also have associated costs to operations and maintenance budgets, as well as the defence Capital equipment program.

In addition to the quantity of uniformed personnel affecting the size of the personnel budget, the quality of personnel employed also has a significant impact. Changes in the quality of combat soldiers, air crew and sailors, combined with the vast numbers of military technicians and tradesmen required in a modern, technology based, military force shifts over time. Indeed, the demands on military personnel in the digitized battlefield, as well as in asymmetric warfare have never been greater. Adjustments to the rank structure and classification system, in addition to the Army, Navy, and Air Force environmental balance can also radically influence costs over the long-term.

Notwithstanding quantitative and qualitative changes that may occur to Canadian Forces personnel, the forecasted decline in numbers of young Canadians in the future is perhaps the most important human resource issue facing the military. The economical consequence of a declining pool of recruits combined with a constant, or increasing, demand for new personnel is likely to be pressure for increased benefits for Canadian Forces personnel in order to attract and retain personnel in the future. Finally, the intense and sustained activity rate of the Canadian Forces has resulted in the partial reversal in the long-term trend towards substitution of capital for labour. Combat operations in a high intensity environment place a premium on technology. Conversely, in peacekeeping operations, trained and experienced soldiers in sufficient numbers have a critical impact on the mission.[9] This recognition of the increased importance of military personnel as a necessary resource available to national governments is reflected in the growing number of Canadian Forces personnel.

OPERATIONS AND MAINTENANCE COSTS

The end of the Cold War was projected to herald a new international era of peace and stability. The loosening of constraints held in check for decades by the Cold War, however, unleashed a number of different ethnic, nationalistic and resource based confrontations. Defence forces and budgets, cut at the end of the Cold War as part of a much welcomed peace dividend, were left to cope with a much higher operational tempo, as evident from the repeated peacekeeping and peace-making operations to which they were assigned. The Canadian peacekeeping deployments that followed were numerous, and destinations included Bosnia-Herzegovina, Somalia, Haiti, and East Timor. The shift to deployed operations was significant. The transition of the long-standing threat of confrontation between the North Atlantic Treaty Organisation (NATO) and the Warsaw Pact to the new defence paradigm of multiple, simultaneous small conflicts, disbursed worldwide, has been a difficult adjustment for military forces. Military supply chains have been stretched to the limits of their capability by the significant distances deployed operations are from home countries. The inhospitable climate and austere locations of many deployed bases have increased national support requirements. The result of the changed type of operations that military forces are now encountering, and the sustained high operational tempo they are maintaining, is that Operations and Maintenance (O&M) budgets have come under intense and sustained pressure.[10] An excess of operational demands on available resources, combined with a limited defence budget to accommodate this surge of demand, has resulted in a continuing sustainability problem for Western defence forces.

Sustainment of the Canadian Forces (CF) has been a recurring theme in Canadian Defence policy since the 1964 *White Paper on Defence*, which was a government response to rapidly escalating defence costs. The 1987 White Paper *Challenge and Commitment* termed the sustainability problem as one of "rust out". In the next decade, the 1994 White paper sharply reduced personnel and infrastructure, in an attempt to bring capabilities in line with affordable resources. The high operational tempo of the smaller Canadian Forces in the decade following the 1994 White Paper again brought prominent attention to sustainment. Consequently, in Budget 2003, defence spending was increased by $800M annually. The Chief of the Defence Staff (CDS) subsequently stated, "with this increase in funding, our sustainability gap can be nearly eliminated."[10] However, funding pressures resulting from deployed operations, aging equipment and infrastructure have continued to hamper attempts to ensure the Defence Services Program (DSP) is sustainable.[11] Budget 2005 recognized the continued sustainability problems. While noting the expanding demands of deployed operations, the government acknowledged, "supplies of spare parts and military equipment have been depleted, and repairs, overhauls and upgrading of equipment have been delayed or missed to support the high operational demands."[12] The government response to this significant pressure resulting from a continuing series of demanding Canadian Forces operations was to increase sustainment funding by a total of $3.220 billion over five years, starting in 2005-06.[13] This was followed by Budget 2006, which increased investment in base infrastructure.[14]

The distribution of Operations and Maintenance expenditures in 2005-06 is presented in Figure 4.4. Equipment and services are the two main categories, with utilities, materials and supplies, as well as transportation and communications as additional significant expenditure categories. Miscellaneous expenditures and facilities are the two remaining categories.

EQUIPMENT LIFE CYCLES AND DEMAND FOR OPERATIONS AND MAINTENANCE FUNDING

Effective management of defence resources requires a focused, long-term strategy. This is particularly relevant for major equipment. The conundrum is that a multitude of immediate and short-term demands divert the attention of senior DND/CF management from long-term issues. One mitigating factor is that the capital stock of equipment and infrastructure within defence only changes marginally from year to year. However, decisions made in the current year have long-term effects on capital stocks.

Figure 4.4: Department of National Defence Gross Operations and Maintenance Estimates FY 2006-07 Main Estimates - $5.5 billion

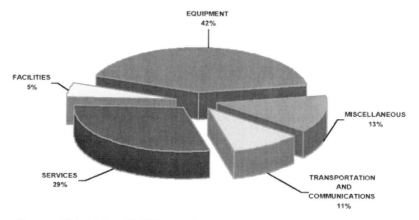

Source: Department of National Defence 2007-2008 Report on Plans and
Priorities and Director Budget 4

A long-term approach to defence decisions is necessarily prominent in decisions regarding the purchase of major weapon systems. Once a decision is made, defence departments incur some research and development costs, and then the multi-million dollar purchase cost is incurred over a short number of years during the trial and delivery
phase. The in-service period for the equipment is the longest phase and can result in
costly requirements for operating and maintenance funding. Finally, there could be
some disposal costs at the end of the useful life of the equipment. This equipment life
cycle is illustrated in Figure 4.5. Costs incurred during the procurement phase are
funded through the capital element of the defence budget. The in-service costs for the
equipment funded through the defence budget are derived from the operations and
maintenance element of the budget. This chart, however, does not include the costs of
upgrading the equipment during the life-cycle, which may occur at single or multiple
times during the use of that equipment. This is dependent on the type of equipment,
level of technological change, and funding available for upgrades.

Figure 4.5: Weapon System Life Cycle Costs

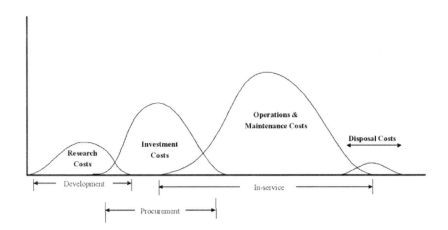

The increasing average age of major Canadian Forces weapon systems will drive the operating cost of those systems, as they approach the peak of the in-service cycle. The increasing cost of operating aging equipment can be estimated fairly accurately for items such as spare parts requirements and DND/CF labour costs. Maintenance and supply personnel have several decades of data on these systems, and they can forecast requirements effectively, based on projected activity levels. The risk of operating older equipment, longer than previous generations, however, is less quantifiable. Other factors, including spare part shortages due to manufacturers closing obsolete production lines and industry consolidation of repair and overhaul facilities, can also significantly affect costs unexpectedly.[15] Furthermore, as military equipment ages, the effects of fatigue and corrosion are both important workload and cost considerations.[16]

A key element of O&M spending is the National Procurement budget (NP), which accounts for approximately forty% of O&M expenditures. The National Procurement budget of the Department of National Defence has recently emerged from obscurity, where it remained for much of the Cold War, to being viewed by defence planners as an increasingly critical element in defence resource allocation. The two main reasons for this re-emergence are the current Post-Cold War strategic environment and the recurring theme of Canadian Forces sustainability.

The National Procurement budget provides a wide variety of support services that allows the CF equipment to function while on deployed operations, during training or in support to Canadians during natural disasters. The National Procurement budget is a consolidated and centralized budget, managed by specialists, which acquires materiel and/or services necessary to support existing equipment, or systems, that are administered centrally. This wide-ranging responsibility includes procurement of spare parts and contracting for such services such as maintenance, repair and overhaul contracts or technical support.[17]

National Procurement in fiscal year 2005-06 funded a wide variety of activities. The distinguishing feature of the National Procurement budget is the support provided throughout the Canadian Forces and Department of National Defence. Consequently, it is important to understand the pervasive influence of NP funding. This funding includes equipment life extension programs, spare parts for major capital equipment, repair and overhaul expenditures for weapon systems, maintenance services and commercial freight. Furthermore, soldiers, sailors and air personnel receive environmental clothing funded by the National Procurement program, and the ammunition they use on training, exercises, or operations is all procured by National Procurement funding. Figure 4.6 shows the diversity of organizations funded through the approximately $1.9 billion central National Procurement budget. The Air Force, a capital-intensive activity, absorbed the largest share. Naval and Army expenditures were also significant. Land and J4 (Logistics) materiel common categories supply materiel to all environments. The Director General Materiel Systems and Supply Chain (DGMSSC) provides management support to the materiel acquisition and support framework, thereby optimizing the delivery of materiel and operational support to Canadian Forces operations and departmental activities.

Figure 4.6: 2005-06 National Procurement Expenditure

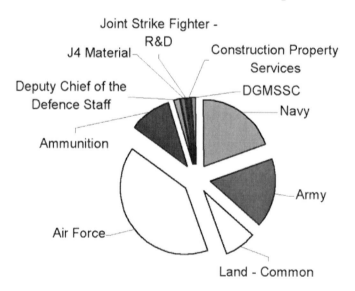

Items procured through National Procurement have several common characteristics. The first characteristic of National Procurement funding is that of an enabler, which provides personnel with the environmental clothing required, and their equipment in an operationally ready state. The second characteristic of National Procurement is immediacy. Without sufficient National Procurement funding, equipment availability degrades over time, and defence capabilities decline. The effect of insufficient National Procurement funding in a single fiscal year is different, depending on the category of expenditure. For example, repair and overhaul of armoured personnel carriers can be delayed for a year or two, but significant long-term effects quickly become evident if refurbishment is delayed indefinitely. Conversely, the ability of the National Procurement program to absorb significant incremental funding in one fiscal year is also limited. For example, additional funding provided to upgrade a specific aircraft fleet requires several years to plan, design, and to schedule instalment of new systems in all fleet aircraft. The third characteristic is the lack of attention National Procurement expenditure receives in the media and with the Canadian public. In large part, this is due to the level of detail and knowledge required in order to understand the complex relationships inherent in defence management. Furthermore, National Procurement is not highlighted in either the DND Report on Plans and Priorities (RPP) or the Departmental Performance Report (DPR), both of which are published on an annual basis.

Figure 4.7 illustrates the demand and the expenditure for National Procurement for the past 15 years.[18] The chart is in Budget Year (BY) dollars, which applies DND Economic Model "Escalation Factors (EFs) to constant dollar cash flows."[19] The chart demonstrates the widening gap between demand for National Procurement funding and actual funds available prior to Budget 2006. The funding gap between demand and budget allocations creates a cumulative negative impact over time, which if left unchecked only increases the risk of catastrophic effects, concurrently with increased sustainability pressures. Demand is measured by requests by Army, Navy and Air Force Commanders, as well as the Commanders of Canada Command, CEFCOM, CANSOFCOM and CANOSCOM in their annual business plans. The recent growth in National Procurement demand has been exceptional with overall growth of National Procurement increasing by 25% between 2001-02 and 2005-06. The major factors responsible for this significant growth have been the addition of corporate information technology and information management, joint operations support requirements, deferred maintenance on major surface vessels and increased costs for Command, Control, Computers, Communications (C4), Intelligence, Surveillance, and Reconnaissance (C4ISR) systems. Increased defence funding announced in Budgets 2005 and 2006 will mitigate some of the existing National Procurement funding pressures. Work is also in progress at National Defence Headquarters to prioritize and rationalize existing National Procurement demand.

Figure 4.7: National Procurement Expenditure 1990-2006

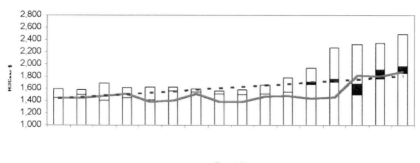

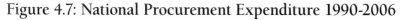

Over the period from 1996 to 2006, National Procurement has gradually increased from 12% of total annual defence funding to 14%. This trend reflects continued O&M pressures on the defence budget and can be viewed as a microcosm of changes occurring overall within the budget. It does not, however, reflect other equally important pressures and changes to the supply system. The mid-1990s was a period of significant rationalization in the Canadian Forces Supply System (CFSS). The department and Canadian Forces made the transition from a supply system based on maintaining stocks of supplies and spare parts in warehouses, to an emphasis on procuring spare parts as required. Two central supply depots were closed and stock levels gradually declined. Although this allowed for a more cost-effective operation, the changes increased demand on the Canadian Forces Supply System for greater responsiveness in dealing with critical high-value spare parts. The nature of spare parts for major military capital equipment is that the source of supply is very limited. In fact, often the only procurement source is the original manufacturer. As a consequence, this puts a premium on forecasting future spare part requirements. Stock availability on the part of the manufacturer is also important. The absence of significant spare part inventories for Canadian Forces weapon systems means that spare parts need to be ordered when required. The Canadian Forces was able to save money as spare part inventories were drawn down in the 1990s. This source of cost savings has now largely been exhausted. Current limited National Procurement funding means that choices have to be made regarding which equipment fleets and associated spare parts take priority.

CAPITAL

Armed forces in Western countries are highly mechanized and their equipment includes state of the art technology in a number of integral systems. Advanced military equipment has a number of unique characteristics. Most important is capability. Indeed, better-equipped military forces generally do better in conflict situations than less well equipped military forces. As a result, it is generally acknowledged that "when men of equal worth fight, the side with the better weapons wins."[20] Therefore, the importance to defence planners of procuring and maintaining leading edge military equipment is paramount. Nevertheless, the considerable cost of major defence procurement programs places significant cost pressures on the capital programs, with many large projects valued at up to several billion dollars each in progress at any one point in time.[21] Although armed forces initially require well-trained and capable soldiers, sailors and air personnel, their effectiveness is multiplied by the quantity and quality of equipment available to them.

The level of defence expenditure on Capital has fluctuated significantly over the past four decades, as indicated in Figure 4.8. The periods of low capital procurement are generally followed by a significant period of recapitalization, and then back again to limited procurement. This cycle exacerbates differences in age among different weapon systems.

Figure 4.8: Percentage of the Defence Budget Spent on Capital

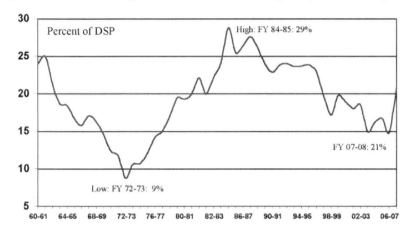

The effect of aging equipment on defence forces is significant. As equipment ages, the frequency of equipment failures increases and the cost of maintaining that equipment grows.[22] Studies in the United States have found that the time between breakdowns in US Air Force aircraft increases 1 to 7% annually, with operating and maintenance costs increasing between 1 to 3% per year.[23] Similar studies have also found that age has an impact on American Army equipment.[24] Figure 4.9 illustrates the effect of aging equipment on the Canadian Forces. The chart measures the operational effectiveness and forecasted time remaining in the life cycle of all in-service major weapon systems.

Figure 4.9: The Effect of Aging Defence Equipment

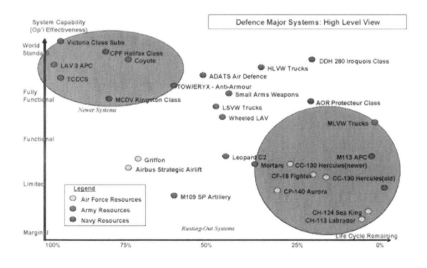

The Canadian Forces owns and maintains a massive inventory of advanced weapon systems. Equipment, once purchased, can undergo extensive use for 20 to 40 years. The high cost of new defence equipment results in a relatively small quantity of weapons purchased annually, which are then operated intensely for many years. As such, the CF equipment inventory only changes marginally each year. Consequently, the overall age of the inventory changes slowly. Conversely, decreasing the overall age of the inventory, even in times of high procurement, can also take years.[25] Governments must continually confront the dilemma of the degree of funding the current force and the future force. Current forces consist of expenditures on Personnel and O&M. These expenditures produce immediate capabilities. Conversely, Capital expenditures produce future capability. However, the benefits are not available for several years. Defence expenditures need to maintain a difficult balance between ensuring that current forces have sufficient funding to effectively conduct current operations and the procurement of military equipment in sufficient quantity and quality to ensure operations in a forecasted future international strategic environment. Defence capital programs are inherently difficult to develop and maintain due to the considerable number of competing interests and assigned tasks.[26] Furthermore, cost growth in weapon system programs is a recurring problem in Canada, as with other allied nations. A recent RAND Corporation study determined that there is a "systematic bias towards underestimating the costs and substantial uncertainty in estimating the final cost of a weapon system."[27]

In addition to large equipment holdings, the Department of National Defence is one of the most significant landowners in Canada. At the end of the 2005-06 fiscal year, the department had an inventory of land, buildings and works valued at $7.1B. As illustrated by Figure 4.10, the age profile of DND realty assets is quite distinctive and problematic. Specifically, 81% of DND realty assets were designed, constructed, or acquired in response to the First World War, the Second World War or the Cold War Threat. Based on a facility life cycle of approximately 50 years, more than half of DND realty assets will need to be rebuilt over the next decade. This will increase demands for Capital funding during a period when a significant number of weapon systems will also be nearing the end of their expected life cycle. This state of affairs of significant forecasted demand for capital replacement is now relatively common among Western military forces.[28]

Figure 4.10: Defence Realty Asset Allocation and the Purpose of Acquisition/Construction

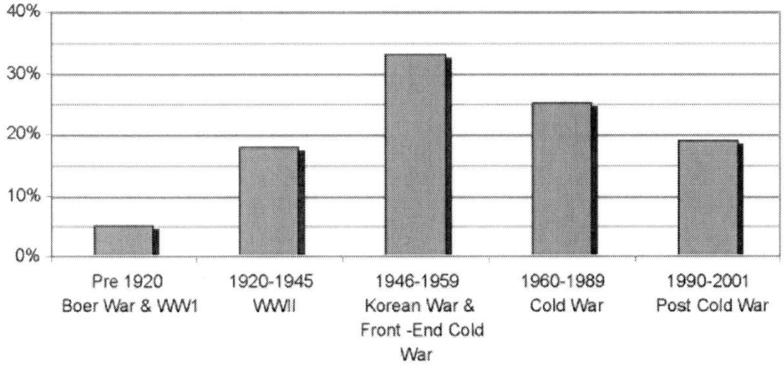

The construction of buildings has several important different characteristics from that of purchasing major weapon systems. Approval processes are largely departmental, with the Minister of National Defence authorized to approve individual construction projects under $60 million, which in essence results in the Minister normally approving most such projects. The other distinguishing feature is that the timeline from conception to construction of buildings is relatively short. Nevertheless, construction costs are very sensitive to market conditions for materials and labour.[29] Finally, although facilities are relatively easy to build, realty assets are exceptionally difficult to dispose of or rationalize.

DEFENCE SPECIFIC INFLATION

Inflation in the defence sector in Canada has been a concern of defence planners for several decades. Defence Specific Inflation (DSI) became a prominent issue in Canada in the 1950s with the rapid rise in the cost of defence equipment. The impact of the Defence Specific Inflation on the defence budget was highlighted in the August 1963 report on the defence budget by the *Ad Hoc Committee on Defence Policy*, commissioned by the Defence Minister Paul Hellyer, which found that although defence expenditure declined by 13% when measured in dollars between 1952-53 and 1962-63, it shrank by 38% when measured in purchasing power.[30] Although in subsequent decades the decline in defence purchasing was not as significant, this trend has continued. Figure 4.11 compares Defence Specific Inflation with the overall inflation in the Canadian economy between 1972 and 2007. Over this period, Defence Specific Inflation averaged 5.4% annually, whereas the GDP deflator was 4.7%. Although over a single year this decline in defence purchasing power many not be material, over a number of years the cost can be notable. Figure 4.12 compares the effect of inflation on the defence budget, in real terms, between the Consumer Price Index, GDP Deflator and Defence Specific Inflation using 1972 as a base year. Figure 4.13 portrays the accumulated difference of $2.5 billion between Defence Specific Inflation and the GDP deflator between 1972 and 2004.

Figure 4.11: Defence Specific Inflation and Gross Domestic Product Deflator (1972-2006)

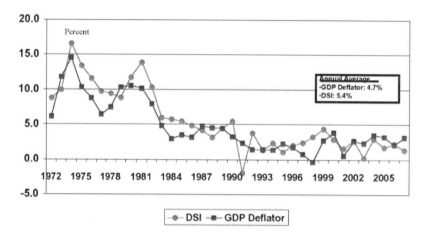

The effect of inflation on defence purchasing power is recognized by central agencies. Compensation is provided by funding for the Department of National Defence that explicitly includes an "inflation factor" to the Defence Services Program baseline funding of 1.5% on an annual basis. In addition the Department of National Defence, as with other departments, also receives compensation for public servant collective bargaining wage increases and associated compensation enhancements for military personnel. The defence basket of goods is unique within Canada. As a consequence, Defence Specific Inflation is focused on cost growth in a narrow band of goods dominated by high value limited quantity products with the federal government as the sole market, advanced technology, repair and overhaul of complex weapon systems and an intensive use of fuels. Conversely, the GDP deflator is more broadly based and inflationary effects are spread out across the Canadian economy. Note also that imports are netted out partially eliminating foreign inflation and foreign exchange impacts.

Figure 4.12: Inflation and the Defence Budget 1972-2006 (Real Defence Expenditures in $M)

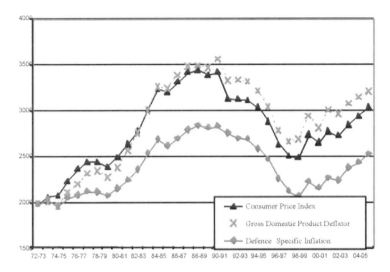

Defence Specific Inflation in Canada is based on three distinct factors. The primary factor is the understanding that national deflators such as the Gross Domestic Product (GDP) implicit index and the Department of National Defence economic model basket of goods can provide appreciably different outcomes during periods of extraordinary inflation. The second factor is an appreciation that government policies affecting defence procurement, combined with the distinctive structure of the defence market, have an impact on defence inflation. The third factor is acknowledgement by government officials and ministers that the high foreign content of defence goods purchased have a follow-on influence on the cost of defence goods resulting from both inflation in supplier countries and shifting exchange rates.[31]

Figure 4.13: DSI and GDP Deflator 1972-2006 ($Billions)

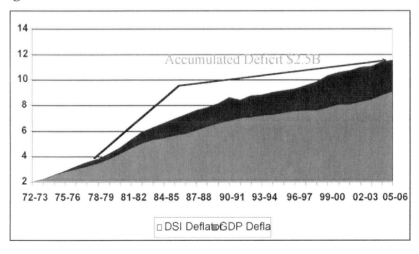

An economic model developed internally in the Department of National Defence is employed to capture the effect of inflation on a designated defence-related basket of goods.[32] This economic model is used extensively throughout the department, and is particularly influential in the planning and development of the Capital program. Specifically, estimated defence specific inflation from the DND economic model is applied against planned capital projects as a cost management and forecasting tool. The multi-year funding required for defence procurement projects places a high importance on incorporation of anticipated inflation effects.[33] Employing economic model forecasted inflation for capital projects allows the department to more accurately predict funding demands in future fiscal years.

Deployed Operations Costs

Canadian military forces are continually engaged in a wide range of activities, all of which must be supported, managed and coordinated within one national organization, spread out across several thousand kilometres and active in every province and territory. Military forces operate a variety of training institutions, engage in military operations, manage army, navy and air force equipment programs and life-cycle management, support national objectives, maintain and support infrastructure at bases and units, provide search and rescue services throughout the country and also respond to aid of the civil power requests from provincial governments. Deployed operations, then, are only one of a myriad of different, but related, defence activities.

The Department of National Defence, as with other federal government departments, falls under the Federal Expenditure Management System (EMS), and must manage budgets in accordance with federal management policies, practices and procedures. Determination of deployed operation expenditures must, therefore, be derived from the accounting system used by the Department of National Defence. However, the cost to the Department and the Canadian Forces of deployed operations does not fall along neat functional lines, or fit into convenient expenditure categories. In fact, the cost of deployed operations is derived from a wide variety of organizations that undertake activities in direct and indirect support, including personnel, materiel, training, capital and operational expenditures. In this regard, deployed operations related costs could be incurred by the Army, Navy or Air Force, Chief of Military Personnel, Assistant Deputy Minister (Materiel), Assistant Deputy Minister (Information Management), as well as the Commanders of Canadian Expeditionary Force Command (CEFCOM), Commander of Canadian Special Operations Forces Command (CANSOFCOM) and the Canadian Operational Support Command (CANOSCOM). Actual deployed operations expenditures occur at a multitude of locations and levels in both DND and the Canadian Forces. All these expenses must be accounted for separately and are charged to different budgets. The difficulty is to capture all deployed operations expenditures incurred by organizations that undertake many concurrent activities.[34] This is further complicated by activities that support both deployed operations and other defence missions simultaneously.

Deployed operations are not activities that fit uniquely into traditional army, navy or air force activities. Indeed, peacekeeping is an activity that cuts unevenly and at different rates through all major functions in defence, consuming resources and potentially utilizing thousands of military personnel for long periods of time. Although the Army, Navy and Air Force are allocated funding for certain activities, DND does not currently report deployed operations expenditures separately. The format of DND financial budgets are prepared in accordance with Treasury Board direction and have as their objective the provision of meaningful information to Parliament on defence spending in general. Clearly, the costs of deployed operations are felt throughout the Department of National Defence and Canadian Forces. As a consequence, the financial management of deployed operations costs in defence at the departmental level presents a unique challenge to senior military officers and public servants. The budgetary process to reimburse DND for incremental deployed operations in a specific fiscal year presents another distinct predicament to defence planners.

Deployed operations undertaken by the Canadian Forces are one of the most prominent activities of the Canadian military. Consequently, the cost to DND and the Canadian Forces of these international activities are of interest to the government, Canadians, and the academic community. Indeed, the Chief of Defence Staff in his 2002-03 Annual Report stated that "operations are our business and the most important and visible expression of how we make a difference and why we serve."[35] Table 4.2 provides the full and incremental deployed operations cost estimates from the end of the Cold War through to 2006-07. Peacekeeping costs exploded in 1991-92 with Canadian participation in the Gulf War, followed by a series of peacekeeping and peace support operations to conflicts in diverse areas of the world such as the Former Republic of Yugoslavia and Haiti.

Table 4.2: Deployed Operations Cost Estimates 1989-2007 ($M)

Fiscal Year	Full Cost	Incremental Cost
1989-1990	$72.1	$22.6
1990-1991	$68.6	$21.4
1991-1992	$773.6	$159.0
1992-1993	$643.6	$255.4
1993-1994	$698.0	$231.0
1994-1995	$738.0	$211.0
1995-1996	$697.0	$218.0
1996-1997	$494.9	$147.1
1997-1998	$482.0	$138.3
1998-1999	$639.5	$148.9
1999-2000	$1,418.2	$390.2
2000-2001	$924.6	$266.3
2001-2002	$1,181.0	$391.9
2002-2003	$1,224.6	$425.6
2003-2004	$1,704.6	$829.9
2004-2005	$927.2	$396.3
2005-2006	$1,526.1	$656.2
2006-2007	$2,003.5	$833.9
Total	$15,950.5	$5,608.1

Source: DND, Peacekeeping and Humanitarian Cost Estimates 1989-1990 to 2005-06 (Ottawa: Assistant Deputy Minister (Finance and Corporate Services), 2006

Figure 4.14 shows both the significant annual variation in the number of troops deployed and the changing geographical locations of deployments. Despite the short timeframe, deployed operations were first deployed in response to the Post-Cold War strategic environment and then in response to the asymmetrical threat of terrorists.[36] With the increase of the size of the Canadian contingent in Afghanistan to approximately 2,500 in late 2006, deployed operations expenditures can be expected to remain high through to the end of the current mandate in 2011.

Figure 4.14: Personnel Deployed on International Operations Since 1980

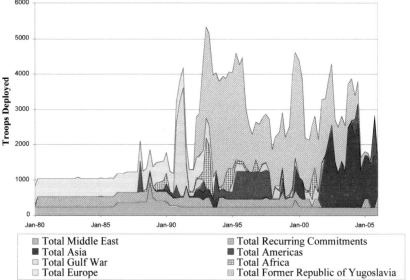

The costs associated with deployed operations as illustrated in Table 4.2 are significant, yet are not explicitly captured or analyzed for their long-term impact on the defence budget. In particular, the increased use of vehicles and equipment on deployed operations has a follow-on inflationary influence on subsequent requirements for spare parts, repair and overhaul, and the timing of equipment replacement programs. In essence, the cumulative effect of the decade-long high level of deployed operations will impact the near term defence budget. The negative impact of these pressures will be felt in capital, as well as, operations and maintenance budgets for the next fifteen years. In effect, the entire length of the long-term capital program. The impacts need to be understood, their influence recognized and problems addressed within the defence-funding envelope. As with equipment, the high participation of military personnel in deployed operations has brought increased costs that will be felt over the next ten to fifteen years. Specifically, illnesses such as Post-Traumatic Stress Syndrome, or diseases such as malaria, and other medical problems resulting from the conditions under which military personnel have served outside Canada will result in increased medical and disability costs to the department.

The medium-term cost to DND from the Afghanistan mission will be significant. In addition to the unfortunate death and injury to soldiers, the damage and destruction of high-value vehicles and equipment, as well as the intense daily use of all vehicles in an austere and difficult environment, will place additional demands on the defence budget. DND will have the difficult task in upcoming years of planning and funding the repair and overhaul of equipment in use in Afghanistan in a demanding combat environment, as well as the replacement of unsalvageable equipment. For example, a recent American study on the US Marine Corps in Iraq concluded that Marine Corps "equipment is used at as much as nine times its planned rate, abused by a harsh environment, and depleted due to losses in combat."[37] Although the situation of the Canadian Forces in Afghanistan and the US Marine Corps in Iraq have numerous significant differences, the report does point out the importance of recognizing and addressing the long-term equipment effects of military operations in a conflict situation. Future DND budgets will need to incorporate funding for repair or replacement of equipment rotated back from Afghanistan.

Managing Defence Resources Effectively

The fundamental tenets of Canadian defence management in the 1970s and 1980s are no longer valid. The well-defined Soviet threat to Western nations allowed defence planners the ability to control expenditures, in that they could actually control personnel and equipment activity rates. The result was that, excluding the impact of Defence Specific Inflation, defence managers could largely control personnel related costs, the Operations and Maintenance budget, and the capital equipment budget. However, starting in fiscal year 1990-91 the number and difficulty of deployed operations exploded, and has continued at an exceptional level through into the 21st century. The result was that these new circumstances destroyed the effectiveness of management practices that had developed over the preceding decades to control defence expenditure. The response to these changed circumstances has been a series of management initiatives that will be discussed in this section. This will include business planning, development and management of a Strategic Capability Investment Plan, modern comptrollership, the 30-year strategic costing model, the Financial Decision Support Initiative, supplementary funding, quarterly financial reviews and finally corporate over-programming.

OFFICIALS RESPONSIBLE FOR RESOURCE MANAGEMENT IN DEFENCE

In all government departments, the Deputy Minister (DM) of a department is provided with financial responsibility and accountability for that department. In Defence, the DM has delegated the responsibility for financial management of the department to the Assistant Deputy Minister (Finance and Corporate Services). In turn, the Director General Financial Management, the senior full-time finance officer, has been assigned key financial responsibilities within the department. Unique to defence is the position of Vice Chief of the Defence Staff (VCDS) and that position has the responsibility of departmental strategic resource manager. These officials, as well as other senior managers at National Defence Headquarters, work together in an integrated system of operational and managerial committees. This work culminates in the Defence Management Committee (DMC) and the Program Management Board (PMB), where decisions regarding resource allocation within DND/CF are made and the Defence Services Program managed.

Business Planning & The Strategic Capability Investment Plan

Business planning is the central unifying feature of Canadian defence management. Business planning provides defence planners with a systematic process to organize and prioritize the allocation of defence resources. Business planning fits well into the military culture because it is a results orientated cyclical activity that applies defence resources towards military operations and their related support activities. The Investment Plan is complimentary to business planning and provides a long-term framework for the Canadian defence planning process. The purpose of the Investment Plan is to provide a document that integrates the requirements needed to build Canadian Forces capabilities. This document includes annexes for major capital equipment, infrastructure, personnel, technology development and finally experimentation. Approval of an Investment Plan by the Minister of National Defence would be a significant guidance document for defence planners. Business planning in defence and the Investment Plan were discussed earlier within the context of the overall defence management system.

Modern Comptrollership

The mid-1990s was a period of significant change, distinguished by sharp funding reductions, a growing operational tempo, and increased deployments from within a smaller military force. Improved financial management in government provided an essential foundation to enable better decision-making during a period of significant transition within the federal government. The importance of modern comptrollership became evident during the examination of controls in government by an independent panel report in 1997 that resulted in the call for informed decision-making through risk identification and support for values and ethics.[38] DND was one of five departments selected to test the concept and the department embraced modern comptrollership as one key method to improve departmental processes. Modern comptrollership reinforces the management framework set out in the federal document *Results for Canadians*, which emphasizes fostering a citizen focus within government programs and services, clear public service values, responsible spending and finally habitual measurement and evaluation of program results.[39] Modern comptrollership provides for the integration of five core elements which contribute to the renewal of the functional finance chain through enhanced professional direction, effective finance community management and revitalization, training of resource managers, the Financial Information Strategy (FIS) and finally integration of financial and non-financial performance. Modern Comptrollership will remain at the forefront of management, as the trend in public sector management is to "provide long-term advice, contribute to business decisions and develop effective strategies."[40]

30-YEAR DEFENCE STRATEGIC COSTING MODEL

An economic perspective on defence views the production of defence capabilities from the perspective of constrained maximization. When provided with the combination of a given budget, defence technology base and set of cost estimates; the maximum potential military capability of a defence establishment can be approximated. This requires a process, or model, that can forecast the system-wide cost of producing military capabilities. Officials within the Vice Chief of the Defence Staff and Assistant Deputy Minister (Finance and Corporate Services) organisations began work on developing a strategic costing model in September 2005. The model, which is still under development, depicts the full, unmitigated capability demands of the entire defence enterprise across all DND/CF organisations, and compares this demand against an established fiscal planning framework to create a 30-year view.[42] Future versions of the model will be refined and used to assist in development of the Defence Capabilities Plan (DCP). The 30-Year Defence Strategic Costing Model will be used in subsequent defence planning to shape and inform program and budget decisions.

THE FINANCIAL DECISION SUPPORT INITIATIVE

The Financial Decision Support (FDS) Initiative is the foundation of a decision support system that will support management planning within DND/CF. The DND Financial and Managerial Accounting System (FMAS) is the official accounting system of the department. The focus, however, of FMAS, is to perform financial accounting and reporting. Conversely, the focus of FDS is to perform management accounting. The Financial Decision Support (FDS) Initiative is not a replacement for FMAS, but uses financial accounting data as a foundation that is then manipulated to meet management requirements. FDS will build and develop a data warehouse that will use Business Intelligence software to increase the usefulness and employability of data to management. With the availability of a data warehouse that is regularly updated, decision-makers have the capability of managing with the data they need, rather than with the data they can obtain. This data warehouse will provide DND with the means to compare financial information in a dynamic environment. In addition the data warehouse will provide DND/CF personnel with aggregated information to support strategic decisions, as well as granular information to support daily operations.

SUPPLEMENTARY FUNDING

The uncertainty in the international security environment and change brought forth by the end of the Cold War has resulted in frequent unexpected and unplanned deployments of Canadian Forces personnel during a fiscal year. The potential for large fluctuations in Canadian Forces activity levels can have significant cost implications. The incremental – and unfunded – costs of unexpected Canadian Forces deployments are submitted to the Treasury Board through the Supplementary Estimates process for reimbursement to DND, with the support of the Treasury Board Secretariat. Indeed, DND is one of the significant annual beneficiaries of the Supplementary Estimates funding process. Consequently, forecasting, tracking and reporting on the cost of incremental activities is an important managerial function at National Defence Headquarters.

The Department of National Defence and Treasury Board Secretariat have developed a professional and effective working relationship over the past decade. Prior to the end of the Cold War, Treasury Board Secretariat analysts dealt mainly with DND capital projects and other relatively stable on-going activities. Starting in 1990-91 with the dramatic growth of Canadian Forces deployed operations, Treasury Board Secretariat analysts had to react to an ongoing change in Canadian Forces deployed operations during the fiscal year. The resulting changes in activity levels at various times during the fiscal year led to the requirement for supplementary funding. From the perspective of DND, this demanded: the capability to forecast the cost of operations before deployment, the detailed cost capturing of all incremental costs, and the provision of well-documented submissions to Treasury Board Secretariat that supported requests for supplementary funding.[41] Financial management of these operations is a priority within the VCDS, CEFCOM and ADM (Fin CS) organisations. From the perspective of Treasury Board Secretariat, increased staff effort had to be devoted to monitor peacekeeping costs and to liaise with other central agencies. One positive result is that a close working relationship developed, at several levels, which ensured that both DND and Treasury Board Secretariat passed information quickly and effectively. As a consequence, both parties generally had a common understanding and agreement of incremental costs and recommended supplementary funding.

The DND funding baseline includes a threshold for incremental O&M peacekeeping expenses. Historically, "defence has been able to absorb incremental costs, net of revenues, in the order of 1.25% of annual defence funding."[42] Incremental deployed operations funding is normally only provided to DND after they exceed this threshold. When estimated costs of known deployed operations are known at the time the government tables its annual budget, these costs are generally included in the budget. Funding of incremental costs incurred on deployed operations that arise following tabling of the annual budget is generally accomplished through the federal supplementary funding process near the end of the fiscal year. As a consequence, DND must "cash manage" expenditures from within the original funding envelope allocated at the start of the fiscal year until Parliament approves the federal supplementary funding package.

The cash management of incremental deployed operations costs in a defence budget in fiscal year 2006-07 of approximately $15.5 billion could amount to several hundred million dollars.[43] Indeed, during the first three quarters of the fiscal year, defence expenditures are normally well below DND funding allocations. Nevertheless, cash management of unfunded deployed operations expenditures becomes an important consideration in the fourth quarter.

CORPORATE OVER-PROGRAMMING

Corporate over-programming in DND complements the formal business planning process. In the federal government, spending authority is allocated to departments through the budget process. Effective spending of a multi-billion dollar defence budget is a complex process. In any given year, unexpected delays may occur in the capital program, activities may be cancelled and approval of expenditure programs may be shifted to the following fiscal year. In 1997-98, DND began incorporating over-programming into the internal departmental funding allocations to the Army, Navy, Air Force, ADM (Materiel), and other senior level managers. This institutional over-programming is managed and drawn down to zero during the fiscal year to equal spending authority by the end of the fourth quarter. In effect, defence officials plan at the start of the fiscal year to spend conservatively. This management of defence resources has enabled defence planners to keep the Treasury Board approved carry-forward of unexpended funds to the next fiscal year to a minimum.

QUARTERLY FINANCIAL REVIEWS

In-depth reviews of all DND financial accounts are undertaken quarterly at National Defence Headquarters. The objective is to systematically review spending to that point in the fiscal year and then identify funding pressures, program slippage and account surpluses. The Defence Management Committee (DMC) provides oversight of this process, with funding reallocation decisions made by the Program Management Board (PMB), to realign departmental funding in order to better reflect the demands and pressures experienced by DND and the Canadian Forces. This serves three main objectives. First it ensures that senior management is kept up to date regarding the current budgetary position of the department. Second it ensures that funding is brought into line with immediate and short-term requirements. Finally it is an in-year reallocation process that systematically moves funding from lower priority activities to higher priority activities.

YEAR-END CARRY-FORWARD

Funds that are not spent in government budgets traditionally lapse at the end of the fiscal year. This has, at times, resulted in inefficient spending at year-end in order to spend the remaining funding. Consequently, in recent years, Treasury Board has permitted government departments to "carry-forward" a certain amount of current fiscal year funding to the following year, should the department anticipate that it would not be able to spend all remaining funding. The objective of the carry-forward is to foster enhanced resource management. It puts the responsibility on the department to identify spending shortfalls on a timely basis and to discuss this forecasted under expenditure with the Treasury Board Secretariat. This allows for better corporate cash management within the federal government and ensures that the department is not penalized by not spending those funds. In addition, it provides a mechanism for the department to spend an agreed carry-forward amount in the next fiscal year. This is achieved through the supplementary funding process, and the funds are distributed internally at the start of the fiscal year within the department as one element of over-programming. The ability for DND to carry-forward unexpended funding to a subsequent fiscal year is important to an organisation coping with both a high operational tempo and significant activity in the defence Capital program, where uncontrollable events, slippage and delays in approvals can occur. The authorized Treasury Board carry-forward for DND at 2005-06 year-end was $155.6 million.

Long-term issues affecting the defence budget

In order to conclude this discussion on the how defence allocated its budget within the department, it will be useful to raise three long-term issues. The first issue is the need for long-term stable funding for defence. This includes funding for a defined Capital program and also for sustainability of the Canadian Forces equipment and infrastructure. The second issue is the implementation and management of the Capital program under accrual budgeting. The third issue is the troika of the simultaneous bow-wave of capital projects, Regular and Reserve Force expansion and high tempo of deployed operations

LONG-TERM STABLE FUNDING

Defence Management must simultaneously address a myriad of short-term and long-term issues. Change comes slowly to defence, yet conversely long lead times are required to procure new or replacement equipment fleets. Consequently, long-term stable funding is a key enabler toward this process. In recent years, the federal government has contributed to medium-term stability in defence funding by projecting defence funding out five fiscal years in Budgets 2005 and 2006.

ACCRUAL BUDGETING FOR CAPITAL PROJECTS

The Department of National Defence has historically accounted for the cost of purchasing capital equipment on a cash basis. However, as part of changes within the federal government, the department has now moved to account for procurement of capital equipment on an accrual basis. This is a significant change within the department, and reflects a move to adopt accounting practices for capital assets generally used in the private sector.[44]

The federal government has historically accounted for the procurement of Capital assets on a cash basis. This accounting method records economic events when revenue is received and expenses paid. In contrast, under accrual accounting, revenue is re-corded in the fiscal period in which it is earned: regardless of when the revenue is ac-tually received. Similarly, notwithstanding whether expenses incurred in a particular fiscal period are paid or not – they are charged to that period. The general principles for the two types of accounting are shown in Table 4.3.

Table 4.3: General Principles for Accounting Methods

Cash Basis	Accrual Basis
Revenue is recorded when you receive cash	Expenses are recorded in the period when goods or services are consumed
Expenses are deducted when they are paid	Revenues are recorded in the period when they are earned
	Capital assets are recognized by being expensed (amortized) over the time they are expected to be used

The Financial Information Strategy (FIS), which was initiated in 1989 and re-launched in 1995, "aims to modernize federal government accounting by bringing it in line with practices in the private sector and in other public sector jurisdictions. Among other things, its full implementation would see the costs of programs linked to the results, giving government managers better financial information to use in making day-to-day decisions."[47] Treasury Board approved the Financial Information Strategy in 1995 as an initiative to improve government decision-making and accountability, as well as gov-ernment performance through the considered use of both financial and non-financial performance information. The intent of the Financial Information Strategy is to pro-vide decision makers within government with the appropriate tools and information to make good decisions. This initiative included the change in government accounting from cash to accrual accounting. This change in accounting methodology was iden-tified in Budgets 1995 and 1996 as a government priority. Accrual accounting was implemented in all federal government departments at the start of the 2001-02 fiscal year as a key pillar of the Financial Information Strategy (FIS).[45]

The Federal Budget, as well as the Government of Canada summary financial statements are now prepared on a full accrual basis. Accrual accounting is based on the following principles. First, expenses are recorded in the period when goods or services are consumed. Second, revenues are recorded in the period when they are earned. Third, capital assets are recognized by being expensed (amortized) over the time they are expected to be used. The decision by the government to adopt accrual accounting is an important shift towards greater use of private sector accounting practices. The benefits of accrual accounting are generally viewed in the reporting and in the more comprehensive information it provides for management decision-making.

The Federal government defines Capital assets as generally including "any asset which has been acquired, constructed or developed with the intention of being used on a continuous basis and is not intended for sale in the ordinary course of business.

Capital assets also include betterments. Betterments are expenditures relating to the alteration or modernization of an asset that appreciably prolong the item's period of usefulness or improve its functionality."[46] Capital assets held by government departments as of 1 April 2001 had to be identified and valued by use of an appropriate cost base.[47] Where practical, this involved the use of historical costs – less the portion of useful life of the asset that had already been consumed.

The cost to the Department of National Defence for the use of capital assets is in effect an advance payment for the long-term use of those assets. From this perspective, as the economic life of that asset expires, the cost of that asset should be apportioned to that organisation as an expense over time. This expense is referred to as amortization. The maximum amortization period is limited to 40 years. The service life of the asset is generally measured in years, although for assets such as aircraft, flight hours may be a more suitable measure of service life. The Financial Managerial Accounting System (FMAS) is the financial system of record for the Department of National Defence. The source systems of record "are the Department's subsidiary ledgers where individual, detailed records are held for all capital assets and related capital asset transactions."[48] Table 4.4 lists the source system of record for capital assets.

The process to purchase and then account for major capital equipment in defence under accrual accounting is as follows. The process starts with a submission to Cabinet requesting policy approval to purchase the equipment for large capital projects. This memorandum to Cabinet includes an accrual accounting table. This table is used by Treasury Board and the Department of Finance as part of their fiscal framework management. Subsequent Treasury Board submissions from the Department of National Defence for funding authority at the Preliminary and Effective Project Approval stages include an updated accrual accounting table.

Table 4.4: Source Systems of Record for DND Capital Assets

Source System	Office of Primary Interest (OPI)	Assets on Record
Material Acquisition and Support Information System (MASIS)	ADM (Materiel)	All capital equipment assets except those held by other OPIs in this table
Realty Asset Accrual Accounting System (R3A)	ADM (Infrastructure)	All realty assets (land, buildings, works, and leasehold improvements) except those in HAMIS
Computer Assisted Material Management System (CAMMS)	Canadian Forces Medical Group (CFMG)	Capital medical equipment assets
Financial Accounting Management Information System (FAMIS)	Communications and Security Establishment (CSE)	All capital assets held by CSE that are not recorded in other systems of record
Housing Agency Management Information System (HAMIS)	Canadian Forces Housing Agency (CFHA)	All CFHA managed residential assets
FMAS Project System (PS) Module	ADM (Finance and Corporate Services)	All capital assets under construction

Once the contract is awarded and the contract signed, the Department of National Defence accounts for the purchase in the Financial Managerial Accounting System. For example, if the department purchases 100 heavy-duty military pattern logistics trucks in one fiscal year for a purchase of $200,000 each, plus other associated costs of $100,000 each, for a total cost of $30,000,000, with an estimated expected life of the asset of 15 years, then amortization would be $2,000,000 per year.[49] In the event that the assets were purchased over two fiscal years, the table would be reflected to account for the vehicles purchased in each year. During the life of the asset, any betterments would be accrued and adjustments would be made for any gain or loss on disposal. This process is shown at Figure 4.15.

Figure 4.15: Illustration of Accrual Accounting

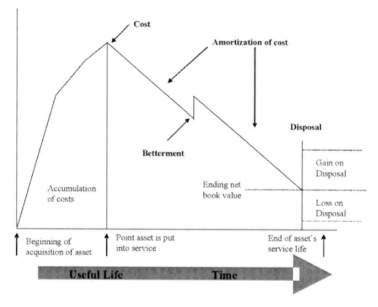

Although the accrual-based budget is one output of the federal budgetary process, the means that produces that budget is still largely cash based. Within the federal estimates process, Department of National Defence expenditures continue to be recorded in the period in which they are incurred. This includes such items as salaries, fuel and maintenance. In this situation, cash equals accrual. In addition to the federal estimates process, departments and agencies also have a requirement to produce financial statements on an accrual accounting basis. In terms of capital purchases $30,000 and over, expenditures are capitalized and recorded as an expense over the period in which amortization occurs. In this situation, cash does not equal accrual. The department is now in a period of transition. Although the Department of Finance has prepared the budget on an accrual basis since Budget 2003, the Assistant Deputy Minister (Material), Capital Project offices and the Chief of Program (CProg) are using a cash basis for capital planning. In essence, a cash basis is still required for the legacy capital program and an amortization view is necessary for capital programs announced in Budget 2005 and subsequent budgets, although this is presently done on an ad hoc basis by the Department of Finance and Treasury Board Secretariat on a project by project basis.

New future capital projects, assets will be essentially purchased using "investment cash". Control by central agencies will be allocation of a ceiling to DND on how much it can expense. The expense-ceiling total will consist of cash expenses and amortization expenses. It should be noted that "investment cash" does not count against DND's budgetary ceiling. This is because the allocation of investment cash to DND is a treasury function that requires departmental negotiation with the Department of Finance and is separate from DND's expense budget. Investment cash for Capital projects can be requested in Memoranda to Cabinet, Treasury Board Submissions, the Annual Reference Level Update (ARLU) or Supplemental estimates.

Parliamentary control over disbursement of public funds flows from the use of an annual appropriation (12 months), as well as the use of a vote structure to control how the appropriated funds are spent. It is important to note that investment cash can only be requested from Parliament in the estimate process. In this regard, Memoranda to Cabinet provide policy coverage and earmark the funding in the federal fiscal framework. The subsequent Treasury Board Submission gives project approval and the authority to ask Parliament for the release of funds through the estimate process. The Annual Reference Level Update incorporates the Treasury Board decision into an updated reference level for the department, which will appear in future Main estimates. Finally, the Supplementary Estimates are used to ask Parliament for funds not included in the Main Estimates.

TROIKA OF CONCURRENT MAJOR CROWN PROJECTS, PERSONNEL GROWTH AND OP TEMPO

Defence priorities are established on an annual basis in order to guide initiatives developed in response to both the government agenda and the operational requirements of DND and the Canadian Forces. The 2007-2008 Defence Priorities are focused on generating and sustaining operational forces in Afghanistan, increasing the size of the Regular and Reserve forces and moving forward on a wide variety of major Capital projects.[50] Each of these three major defence efforts alone will demand a significant effort from the Canadian defence establishment. Taken together, the difficulties in personnel staffing and in resources will be substantial. This will be the major challenge to defence through into the next decade and effective resource management and allocation will be a major contributor to ultimate success or failure.

Conclusion

The objective of Defence administration in a nation has been portrayed as "the building and sustaining of combatant capabilities."[51] Effective management of defence budgets is complicated by the fast paced and changing international security environment, which is dominated by asymmetric threats. The reality of simultaneously maintaining aging equipment, supporting new equipment, adapting to a transforming military force, and coping with shifting activities and activity levels compounds budgetary difficulties. These effects, both internal and external to defence, will continue notwithstanding increased funding levels provided in Budgets 2005 and 2006, or commitments to move forward a number of Capital projects announced by the government following the 2006 Budget. The most effective approach to mitigating these issues is to develop an institutional level in-depth knowledge and understanding of defence costs, as well as the establishment of a prioritized capability plan. Then, armed with this knowledge, subsequently develop a long-term affordable plan to manage allocated resources.

One key element required to enhance defence resource management is the development of a more comprehensive approach to cost management within DND. A United States Government Accountability Office (GAO) report on cost growth in American defence acquisition stated, "the goal is to get a better match between budgeted funds and costs in order that the true impact of investment decisions is known."[52] This conclusion is taken further in a recent Center for Strategic and International Studies (CSIS) study in which one of the major findings is that "resource constraints require a more integrated approach to defense."[53] Indeed this approach is now gradually starting to become a significant focus for planning staffs at National Defence Headquarters. Although this work occurred between 2004 and 2006 and began to take shape in planning for the Defence Policy Statement, it is now beginning to change the way defence administration is undertaken in Canada.

This shift in emphasis towards a more integrated approach to defence administration in Canada is most evident in the priority that leaders in National Defence Headquarters have assigned to financial management of defence resources. This has resulted in senior management at National Defence Headquarters now demanding more comprehensive cost information when making decisions. This, in turn, alters and challenges the manner in which the various staffs prepare Assistant Deputy Minister level officials for decision making forums. Three developments, which can be categorized as conceptual, structural and financial in nature, illustrate the resulting changes. In essence, these developments are related to changes in how DND decides to purchase new capital equipment, what DND purchases, and how DND manages the acquisition process for what they have bought.

First, an important priority is ongoing work in support of developing a management framework that supports an Investment Plan and clearly responds to the direction provided in the 2005 Defence Policy Statement. This work includes developing a long-term cost model that integrates procurement and operating costs in order to support the estimated affordability of future plans. Second, structural changes are illustrated by the creation in October 2005 of a Major Project Delivery Division within the Materiel Group to consolidate the management and oversight of many of the large complex capital projects under one organization. This new organization will support the development of more experienced project managers and allow for more flexibility in the planning, acquisition and delivery of Major Crown Projects. Finally, the most significant financial change was establishment of the Directorate of Strategic Finance and Costing three years ago to improve Comptrollership and financial management within DND. One of the mandates of this organization is to independently validate the costs of all capital projects before decisions on those projects are made at a Senior Review Board, or the departmental Program Management Board. Completed project cost validation reports are now an essential prerequisite before resource commitments are made. This includes validation of not only the purchase costs, but also the downstream operating and maintenance costs.

The common linkage of these conceptual, structural and financial changes now occurring within National Defence Headquarters is a greater degree of integration within strategic level defence decision-making. This strengthening of defence administration processes is also extending beyond National Defence Headquarters. Specifically, greater integration in planning and decision-making is also becoming more prevalent between defence and the central agencies. This was particularly evident in the work leading up to Budgets 2005 and 2006, as well as in the ongoing work in developing the Defence Capability Plan.

Endnotes

1. Treddenick, John M., "Distributing the Defence Budget: Choosing between Capital and Manpower", in *Issues in Defence Management*, edited by Bland, Douglas L. (Kingston: Queen's University School of Policy Studies, 1998), 43

2. DND, *Defence in the 70s* (Ottawa: Information Canada, 1971).

3. Treddenick, John M., "Distributing the Defence Budget: Choosing between Capital and Manpower", in *Issues in Defence Management*, edited by Bland, Douglas L. (Kingston: Queen's University School of Policy Studies, 1998), 43

4. For a detailed discussion on this issue, see Keating, Edward G. and Dixon, Matthew, *Investigating Optimal Replacement of Aging Air Force Systems* (Santa Monica: RAND, 2003) http://www.rand.org/pubs/monograph_reports/2005/MR1763.pdf accessed 12 April 2007, and CBO, *The Effects of Aging on the Costs of Operating and Maintaining Military Equipment* (Washington: Congressional Budget Office, 2001) http://www.cbo.gov/ftpdocs/29xx/doc2982/AgingCostsO&M.pdf accessed 12 April 2007. Korb, Lawrence J., Bergmann, Max A. and Thompson, Loren B., *Marine Corps Equipment After Iraq* (Arlington: Center for American Progress, Washington and Lexington

Institute, 2006). http://www.americanprogress.org/issues/2006/08/marine_equipment.pdf accessed 12 April 2007.

5. Figure 4.3 also shows 1% allocated to Statutory costs are costs that have been authorized by legislation. Grants and contributions are an element of the category of expenditure referred to as transfer payments. Transfer payments are transfers of money from the federal government to individuals or organizations of various forms, including businesses or other governments. Goods or services are not directly received in return by the federal government.

6. DND, *Cost Factors Manual 2006-07* (Ottawa: Department of National Defence, 2006) Chapter 1 (Personnel). The average cost from Private to General in 2006-07 is $87,000.

7. Fetterly, Ross (2006) "The Demand and Supply of Peacekeeping Troops" *Defence and Peace Economics* 17:5:457-471 (October 2006).

8. Ankerson, Christopher, "The Personnel Crisis" in *Canada without Armed Forces?* Edited by Bland, Douglas L., (Kingston: Queen's University School of Policy Studies, 2003), 55-82.

9. Sloan, Elinor C., *Security and Defence in the Terrorist Era.* (Montreal: McGill-Queen's Treddenick, John M., "Distributing the Defence Budget: Choosing between Capital and Manpower", in *Issues in Defence Management*, edited by Bland, Douglas L., (Kingston: Queen's University School of Policy Studies, 1998), 43. Press, 2005).

10. For example, see Groves, Richard and Fetterly, Ross (2008) "An Imperfect Storm: Air Force Operations and Maintenance Cost Trends" *Canadian Air Force Journal* 1:1:16-29. http://www.airforce.forces.gc.ca/CFAWC/eLibrary/Journal/Vol1-2008/Iss1-Spring/Sections/05-An_Imperfect_Storm-Air_Force_Operations_and_Maintainance_Cost_Trends_e.pdf Accessed 12 June 2008.

11. Henault, R., *Annual Report of the Chief of Defence Staff 2002-2003* (Ottawa: Department of National Defence, 2003). http://www.cds.forces.gc.ca/pubs/an-rpt2003/intro_e.asp. Accessed 26 September 2006.

12. The Defence Services Program is defined as departmentally approved activities and projects in fulfilment of government policy.

13. Department of Finance, *The Budget Plan 2005* (Ottawa: Department of Finance, 2005), 220. http://www.fin.gc.ca/budget05/pdf/bp2005e.pdf accessed 12 April 2007.

14. *Ibid.*

15. Department of Finance, *The Budget Plan 2006: Focusing on Priorities* (Ottawa: Department of Finance, 2006), 135. http://www.fin.gc.ca/budget06/pdf/bp2006e.pdf accessed 12 April 2007.

16. Greenfield, Victoria A. and Persselin, David M., *An Economic Framework for Evaluating Military Aircraft Replacement* (Santa Monica: RAND, 2002). http://www.rand.org/pubs/monograph_reports/2005/MR1489.pdf accessed 12 April 2007.

17. CBO, *The Effects of Aging on the Costs of Operating and Maintaining Military Equipment* (Washington: Congressional Budget Office, 2001). http://www.cbo.gov/ftpdocs/29xx/doc2982/AgingCostsO&M.pdf accessed 12 April 2007.

18. DND, *National Procurement Program Expenditure* (Ottawa: (ADM (Material) Director Materiel Group Comptroller 5), 2005).

19. *DND, National Procurement Program Forecast* (Ottawa: (ADM (Material) Director Materiel Group Comptroller 5), 2006).

20. DND, *Cost Factors Manual - 2006-2007 Edition* (Ottawa: Director Strategic Finance and Costing, 2006).

21. Keegan, J., *A History of Warfare*, (London: Hutchinson, 1993), 38.

22. The most expensive weapon system is the United States nuclear powered aircraft carrier. A recent RAND study examines options for funding aircraft carriers. See Birkler, John et al., *Options for funding Aircraft Carriers* (Santa Monica: RAND, 2002). http://www.rand.org/pubs/monograph_reports/2005/MR1526.pdf accessed 12 April 2007.

23. See for example, Peltz, Eric, Colabella, Lisa, Williams, Brian and Boren, Patricia M., *The Effects of Equipment age on Mission-Critical Failure Rates: A Study of M1 Tanks* (Santa Monica: RAND, 2004). http://www.rand.org/pubs/monograph_reports/2005/MR1789.sum.pdf accessed 12 April 2007.

24. CBO, *The Effects of Aging on the Costs of Operating and Maintaining Military Equipment* (Washington, Congressional Budget Office, 2001), 26. http://www.cbo.gov/ftpdocs/29xx/doc2982/AgingCostsO&M.pdf accessed 12 April 2007.

25. Peltz, Eric,Colabella, Lisa, Williams, Brian and Boren, Patricia M., *The Effects of Equipment age on Mission-Critical Failure Rates: A Study of M1 Tanks* (Santa Monica: RAND, 2004). http://www.rand.org/pubs/monograph_reports/2005/MR1789.sum.pdf accessed 12 April 2007.

26. Treddenick, John M., "Distributing the Defence Budget: Choosing between Capital and Manpower", in *Issues in Defence Management*, edited by Bland, Douglas L., (Kingston: Queen's University School of Policy Studies, 1998).

27. Sloan, Elinor, *The Strategic Capability Investment Plan: Origins, Evolution and Future Prospects* (Calgary: Canadian Defence & Foreign Affairs Institute, 2006).

28. Arena, Mark V., et al, *Historical Cost Growth of Completed Weapon System Programs* (Santa Monica: RAND, 2006), xii. http://www.rand.org/pubs/technical_reports/2006/RAND_TR343.pdf accessed 12 April 2007.

29. United States Congressional Research Service (2005) *Defense Budget: Long-Term Challenges for FY2006 and Beyond* (Washington: Congressional Research Service, 2005). http://www.fas.org/sgp/crs/natsec/RL32877.pdf accessed 12 April 2007, and United States Congressional Budget Office, *The Long-term Implications of Current Defense Plans and Alternatives: Summary Update for FY2006* (Washington: Congressional Budget Office, 2005).http://www.cbo.gov/ftpdocs/67xx/doc6786/10-17-LT_Defense.pdf accessed 12 April 2007.

30. DND, *DND Economic Model 2006-2007* (Ottawa: Director Strategic Finance and Costing, 2006).

31. DND, "The Canadian Defence Budget" *Ad Hoc Committee on Defence Policy* (Ottawa: Department of National Defence, 1963), i.

32. Solomon, Binyam, "Defence Specific Inflation: A Canadian Perspective" *Defence and Peace Economics* 14:1:19-36 (2003).

33. DND, *DND Economic Model 2006-2007* (Ottawa: Director Strategic Finance and Costing, 2006).

34. Wise, Gregory and Cochran, Charles, *DoD Inflation Handbook* (McLean: MCR Federal LLC, 2006), 12.

35. Fetterly, Ross, "The Cost of Peacekeeping: Canada" *The Economics of Peace and Security Journal* 1:2:47-53 (2006).

36. Henault, R., *Annual Report of the Chief of Defence Staff 2002-2003.* (Ottawa: Department of National Defence, 2003). http://www.cds.forces.gc.ca/pubs/anrpt2003/intro_e.asp accessed 26 September 2006.

37. Pollick, Sean, *Personnel Deployed in Operations Spreadsheet 1980 – 2006* (Ottawa: Department of National Defence, 2006).

38. Korb, Lawrence J., Bergmann, Max A. and Thompson, Loren B., *Marine Corps Equipment After Iraq* (Arlington: Center for American Progress, Washington and Lexington Institute, 2006), 1.

39. Independent Review Panel on Modernization of Comptrollership in the Government of Canada, (Ottawa: Supply and Services Canada, 1997).

40. Treasury Board of Canada Secretariat, *Results for Canadians* (Ottawa: Supply and Services Canada, 2000). http://www.tbs-sct.gc.ca/report/res_can/rc_e_pdf.pdf accessed 12 April 2007.

41. Conference Board of Canada, *Strategy, Accountability and the New Role of the CFO: Modernizing Financial Management in Government* (Ottawa: Conference Board of Canada, 2006).

42. Chouinard, P. and Wood, I.D.H. (2007) *The Department of National Defence Strategic Cost Model: Development - Technical Report 2007-14* (DND Centre for Operational Research & Analysis, Ottawa).

43. Fetterly, Ross, "The Canadian Defence Peacekeeping Cost Estimation Process" *US Army - Resource Management* (Spring 2005) 28-32. http://www.asafm.army.mil/proponency/rm-mag/fy2005/1stQ.pdf.

44. Bland, Douglas L. and Maloney, Sean M., *Campaigns for International Security* (Montreal: McGill-Queen's University Press, 2004), 181.

45. DND, *Report on Plans and Priorities 2006-2007* (Ottawa: Department of National Defence, 2006), 86.

46. For more detail on accrual accounting and budgeting in defence, see Fetterly, Ross and Groves, Richard (2008) Accrual Accounting and Budgeting in Defence - *Claxton Paper 9* (Queen's University School of Policy Studies, Kingston).

47. Auditor General, *2001 Report of the Auditor General – Chapter 1: Financial Information Strategy - Infrastructure Readiness* (Ottawa: Office of the Auditor General of Canada, 2001) http://www.oag-bvg.gc.ca/domino/reports.nsf/html/0101ce.html accessed 5 March 2007.

48. Treasury Board, *Treasury Board President Announces the Successful Implementation of the Financial Information Strategy Across Government* (Ottawa: Treasury Board Secretariat, 2001) http://www.tbs-sct.gc.ca/media/nr-cp/2001/0402_e.asp accessed 5 March 2007.

49. Treasury Board, *Treasury Board Accounting Standard 3.1 – Capital Assets* (Ottawa: Treasury Board Secretariat, 2001) http://www.tbs-sct.gc.ca/pubs_pol/dcgpubs/accstd/capasset1_e.asp#_Toc510490914 accessed 5 March 2007.

50. *Ibid.*

51. DND, *Handbook 201- Accrual Accounting for Capital assets in DND* (Ottawa: Assistant Deputy Minister (Finance and Corporate Services), 2006), 5.

52. Other associated costs can include installation and setup costs, design and engineering costs, architectural fees, legal fees, survey costs, site preparation costs, freight charges, as well as any other significant costs incurred to make that particular asset operational.

53. Hillier, Rick and Elcock, Ward, *2007-2008 Defence Priorities* (enclosure to Vice Chief to the Defence Staff memorandum 1000-1 (DDSM 5) dated 1 February 2007).

54. Bland, Douglas L., *Transforming National Defence Administration* (Kingston: Queen's University School of Policy Studies, 2005).

55. GAO (2005) *Defense Acquisitions: Improved Management Practices Could Help Minimize Cost Growth in Navy Shipbuilding Programs* (Washington: Government Accountability Office, 2005).

56. CSIS, *European Defense Integration: Bridging the Gap between Strategy and Capabilities* (Washington: Center for Strategic and International Studies, 2005). http://www.csis.org/media/csis/pubs/0510_eurodefensereport.pdf accessed 12 April 2007.

Chapter 5

DEFENCE PROCUREMENT AND THE NEED FOR DISCIPLINED CAPITAL INVESTMENT

CRAIG STONE

> The production and supply of defence items have undergone dramatic changes since the time of the Second World War. For example, advancements in the technological and sophistication of weapon systems have served to lengthen the necessary lead times required for production.[1]

This observation was made in late 1987 by the Defence Industrial Preparedness Task Force (DIPTF) as part of the overall governmental review of foreign and defence policy. The essence of the comment was that weapon systems were getting more complex and required even longer lead times to move from the initial identification of a capability deficiency through research and development, and finally to the fielding of a specific piece of equipment. Within the context of the DIPTF report, the implication was that there was a need for a long-term industrial preparedness policy that remained consistent over time. In the broader context, the increased costs and time requirements associated with new weapon systems that the report implies continues to be an issue for Canada and most nations some 20 years later.

In addition, there is considerable discussion and debate about the Revolution in Military Affairs (RMA) and how it will influence all aspects of the military. This issue is particularly challenging when many of the new computer based technologies are changing at speeds significantly faster than the time frame taken for defence procurement projects in the past. Of particular interest is a notion that the future of defence and material acquisition will be based on the rapid development and fielding of prototypes completed in the context of production lines designed for adaptability.[2] As Robert Leonhard argues, "Even the idea of "wartime production" is outdated, because future wars will be fought at a tempo and in a political context that will not allow formal transition to war either economically or politically."[3]

Although one might not agree with Leonhard's argument that wartime production is outdated, an examination of the literature on the nature of future war clearly indicates the need for militaries to adapt quickly in an uncertain environment. The lengthy lead times discussed by the DIPTF will not meet the needs of the nation should Canada become involved in a future conflict that requires the rapid development advocated by Leonhard. As well, an argument could be made that certain aspects of future warfare will require considerable flexibility and adaptation in the normal day to day running of a nation's standing army, regardless of size.

In a related context, Dan Middlemiss argues that defence procurement is a vital component of Canadian defence policy. "It is what puts the "arms" into the armed forces and because of the many (sometimes very large) contracts and jobs involved, it is also "big business" in Canada."[4] Despite this argument, the overall impact of defence procurement as a factor in the Canadian economy is marginal at best. "Total defence production accounts for considerably less than 1 per cent of both gross domestic product (GDP) and total employment."[5] Fundamentally, both the above arguments are valid; it is the context that is important. Although defence spending is a very small part of the overall economic activity in the nation, procurement is an important aspect of our defence policy, especially when major capital equipment is being considered. The intent of this chapter is to explore the procurement challenges facing the Department of National Defence with specific emphasis on major capital equipment projects. The chapter will begin with some of the basic theory that applies to military procurement and then discuss the Canadian context. Based on this Canadian context, the current procurement process will be reviewed followed by some observations about why future procurement opportunities will need to be conducted in a much more disciplined way than previous years. In other words, there must be a coherent long term investment plan that will allow for the investment in defence without the huge swings in dollar amounts that are shown at Figure 5.1.

Figure 5.1: Capital Expenditures 1960 to 2007

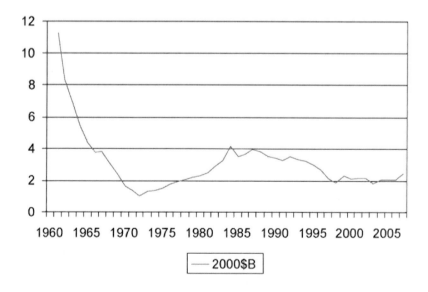

The Defence Procurement Market

In most nations the resources required to provide weapons systems to military forces are second in cost next to manpower. Years of defence procurement, particularly during the Cold War, has created a thriving field for analysis, including contract incentives, budgetary issues, research and development, organizational productivity and political military relationships. There is an ample supply of literature that discusses this collection of issues within the context of military procurement projects.

The weapons procurement process is important because the cost of weapons continues to rise, the procurement process itself is very long and enough data and research exists to indicate either that money is often wasted or that weapons systems often do not meet the performance expectations originally planned for. There are a variety of reasons for this but the most important realization for any examination of the process is the need to set aside any belief that defence procurement can be achieved in a competitive market environment. This is just not the case.

Defence procurement is conducted in a unique environment with some very distinguishing features. Two of the definitive economic texts in the field of procurement are *The Weapons Acquisition Process: An Economic Analysis* written be Merton Peck and Frederic Scherer in 1962 and *The Weapons Acquisition Process: Economic Incentives*, written by Frederic Scherer in 1964.[6] These seminal works indicate that there are four key features of the acquisition process. First, the development work for weapons is characterized by uncertainty and risk. Often, the cost of this risk is shifted from the contractor to the government through cost reimbursement contracts. Second, when a project starts the contractor acquires specialized knowledge, information and assets unique to the weapons system. This restricts the government's ability to shop around for other contractors. Third, the features of the weapons acquisition process lead to a nonconventional market system. It is a quasi-administrative buyer-seller relationship. Finally, in the absence of market forces, successful weapons systems acquisition requires government intervention through controls on contractors or through incentives to reward good performance and penalize poor performance.

More recently, in analysing US procurement, Jacques Gansler's *The Defense Industry*, provides an excellent list of differences between free market theory and the defence market.[7] Perhaps the most important issue is that the defence market is a market with one buyer and very few, and often very large suppliers as opposed to the free market structure of many buyers and many sellers. Also, despite the similarity to oligopoly and monopoly market structures, the defence market is one where the buyer and seller (defence firm and government) have a mutual interest in the weapon system. Price plays a minor role when a weapon system is required for national security.

However, the issue of pricing and related cost/profit issues is one of the major sources of dissatisfaction with defence procurement and the defence industry. Governments are central to understanding defence equipment markets. The government determines technical progress, whether to import equipment or purchase domestically, industrial policy through its defence purchases and determines the size of the defence industry by establishing entry and exit barriers. Furthermore, the trend is that new high-technology defence equipment is costly and is rising in real terms.[8] In his 2004 work, Kirkpatrick observed that the two main trends in weapon system costs were the increasing unit cost of weapon systems and the increasing dominance of the fixed costs associated with those weapon systems.[9] Later in the same article he states that the "Analysis of cost trends in recent decades has shown that, within each class of weapon system, successive designs have progressively higher unit costs associated with improvements in their performance."[10]

In essence then, the real unit production cost of new generations of equipment is much more costly than that of the previous generation. In addition, technical progress is perhaps one of the most distinguishing features of defence equipment markets. In order for a defence firm to achieve the technical progress required, it needs to devote resources to research and development, an expensive and risky proposition without guarantee of success. Consequently, as the need for new and better technology has advanced, defence firms have become larger and fewer in number. This is the only way to achieve economies of scale, reduce production costs and maintain a large research and development organization. A single source with long run production can spread the research and development costs out over larger volume thereby contributing to the reduction in unit cost.

Defence procurement is the demand side of the defence equipment market and requires militaries and governments to make choices between defence contractors and also between services. In the context of choosing between services the national security requirements should dictate who gets what, but more often than not, particularly in Canada, decisions are made based on the principal of Buggin's Turn. In other words, last year the navy bought ships, this year the army bought APC's and next year the air force buys planes.

Also, the selection of a defence contractor is a complicated and lengthy process. Decisions are required on whether or not to source the equipment from a domestic supplier or a foreign supplier. Any decision to open the contract to foreign suppliers will likely be opposed by domestic suppliers and those who advocate the use of defence purchases for other economic and political goals. As well, both the type of contract to be awarded and how the choice will be made must be decided.

In general, defence procurement that involves recurring purchases or items readily available in the market are tendered using a fixed price contract. There is little risk to the contractor or the government with respect to cost changes and quality. Although most defence procurement is done on a fixed contract basis, new weapons systems seldom fall into this category. New weapon systems are generally contracted using a cost-plus or incentive type contract. Cost plus contracts are often used when development work is exploring leading edge technology with significant risk. Governments will pay the costs of such research and an additional agreed level of profit, either a flat fee or a percentage of costs. Unfortunately, this type of contract has often led to accusations of profiteering, inefficiency and gold plating. From a free market perspective the argument is that there is no incentive for the defence firm to control or reduce costs, improve management efficiency and production efficiency. Nevertheless, the nature of the contract is useful, particularly when changes are made to the requirements as new discoveries are made during research and development.

More recently, the incentive contract has become commonplace. This type of contract falls between the fixed price and cost plus contracts and is designed to reward those defence firms that can reduce unit costs. For example any saving made during production may be kept by the firm or alternatively, any costs overruns will be shared by both the government and the firm. There are many variations and each contract will be designed to meet the needs of both the defence firm and the military/government. In Canada, versions of all of these methods have been utilized in the past but procurement in the late 1990s and early 2000s is generally connected to the notion of *best value*.

There are difficulties in determining exactly what best value means and how a nation would actually evaluate a proposal. Alan Williams' recent examination of Canadian defence procurement looks at these issues and suggests that best value should be achieved through a compliant lowest cost methodology.[11] Under this method, the actual requirements of the military are being met at the lowest cost and that is therefore the best value. Others may have different views on this issue but Treasury Board defines best value as:

> the combination of price, technical merit, and quality, as determined by the contracting authority prior to the bid solicitation and set out in the bid solicitation evaluation criteria, and which forms the basis of evaluation and negotiation between buyers and sellers to arrive at an acceptable basis for a purchase and sale.[12]

In this context Treasury Board notes that achieving best value is not to be limited and confined to just the actual procurement. It should include all aspects of the process including such activities as the planning and appraisal of alternatives, the definition of requirements, evaluation of sources, selection of contractor, and contract administration.[13] Cost estimation is perhaps the most complex areas of defence procurement. In addition to providing data for forecasting costs, it is closely linked to the decision-making process for choosing between competing options. It is an area that involves both systems analysis and cost benefit analysis. Many of the pioneering contributions emerged in the 1960s with the Rand Corporation and Secretary of Defense Robert Mc-Namara. The introduction of the Programming Planning Budgeting System (PPBS) by McNamara was intended to improve the decision making process for weapon systems by utilizing systems analysis.[14]

Since the seminal work of Scherer, a number of theoretical developments using modern economic methods have been incorporated into the literature on defence contracting. Sandler and Hartley refer to this as the new economics of defence procurement and contract. The buyer-seller relationship can be treated in a principle-agent framework with the defence department as the principal buyer and regulator of the defence firm acting as the agent. As well, game theory is now being used to analyze strategic behaviour in interaction between the defence department and defence firm.[15]

In essence, the use of more formal models of incentive contract have contributed to the understanding of defence procurement by forcing militaries to think more explicitly about costs.

In looking more specifically at Canada's position with respect to procurement, Dan Middlemiss indicates that the major determinants of Canadian defence procurement fall into the two categories of domestic or external. In essence he argues that there has always been a tension between the military oriented external determinants and the political oriented domestic determinants. Without getting into a lengthy discussion on the nature of these determinants, the end result is that today any company trying to win a procurement contract must have a viable industrial and regional benefits package associated with the bid, particularly if they are a foreign company. Adding to this difficulty is that the requirements for the Canadian Forces are not large enough to sustain a domestic industrial base. Although there are a few exceptions to this situation, major weapons systems generally have to be purchased abroad.[16] Once the current situation with global defence industry stabilizes with a smaller number of larger companies, Canada may find that larger companies are less generous when dealing with the small numbers that Canada requires.

At the end of the day politics will always be an important part of defence procurement, in Canada and elsewhere. The difficulty in Canada is that there is no coherent defence industrial policy, and often no clearly articulated defence policy in general, in which guidance for major capital investment can be found. Too often, procurement decisions become mired in the issues surrounding regional industrial benefits and a perception that the established rules are not followed consistently.[17] This makes it difficult for the military and the defence contractors to plan and, more importantly, for the maintenance of public support to spend taxpayer dollars on major capital investment projects. This has historically been the situation for Canadian defence procurement.

A more critical issue in terms of the future requirements of the Canadian Forces is that despite thirty years of unification, the three environments have only marginal capabilities to work together in a joint environment. More important, operational tasks continue to be environment specific with other nations rather than joint between the environments. The exception to this is the normal operational relationship that exists between the air force and the navy when CH-124 Sea King helicopters are on board a ship and between the air force and the army when the Griffin utility tactical helicopters are deployed with the Army.

As well, Canada's strategic and alliance choices have not been the only determinant of defence procurement choices. In addition to procuring equipment for Cold War and domestic use, Canadian politicians have also exercised their freedom of choice in overall levels of funding and equipment purchases in order to meet what is commonly referred to as domestic influences.

More specific to the actual capital acquisition process, the purchase of major equipment has been influenced by many government policy and organizational changes in the past. The acquisition process utilized within the Department of National Defence has evolved over the years based on the budget and planning processes being used by the government of the day. For most of the late 1960s and 1970s the government used a variation of the United States' Planning, Programming and Budgeting System (PPBS) discussed in Chapter 3.[18]

Within DND the process for identifying capabilities and identifying solutions was referred to as the Capabilities Planning Process. This process shown at Figure 5.2 began with a strategic assessment and ended with the existence of a defence capability. In between the start and end points there were a number of steps including defence posture assessment and strategic overview, capabilities planning guide, force development guides, project and force proposals, capital equipment screening, defence services plan and project implementation.[19]

Figure 5.2: Capabilities Planning Process

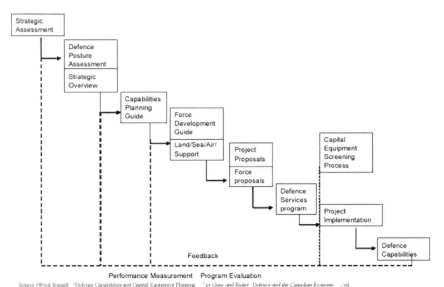

Source 18Neil Russell "Defence Capabilities and Capital Equipment Planning "in *Guns and Butter: Defence and the Canadian Economy* , ed. Brian MacDonald (Toronto: Canadian Institute for Strategic Studi   es, Spring 1984), 59

Procurement Today

The detailed process followed by DND for major capital investments in today's environment has been influenced by many of the government's policy and organizational changes during the past. From a Canadian Forces perspective the changes that then Minister of National Defence Paul Hellyer introduced in early 1960s, which stemmed from a general belief that there was waste and inefficiency in departmental affairs, continue as issues some 40 years later.[20] The programme study group set up in 1964 looked at the requirement for a rational and realistic programming system and a Seven Year Integrated Defence Program (IDP) was introduced in 1966.[21]

Much has been written on defence procurement in Canada and many argue that this formal system, which has been developed over a period of more than twenty years, has not worked. For example, in reviewing the Defence Programme Management System (DPMS) in 1992, the Auditor General noted that the DPMS was found to ineffective and cumbersome, and very expensive in terms of resources devoted to following all the steps in the process.[22] After a variety of reports by the Auditor General criticizing the DPMS, which included the capabilities planning process, the DPMS evolved into the Defence Management System (DMS). Changes to the process were based on recommendations by the Auditor General and other changes made by the Government to move from the Policy and Expenditure Management System (PEMS) to the Expenditure Management System in 1995.[23] The most important point is that the DPMS was a very lengthy process inside an overall process that decided what was needed, what was bought and how funds were allocated.[24]

Since 1992, DND, along with most other government departments, has undergone significant changes in size, organization and structure. One of the major initiatives during this period of change during the 1990s was Defence 2000 which was "a departmental-wide strategic framework providing the foundation for continuous improvement in the way DND/CF manages and conducts business in support of defence missions and task objectives."[25] Defence 2000 established the core product of the CF to be operational capability.

In addition to outlining the management principles for Defence 2000, a series of accompanying pamphlets outlined how defence dollars were to be spent. The intent was to pass on to the private sector those activities that could be accomplished more efficiently in the private sector.[26] All these changes were designed to allow DND to allocate resources more effectively and more closely align the new processes with the government's Expenditure Management System (EMS).[27]

Before discussing the process being used in the early 2000s in more detail, it would be useful to have a general understanding of what was wrong with the old processes. The original DPMS was a sequential process that included five phases: policy planning, project identification, project development, project definition, and project implementation.[28] The process shown at Figure 5.3 was keyed around several documents structured to encourage the orderly and logical development of proposals into solutions. Haglund noted that it evolved to the point whereby it could be viewed as a perfect system designed not to accept risk.[29]

The DPMS was, in fact, a validation process that provided a paper trail that was time consuming and cumbersome. More importantly, the approval process that accompanied the paper trail was just as complex and cumbersome. The Auditor General found it took on average, 6,280 days, or 17 years to take a proposal from inception to Treasury Board approval.[30] The requirement for change was obvious to most of the senior leadership and the new DMS is intended to address many of the shortcomings identified by previous Auditor General and Departmental reports. A new Defence Management System Manual (CFP125) released in the very late 1998s provided the detail on how the Department would deliver the defence services programme in this new environment.

Figure 5.3: The DPMS Process 1995

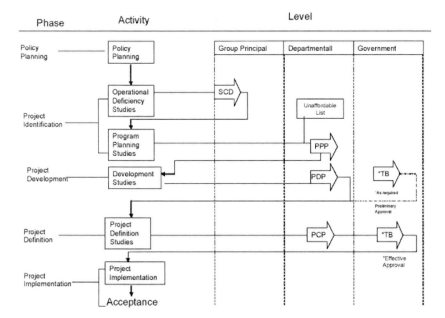

The 1998 version of the DMS argued that the old DPMS "was based on the principle of centralized control, was almost entirely "demand" driven and relied heavily on the maintenance of large central reserves of cash and personnel. This system was very "process" bound, tended to be overly bureaucratic and fostered the growth of large central staffs."[31]

The 1998 DMS was improved and adjusted over time and remained the departmental framework that ensured the effective and efficient delivery of the DSP. It featured clear strategic direction, defined resource levels and business planning as key tenets. The system provided managers with greater financial stability, increased control over expenditures and the flexibility to transfer funds from one resource planning element to another (principally through the business planning process). This system, which was based on a codified system of accountability and responsibilities, was much more decentralized and maintained very small reserves. Instead of large central reserves, it relied on the preparation and implementation of approved level one business plans by the senior departmental heads for the implementation of the Department's defence program. In addition to being linked to the Government's EMS, the new DMS shortened the process, reduced the layers of committees for approvals and the amount of documentation necessary at each step.[32]

Notwithstanding the improvements over the old system, the DMS remained a bureaucratic process tied to the governments' EMS. More important in the context of this chapter, the process that must be followed for the purchase of major capital equipment included six steps. The DMS manual listed effective project management as involving identifiable, phased activity to include:

problem identification - a fully substantiated description of the requirements to be satisfied and a decision to pursue its resolution;

options analysis – examination of a number of options to satisfy the requirement. This examination assesses the rough order of magnitude of costs,
benefits, risks and opportunities of all options against the requirements with
a view to finding the optimum option to be further defined in detail;

definition – activities leading to the creation of a detailed plan, cost and risk
estimate for the implementation of the selected option;

implementation – activities leading to the acquisition and delivery of equipment, infrastructure and/or services which satisfy the requirement defined
during the definition phase. This phase includes the management and monitoring activities needed to ensure that the project delivers the required output
within defined time and cost constraints; and

close out - of the project and the composition of the associated reports.[33]

The DMS provides: a linkage between defence policy and departmental planning;
an overall strategic resource management framework; a department-wide process for
performance measurement; and a detailed framework for reporting to government.
The strategic resource management framework has been centred on defence planning
documents and the annual business plans. The primary Departmental documents,
which now provide annual guidance to the senior management on planning for the
acquisition, organization and maintenance of the military capabilities required to fulfill defence policy are the annual Report on Plans and Priorities and the Defence Plan
On-Line.[34] These documents provide DND's translation of broad government policy
objectives into strategic plans on how those objectives will be achieved.[35]

Despite the improvements, procurement of major new equipment will likely remain a lengthy process. It is not likely that the overall political context for defence procurement will change regardless of how efficient the actual internal process becomes.[36]
The importance of politics and domestic concerns cannot be underestimated. It will always be part of the process and it will generally add additional time to the approval and
development process.[37] That is not say that improvement cannot be made and DND is
making significant efforts to shorten that part of the process that they control.

Shortening The Acquisition Process

In 2001 a conceptual plan to reduce acquisition time by 30% was developed. At that
time the *Defence Planning Guidance 2001* directed the Assistant Deputy Minister Material to prepare a plan on how DND could "shorten the acquisition cycle from Preliminary Project Approval to Initial Operating Capability for capital projects by 30 %."[38]
This was further expanded to include the entire cycle time and not just the portion
identified in the Defence Planning Guidance.

In recent months, the Deputy Minister has agreed to extend the 30% reduction to the entire cycle time from the Identification of an Operating Defi-

ciency to project Close Out. This decision was prompted by the realization that a 30 % reduction between PPA [Preliminary Planning Approval] and IOC [Initial Operating Capability] is not a significant enough reduction to adequately address the fundamental objective of getting systems capability to operators sooner.[39]

As a first step, a baseline cycle time was established as 15.8 years as indicated in Figure 5.4. The significant issue from the analysis conducted to establish this baseline timing was that more than half the time was spent approving the project and getting it to contract.

Figure 5.4: Historical Cycle Times in Defence Procurement Process

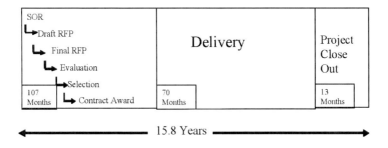

Sourrce: Alan S. Williams, *Canadian Defence Procurement: A View From Inside* (Montreal and Kingston: Breakout Education , 2006). 96.

The difficulty of course is that project approval includes participation by other government departments and politicians. The more complex and the larger the size of a capital project the more time it will take to get approval. Projects over $1B, which basically includes all the major weapon systems for the military, can take over 12 years to get effective approval. The same analysis conducted for establishing the baseline also determined that 13% of the projects sought approval three or four times to accommodate amendments in funding and scope of a project.[40] This type of delay will not support the kind of acquisition and development process needed to accommodate and support the fast paced operations with high technology, frequently updated, information processing systems that are expected in the future security environment.

Based on the review, a number of actions have been taken within DND to reduce the actual time taken for a procurement project. The target time of just over nine years is shown at Figure 5.5. One of the most significant issues was a move to a new performance standard where projects were to take no longer than three years from the time

"Program Management Board (PMB) decides to pursue a resolution of an identified problem as per the SS (ID) until approval-in-principle is given by PMB . . ."[41]

Figure 5.5: Target Cycle Times in Defence Procurement Process

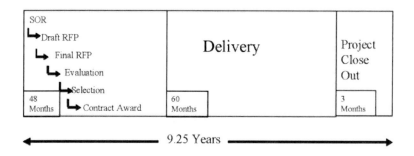

Source: Alan S. Williams, *Canadian Defence Procurement: A View From Inside* (Montreal and Kingston: Breakout Education , 2006), 97.

Related to this issue is the ability of industry to meet the many changes being proposed for shortening the cycle time. In addition to encouraging off the shelf products, DND is planning to: make contractors responsible for producing equipment and then maintaining that equipment for a specific period of time; using more simulation based acquisition and acquisition related modeling and simulation; and, making more use of performance based specifications.[42] It remains to be seen whether or not industry will support these initiatives.

Figure 5.6 shows the procurement process in effect in 2006. The governance structures discussed in Chapter 2 and expanded upon in the Appendix 2 make the decisions at each of these steps.

Figure 5.6: Major Steps in the Procurement Process 2006

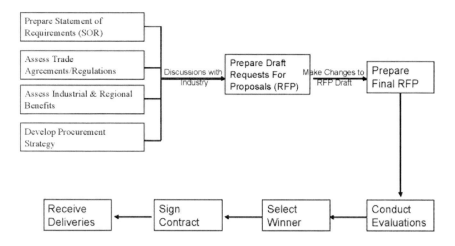

Source: Williams, *Reinventing Defence Procurement*, 38.

At the end of the day, despite different governments and an ever changing world, Canada has generally postured its forces to support its participation in the NATO Alliance and more recently the United Nations.[43] Our selection of major equipment has been designed both to counter Soviet threats and to meet domestic economic concerns. Domestic economic factors are generally more important than the external determinants despite the small overall impact on the Canadian economy. As the largest single element of government discretionary spending, defence spending has important regional and industry specific importance. Therefore, the Department has no choice but to ensure that the process it uses to purchase equipment and supplies satisfies all these variables

The internal and external influences found in Canada's defence procurement environment exist, to varying degrees in most modern nations. For senior military officers to advocate that the government provide more specific policy direction and not consider the domestic imperatives of major capital expenditures would be counter productive. They would be viewed as out of touch with reality and any of their recommendations on other issues would be suspect. Those industries involved in defence activities in Canada will continue to seek both domestic and foreign contracts and they will continue to react as quickly as possible within the constraints of whatever system they find themselves in. More importantly, one must carefully observe the new process to see if the reduction in paperwork and committees actually leads to a reduced timeframe for the procurement of equipment.

As well, with the increased focus on efficiency that comes with the Government's EMS, there are opportunities for the Department to purchase off the shelf or end of production if they present the facts at the right time and in the right context. Outside of these types of incremental improvements, the length of time from identification of a deficiency to fielding the new capability will continue to remain longer than the future security environment demands. Such an environment demands flexibility and an industrial base that can react to the changing demand. However, most nations have the same internal influences on defence procurement and they will have similar difficulties should the need for mobilizing their nation's resources arise. Canada will just continue to do the best it can with what it has.

Endnotes

1. Department of National Defence, Defence Industrial Preparedness: A Foundation for Defence – Executive Version of The Final Report of the Defence Industrial Preparedness Task Force (Ottawa: Minister of Supply and Services Canada, November, 1987), 1-1.

2. Leonhard, Robert R., *The Principles of War For The Information Age* (Novato, CA: Presidio Press, 1998), 122/3.

3. *Ibid.*

4. Middlemiss, Dan, "Defence Procurement in Canada," in *Canada's International Security Policy*, ed. Dewitt, David B. and Leyton-Brown, David (Scarborough: Prentice Hall Canada Inc.,1995), 391.

5. Treddenick, John, "The Economic Significance of the Canadian Defence Industrial Base," in *Canada's Defence Industrial Base: The Political Economy of Preparedness and Procurement*, ed. Haglund, David G. (Kingston: Ronald P. Frye & Coympany,1988), 42. See also the same title published by the Centre for Studies in Defence Resources Management, Report No 15 (Kingston, ON: Royal Military College of Canada, 1987), 50. More recently, Brent Lemon's MA Thesis on the economic impact of defence spending on the Canadian industrial base indicates that defence spending in the domestic industrial base accounts for only 0.4% of the Canadian GDP at factor cost. Lemon, Brent K., "The Economic Impact of Defence Spending on the Canadian Industrial Base," (master's thesis, Royal Military College, April 2001), i.

6. Peck, Merton and Scherer, Frederic, *The Weapons Acquisition Process: An Economic Analysis* (Boston: Division of Research, Harvard Business School, 1962) and Scherer, Frederic, *The Weapons Acquisition Process: Economic Incentives* (Cambridge: Harvard University Press,1964).

7. Gansler, Jacques, *The Defense Industry* (Cambridge: MIT Press, 1980).

8. See for example the work by Pugh and Kirkpatrick in various volumes of *Defence and Peace Economics*. P.G. Pugh, "The Procurement Nexus," *Defence Economics* 4 (1993): 179-194; Kirkpatrick, David L. I., "The Rising Unit Cost of Defence Equipment-The Reasons and the Results," *Defence and Peace Economics* 6, no. (1996): 263-288 and Kirkpatrick, David L. I., "Trends In The Costs Of Weapon Systems And The Consequences," *Defence and Peace Economics* 15, no. 3,(June 2004): 259–273.

9.   Kirkpatrick, "Trends in the Costs of Weapon Systems and the Consequences," 259.

10. *Ibid.*, 261.

11. Williams, Alan S., *Reinventing Canadian Defence Procurement: A View From Inside* (Montreal and Kingston: Breakout Education Network, 2006), 45-47.

12. Treasury Board Secretariate, "Appendix A – Definitions," in *Contracting Policy* (Ottawa: Treasury Board, 9 June 2003). Available at http://www.tbs-sct.gc.ca/pubs_pol/dcgpubs/contracting/contractingpol_a_e.asp; internet; accessed 28 Feb 2008.

13. Treasury Board Secretariate, "Chapter 9 Best Value," in *Contracting Policy* (Ottawa: Treasury Board, 9 June 2003), 57. Available at http://www.tbs-sct.gc.ca/pubs_pol/dcgpubs/contracting/contractingpol_a_e.asp; internet; accessed 28 Feb 2008.

14. There are a number of important works that dealt with this issue of systems analysis. See Hitch, C.J., *Decision Making for Defence* (Los Angeles: University of California Press, 1965) and Quade, E.S., *Analysis for Military Decisions* (Chicago: Rand McNally,1964) were the early texts on systems analysis and Mishan, Edward J., *Cost-Benefit Analysis: An Informal Introduction* (London: Unwin Hyman, 1988) was an early text on cost benefit analyisis.

15. Utilizing game theory, defence procurement has three potential agents; the government, the military, and the defence firm. Other economic methods include contract theory, public choice theory and modelling.

16. In Canada, there is a policy that requires ships to be built in Canada. As well, the government pays an annual fee to SNC lavelin to ensure the supply of certain types of ammunition is available when required.

17. Quite often there are arguments made by those not happy with the outcome of a particular contract. It is actually very difficult to not follow the established rules for contracting because companies can take the issue to the trade tribunal, which can direct compensation be paid or the contract retendered.

18. The history of budgeting in Canada as it relates to defence was discussed in Chapter 3. The reader should also be aware that the president of the Treasury Board issued a guide to departments and agencies on how to implement PPBS in 1968. Lemon, Donald J., *The Politics of Public Spending in Canada* (Toronto: University of Toronto Press, 1990), 57.

19. Russell, Neil, "Defence Capabilities and Capital Equipment Planning" in *Guns and Butter: Defence and the Canadian Economy*, ed. MacDonald, Brian, (Toronto: Canadian Institute for Strategic Studies, Spring 1984), 58/9.

20. Bland, Douglas, *The Administration of Defence Policy in Canada 1947 to 1985* (Kingston: Ronald P. Frye & Company, Publishers, 1987), 157.

21. Canada, Department of National Defence, *An Introduction to The Defence Programme Management System (DPMS) (or, A Survival Guide for the DND Program Management Jungle)*, Tenth Edition (Ottawa: Queen's Printer, March 1995), 3.

22. Canada, Office of the Auditor General, *The Report of the Auditor General to the House of Commons for the Fiscal Year ended 31 March 1992* (Ottawa: Minister of Supply and Service Canada, 1992), 411.

23. Bell, George G., "The Policy Process in National Defence Headquarters" in *Canada's International Security Policy*, ed. Dewitt, David B. and Leyton-Brown, David (Scarborough: Prentice Hall Canada Inc.,1995), 331. See also Russell, Neil "Defence Capabilities and Capital Equipment Planning" in *Guns and Butter: Defence and the Canadian Economy*, ed. MacDonald, Brian (Toronto: Canadian Institute for Strategic Studies, Spring 1984), 58.

24. Bland, Douglas, *The Administration of Defence Policy in Canada 1947 to 1985* (Kingston: Ronald P. Frye & Company, Publishers, 1987), 171.

25. Canada, Department of National Defence, *Defence 2000 A Vision for Management Through Innovation* (Ottawa: DM/CDS letter 9 Nov 1992), np.

26. Detomasi, David, "Re-engineering the Canadian Department of National Defence: Management and Command in the 1990s," *Defence Analysis* 12, no. 3 (1996): 332.

27. Canada, Treasury Board, *The Expenditure Management System of the Government of Canada* (Ottawa: Treasury Board Secretariat (TBS) Program Branch, 1995). AS `indicated in Chapter 3 of this text, the EMS came into effect in 1993 and was the most significant overhaul of the government's expenditure management system since the Policy and Expenditure Management System (PEMS) was established in the early 1980s. The reader will recall that the EMS has four guiding principles and several key features which are designed to allow more flexibility at lower levels. More importantly, the EMS forces the department to live within assigned resource levels, pay for new requirements by reallocating resources from existing spending and provides a system whereby performance objectives are to be measured.

28. DPMS Manual, 11/12.

29. Haglund, D.A., *Canada's Defence Industrial Base: The Political Economy of Preparedness and Procurement* (Kingston: Ronald P. Frye and Company, 1988), 167. See also Maj Mark McQuillan, "Capital Acquisition:Trapped by Policy and Process" (Toronto: CFCSC New Horizons Paper 1994), 1.

30. McQuillan, 19.

31. DND, The Defence Management System Manual (Ottawa: DND, 1998),1-3.

32. The DMS Manual, 1-3.

33. The DMS Manual, 7-2.

34. Those familiar with the defence portfolio will recall that this information used to be provided in the annual Defence Planning Guidance or DPG document. In the 2000 to 2003 time period, this document evolved to the Departmental Report on Plans and Priorities and an annual Defence Plan, which is now provided electronically within DND via the VCDS website.

35. The reader should be aware at the time of writing, there was no approved government defence policy document. The Conservative Government under the leadership of Prime Minister Harper is working on a Canada First Defence Strategy that should provide the way forward. However, the last official government policy was released in April of 2005 by the Liberal Government under then Prime Minister Paul Martin.

36. The Maritime Helicopter Replacement Project is a good example of this. The Liberal Government cancelled the Conservative Government's planned purchase of the EH 101 helicopter in 1993. It was not until the mid 2000s that a replacement was announced. Although the Maritime Helicopter Project may be more difficult than others because of the political baggage associated with the EH101 cancellation, the process for acquisition still requires a lengthy period of time for major projects.

37. It is not possible to say the government will always add time to the process because there are examples when the government circumvents the process and makes it shorter. For example, the March 2002 decision to have the Canadian Forces purchase two Challenger jets from Bombardier was done at the government's direction and not at the military's request. However, these types of acquisition decisions add little to the rationality of the capital acquisition process and reduce funding for either higher priority equipment or more militarily appropriate equipment.

38. Department of National Defence, *Defence Planning Guidance 2001* (Ottawa: DND, 11 April 2000), 3-29.

39. Department of National Defence, *Reducing Acquisition Cycle Time by 30%: A Conceptual Plan* (Ottawa: ADM (Mat) 1 April 2001), 1/24. This is the conceptual plan ADM Mat was directed to develop in the Defence Planning Guidance 2001 document.

40. *Reducing Acquisition Cycle Time By 30%*, 4/24.

41. Alan S. Williams, *Reinventing Canadian Defence procurement: A View From Inside* (Montreal and Kingston: Breakout Education Network, 2006), 96.

42. *Reducing Acquisition Cycle Time By 30%*, 10-14/24.

43. Middlemiss and Sokolsky, 24.

Chapter 6

THE DEFENCE INDUSTRIAL BASE IN CANADA

BINYAM SOLOMON

Introduction

Defence economics has emerged as an important field of study since the 1960 classic work The Economics of Defense in the Nuclear Age brought needed analysis and precision to the field of public administration and defence resource management.[1] Currently, the field of defence economics includes not only the study of defence expenditures, disarmament, conversion and peace, but also the study of defence procurement, defence industrial base capacity, peacekeeping operations, conflict and non-conventional conflict.[2] In Canada, however, the economic analysis of defence issues remains relatively unexplored.

Rosenbluth was the first to apply defence economics tools to Canadian defence policy.[3] In his book, he applied various economic models including an Input-Output (I-O) model to estimate the economic significance of the defence industrial base in Canada. His findings and discussions on data constraints (data on defence industries are not readily available), size and characteristics of the Canadian defence industrial base (niche player in sub-components and especially in remote sensing technologies) and economic significance (small and heavily dependent on the US export market and DND) remained fairly accurate until the early 1990s.

The purpose of this chapter is to critically examine the Canadian defence industrial base (CDIB) from an economic perspective. The chapter does not update statistics on the size and composition of the sector nor does it provide a survey of the literature. Similarly, this chapter does not attempt to provide a definition of the CDIB since it is dependent on the research question asked and how one wants to operationalize the definition. Instead, the economic analysis and critical discussions of the chapter utilize the following broad concepts to delineate the boundaries of the CDIB:

1. The Canadian industrial sector is **both** dependent on military production and relevant to the sector. Relevance to sector can be seen as, for example, important suppliers of weapon systems, etc.

2. A firm that is to some extent dependent on defence spending and/or defence exports and the nation state is dependent upon it for self-reliance in the production of defence goods.

3.   The sector may operate in a relatively non-competitive market as a result of economies of scale, technology or government policies.

While the above may constrain the size of the CDIB under consideration, it is appropriate for the examination of Canadian defence industrial policies and for the design of empirical studies and policy prescriptions. To this end, this introductory section will provide some of the stylized facts about the Canadian Defence Industrial Base as well as some basic theoretical issues that characterize a national defence firm.

Based on this theoretical foundation the chapter will then provide a brief overview of defence within the Canadian economy with particular emphasis on impact studies and empirical tools used to assess the relevance of defence to the economy and regions. Next, the chapter will critically examine the literature on the CDIB and the associated government policies to support the sector. In particular, this section of the chapter will examine industrial offset programs particularly the Industrial Regional Benefit (IRB) policy and its impact on the sector and the Canadian economy. Prior to concluding, the chapter will demonstrate some empirical tests related to the cost of IRBs and present some likely future trends for the sector. The chapter will conclude by discussing some future research directions.

Canadian Defence Industrial Base-CDIB: Stylized Facts

The CDIB is largely foreign-owned or subsidiaries of the large European and US aerospace and defence corporations. Exceptions include the shipbuilding sector, now owned by The Irving Group of companies, a Canadian privately-owned business; Bombardier, a diversified transportation company; and CAE, provider of simulators and integrated training services. General Dynamics Land Systems (formerly General Motors Canada Diesel Divison, a subsidiary of the American automotive company, and then General Motors Defence) dominates the military vehicle-manufacturing sector. However, there are a number of small and medium enterprises that support the automotive and military vehicles sector. Similarly, relatively small and medium-sized firms that specialize in the development, manufacturing and repair of radio communications equipment and associated products, acoustic and infrared sensors, and computers for navigation and fire-control systems dominate the defence electronics sector.[4]

Bernie Grover points out that Canada is competitive in markets for flight simulation, space robotics, satellite communication sub-systems and components, and various surveillance and detection products.[5] In addition, Canadian companies do not manufacture large defence and space systems except to meet domestic requirements, and often serve as sub-contractors for large foreign defence and space programs.[6] Thus, inter- and intra-firm investment and trade are important for Canadian companies.[7]

There is anecdotal evidence suggesting that the CDIB labour force is highly educated and specialized in fields of study that are considered crucial for the new knowledge economy. General statements to this effect are made in Grover and trade association magazines such as the Aerospace Industries Association of Canada.[8] There are at least three important policy implications from the assertion. First, the defence sector crowds-out skilled scientific labour with possible negative impact on the civilian economy through lower productivity.[9] Second, this crowding out may impact productivity and inflation since the competition for scarce labour might increase nominal wage growth by putting workers in a stronger bargaining position or lead firms to employ less skilled and more unskilled workers. Third, lobby groups such as the defence industries association claim special consideration as the sector provides high-value jobs important for the Canadian economy. This rent-seeking behaviour might also add to inflationary pressures.

Solomon used the 1996 Census data to examine the above claims and concluded that the evidence for the CDIB crowding-out talented labour is not strong.[10] For instance, in terms of average wages, the CDIB compensates its employees above the industry average but below the selected "Hi-Tech" (Information Technology, engineering, legal and other services) industries. As such, the "Hi-Tech" sector is in a position to attract more talent (or crowd-out) than the CDIB. Extending the labour force characteristics analysis to the government sector, the education attainment level of the business sector is lagging behind the government sector especially for those with a university education. The industry average for university educated in 1996 stood at 17% while the government sector had 25%. The percentages for the other education attainment variables were comparable, with the government sector holding a slight advantage.[11]

The defence services sector lagged behind its other federal departments and other levels of government in every category except in the field of study, particularly engineering and applied sciences. In this category defence employed 20% of its labour force compared to the government average of 11%. This was also above the industry average. The government sector also pays above the industry average but below most of the CDIB sectors and the "Hi-Tech" industries. In fact, the government sector is facing considerable competition from the CDIB and the "Hi-Tech" sector for talent rather than the other way around.[12]

Another important characteristic of a defence industrial base is its R&D-intensity. While this is true for the larger defence industries in the US and Europe, the Canadian context is rather muted. Foreign subsidiaries of US aerospace firms such as Pratt & Whitney Canada, and Honeywell Canada do show up in the top 100 R&D firms list in Canada but information technology (IT) and pharmaceutical companies often dominate the list. About 55% of the top 100 R&D spending was due to IT firms with Nortel accounting for the lion's share. The CDIB is represented by five Aerospace companies and one engineering firm as shown at Table 6.1. As a group they accounted for 8% of total spending, led by Pratt & Whitney Canada, with $472 million of R&D. The aerospace industry's investment in R&D totaled $952 million in 2006.

Table 6.1: Top CDIB R&D Spenders in Canada in 2005

Rank	Company Name	Revenue $M	R&D as % of Revenue
4	Pratt & Whitney Canada Inc (fc)	2700	17.5
10	Bombardier Inc	17842	1.2
21	CAE Inc	986.2	10.9
14	Honeywell Canada (fc)	1302	7.1
48	MacDonald Dettwiler and Assoc.	832.9	5.9
87	SNC-Lavalin Group	3787.8	0.5

Source: Research Infosource Inc. (2006) Canadian Corporate R&D Directory Database
FC-Foreign Parent Company

The final point on the stylized facts about the CDIB is its unique relationship and access to the US military market and the impact of the April 1999 Department of State regulatory changes to the US International Traffic in Arms Regulations (ITAR) which increased the number of items requiring export licenses to Canada. Any future defence industrial policy design in Canada has to explicitly consider ways and means to reduce the general level of insecurity in the US that technological secrets do not find their way into the hands of a non-allied third-party.

General Characteristics of a Defence Firm and Market

As the major buyers of goods and services for their Armed Forces, governments play a unique role to national defence industries. As the monopsonist (single-buyer), the government can influence the size, structure and ownership of the industry. Note for example that Canada's small domestic defence budget has reduced the CDIB into a lean, export-dependent sub-contractor. In addition, the government's decision to tightly integrate the defence market in the 1950s has led to an ownership structure that favours foreign subsidiaries.

As well, the government can also influence the entry and exit of firms in the sector through control over mergers, competition, subsidies and collateral investment. For example, preferential purchasing and restriction on the transfer of technology are typical strategies to limit entry. While some of these policies are designed to guarantee domestic supply of security needs, they are also designed to support wider industrial and national economic goals. Unfortunately, these are competing goals with potential negative consequences.[13]

The government-induced market failure on the demand side also has consequences in the production of military goods and services due to constrained economies of scale, uneven production cycles, and emphasis on performance. Some of the main characteristics of defence production include:

a. Lack of incentive to be risk optimizers. Governments often finance R&D including investment in infrastructure and capital.

b. Elaborate rules and bureaucratic red tape on contracts. In the absence of a competitive market and to satisfy transparency and accountability, contracts often include cumbersome provisions.

c. Coalitions between contractors, bureaucrats and military. This is also known as the "revolving door" policy where procurement executives and retired military move to defence companies, which leads to expertise in rent-seeking as opposed to commercial markets.

d. Since bureaucratic know-how is the goal, firms may "buy in" by understating costs and risks to win contracts and later make up the loss through gold plating.

e. Due to continuous updates to Statements of Requirement to satisfy the military's requirement for technological enhancements, contracts may have to be renegotiated, which may benefit the contractor who could request additional payments.[14]

These are the defining characteristics of a DIB. Although the CDIB is a small niche player in the defence market, the larger firms of the CDIB do exhibit the characteristics discussed above. Thus, questions such as whether Canada should support a domestically-controlled DIB or whether the existing policy of tying military demands with local socio-economic development projects have to be considered within these unique characteristics of defence firms and markets.

Canadian governments have historically been unprepared to spend significant amounts of money on defence. There are a variety of reasons for this but the most significant reason is that the Canadian public does not see a need for increased defence expenditures, particularly when that expenditure is placed within the context of choosing between defence and health care, education or other social programs. Regardless of the correctness of this choice, defence funding in Canada is always based on what the government believes it can afford and not what a government defence policy might imply.[15]

Studies on Defence and the Canadian Economy

The Centre for the Studies in Defence Resource Management (CSDRM) and the Directorate of Social and Economic Analysis (DSEA) were the sole source for defence economics expertise and publications during the 1980s and early 1990s. Both organizations within DND were closed during the Canadian government program review in 1996-97. Between these organizations there have been over 40 project reports mostly on the economic impact of defence expenditures on the national and regional economies or the economic significance of military installations on their host communities. Given DND's extensive presence in several regions of Canada, impact assessment remains an important source of public relations documentation for the Department and a lobbying tool for local politicians.

Most of the impact studies were performed using input-output (I-O) methodology, as the model was found relatively cost-effective and tractable for monitoring impacts across industries and regions.[16] I-O models are to a large extent an accounting tool designed to track inter-industry and regional flows of production. Indeed, in analyzing the economic impacts of an expenditure on the national or local economy, a detailed account of industry production and other macroeconomic variables (such as government expenditures, exports, etc.) have to be taken into account. Moreover, the resulting impacts of the changes in demand on the economy as a result of the expenditure "shock" have to be examined to identify which sectors of the economy are affected directly and indirectly. Those impacts (usually economic) that are typically quantifiable are most readily estimated within an analytical model such as the I-O model.[17]

Solomon provides a cogent summary of the advantages and limitations of the I-O model within the context of impact studies.[18] In general, the limitations stem from the rather restrictive assumptions about production such as: labour and capital are available to the extent required, the labour-capital ratio is proportional hence the cost of the factors will also be proportional and, demand is distributed among industries based on fixed market shares. The assumption that labour and capital resources are available to the extent required is misleading if the economy is near full employment since it fails to show how and where the resources are re-allocated. In addition, the impact on the general price level is also ignored. The fixed and constant ratio assumptions discussed above are also quite restrictive not only because one expects technology and industrial production to evolve through time, but also because the type of economic shock estimated might also induce technological change. The lack of dynamic mechanism in static I-O models does not allow for possibilities of feedback and provision of information on the adjustment process.[19]

These limitations led the two research units within DND, and particularly DSEA, to look for alternative analytical tools or to modify the I-O model and framework considerably. One competing analytical tool was the Computable General Equilibrium (CGE) model.[20] The CGE model is the mirror opposite of an I-O model in some of its assumptions. While the I-O model ignores full employment possibilities, the CGE assumes nothing else. Which model is more realistic depends on how producers and labour assess, for example, the effect of a defence budget cut or a base closure. That is, if they assume the cuts are transitory or they anticipate other regions are not as attractive, they will remain in the region; alternatively, if the cuts are seen as permanent then both labour and capital may migrate outside the region. Ideally, a combination of both models may approximate reality but resource constraints forced DSEA and CSDRM to concentrate their efforts on modifying I-O models.[21]

These observations led to a hybrid I-O model that relied on community level data as much as possible along with inter-provincial trade flow information.[22] In general the hybrid model uses data from military installations such as operations and maintenance expenditures, and wages and salaries data detailed by postal code or by city. Once the expenditures for the host community are obtained, they are verified for consistency by comparing the data to previous DSEA and headquarters level data sources. Margins (mark-ups) are extracted for goods that are retailed but not locally produced, using margins and trade flow data from SC.[23] Trade flow data are used to provide information on provincial demand for goods and services and what proportion of the demand is satisfied locally. For operations and maintenance expenditures, expenditure by commodity is multiplied by the corresponding coefficient of provincial self-sustainment to estimate the direct impact. The remaining income, after adjusting for national and provincial taxes and any capital component, is multiplied by the appropriate family expenditure ratios (for the province) as well as by the coefficients from the trade flow data to estimate the indirect impact.

The military personnel's consumption pattern was approximated using family expenditure survey data partitioned by income quintiles (the average military income was matched to an income quintile in the survey data). The rationale is that consumption patterns are sensitive to income and the military wages and salaries may be different from the community's average labour income. Such methodological enhancements as discussed above, coupled with the upward bias on economic impacts (as a result of using provincial trade flow information) resulted in the acceptance of the DND impact assessments by the local and provincial governments. These same socio-economic impact studies backed the 1994-95 program-reviews, which resulted in the closure or reduction of about 50% of the Canadian military installations. A sophisticated clustering algorithm was developed to classify bases into three groupings (ranging from severe economic impact, the base representing 68% of the host community income, to small, the base accounting for only 0.6%) to facilitate compensation packages.[24]

Nationally, however, the economic impacts of defence expenditures were not as significant. With the exception of the shipbuilding industry and to some extent the aerospace sector, the industrial impact was not as significant either. Given the fact that isolated communities in various provinces and selected industries are the most dependent on defence expenditures, the lobbying for defence tends to be diffused. The relative insignificance of the economic impacts of defence and the lack of visibility of the military in major urban centres may be factors that explain the perceived lack of interest by both politicians and the public. An update of typical regional impact studies is illustrated at Table 6.2. The Navy and Army presence in Nova Scotia and large army base in New Brunswick have relatively significant economic presence in these Atlantic Provinces that still rely heavily on primary industries (fishing, mining, etc.). Not surprisingly, in the highly diversified and populous provinces of Ontario and Quebec, DND's presence is relatively insignificant. This pattern also holds for defence industrial production and exports.

Studies on the Canadian Defence Industrial base and Policy

As indicated at the beginning of this chapter, Gideon Rosenbluth was the first to apply defence economics tools to Canadian defence policy.[25] Other empirical studies conducted on the economic impacts of defence expenditures on the Canadian industrial sector such as Treddenick, Poole and Wall, and Caron began to show the significance and dependence of the Canadian Defence Industrial Base (CDIB) on domestic defence demand waning.[26] For example, the manufacturing sector that includes the CDIB accounted for 57% of the initial defence expenditures in fiscal year 1984. By fiscal 1992 it has gone down to 36%. The lack of reliable defence export data precluded many analysts from assessing the economic benefits that may have been generated from such activity.

Poole and Bernard advanced the economic analysis away from an assessment of the size of the CDIB to an analysis of military production and its impact on productivity.[27] Concentrating on the larger defence industries such as the aerospace, shipbuilding, electronics and chemical (ammunition) manufacturing, the authors constructed an 'innovation stock' from data on defence industrial production in Canada between 1961 and 1985. Using the Seemingly Unrelated Regression Estimates (SURE) regression Poole and Bernard concluded that military production has a negative impact on total factor productivity for the four industries.[28] While the analysis of technical externalities in the defence sector was an important contribution, the authors did not examine likely positive spill over for second tier suppliers and other related industries. For example, the aerospace industry and the likely positive spill over to the simulators manufacturing or airline services sector in Western Canada should have been explored. In addition, the choice of the lag structure in the estimated equations was arbitrary. In particular, the authors could have indirectly inferred the likely lag length from time series data on completed defence projects or by utilizing statistical tests such as the Schwarz Bayesian Criterion.

Against the backdrop of a declining defence budget and domestic demand and to counter an alleged array of policy instruments used by other nations with whom Canada competes, the federal government actively supported an industrial offset policy and its later incarnation, the industrial regional benefit (IRB) program for its aerospace and defence sectors. Industrial offsets are contracts placed in Canada by foreign companies to offset the loss of jobs or other economic benefits to Canada as a result of the external procurement of major defence equipment.[29] These offsets are usually a large percentage of the total dollar value of the original contract (50-100%) and prior to 1985 there were no explicit provisions to distribute benefits regionally. Offsets are a distinctive feature of Canadian defence procurement policy and they have attracted considerable interest in the literature.

Offsets are politically attractive because some of the benefits such as jobs (at least for the short-term), foreign investment and regional development programs are realized quickly. Although there are some potential benefits from offsets particularly technological transfers and development of competitive industries, economically, as will be discussed, such programs may result in higher premiums and marginal benefits. Before discussing the various studies on industrial and regional benefit policy, a brief description of the policy and the process is required.

Table 6.2 Summary of DND Presence by Province

Canadian Provinces & Territories	Population	GDP	DND Spending	Total DND Economic Impact	DND Population	DND Population as % of provincial population	Total DND Impact as % of Provincial GDP	Total DND $ per Capita
	Thousands	$Millions	$Millions	$Millions				
	A	B	C	D	E	E/A	D/B	C/A
Newfoundland and Labrador	516	21,534	124	161	1,679	0.33%	0.75%	241
Prince Edward Island	138	4,142	72	82	367	0.27%	1.99%	524
Nova Scotia	938	31,451	1056	1462	14,351	1.53%	4.65%	1,125
New Brunswick	752	23,727	434	601	6,203	0.82%	2.53%	577
Quebec	7598	274,863	2279	3707	22,740	0.30%	1.35%	300
Ontario	12541	537,604	5119	8266	38,741	0.31%	1.54%	408
Manitoba	1178	41,933	478	751	5,106	0.43%	1.79%	406
Saskatchewan	994	42,490	72	111	1,509	0.15%	0.26%	73
Alberta	3257	215,858	967	1540	11,700	0.36%	0.71%	297
British Columbia	4255	168,011	788	1202	10,981	0.26%	0.72%	185
Yukon	31	1,522	2	2	63	0.20%	0.11%	57
Northwest Territories	43	4,083	16	19	171	0.40%	0.48%	361
Nunavut	30	1,101	14	14	3	0.01%	1.26%	462

Source: Statistics Canada Canadian Economic Observer: Historical Statistical Supplement, Cat. No. 11-210-XPB, 15, (Ottawa: Statistics Canada) Department of National Defence-DND (2006) Estimated Defence Expenditures by Electoral Districts and Provinces, Ottawa: Public Works and Government Services.

Offsets: the IRB Policy and Process

This section critically examines the Industrial Regional Benefit (IRB) policy from an economics perspective.[30] Some of the historical information and narrative is based on Solomon.[31] Procedures for implementing the government's procurement policy involve several departments. DND as the primary department establishes the need for the project, provides the operational and technical specifications and sets funding and scheduling priorities. The Treasury Board Secretariat (TBS) provides general policies and guidelines for all aspects of procurement. Public Works and Government Services (PWGSC) assists in developing procurement and contracting strategy and is responsible for managing the contracting process. Industry Canada and its regional assistance agencies, the Atlantic Canada Opportunities Agency, the Department of Western Economic Diversification and the Federal Office of Regional Development (Quebec) are responsible for industrial and regional development initiatives to be attached to major capital projects.[32]

In terms of formal internal evaluations of the offset policy, Gray and Nielsen are the earliest.[33] In particular, Nielsen's review showed that 57% of the projected $2.45 billion benefit to McDonnell-Douglas would have occurred without the award of the CF-18.[34] This finding was substantiated further by a Department of Regional Industrial Expansion (DRIE) review that showed 78% of all anticipated benefits from 10 major procurement projects surveyed clearly came about through other direct means such as earlier contract action or other Government initiatives.[35]

ECONOMICS LITERATURE ON IRB POLICY

The evaluation techniques for industrial benefits generally differ from one case to another and as such, there is no specific methodology, such as basic cost-benefit analysis, employed to analyze the commitments. In general, the evaluation method employed by the Department of Industry and Gray relied heavily on subjective considerations and consequently failed to resolve some important considerations.[36] For example, the additional costs for administering offsets are not examined or are unknown. Without such information one cannot make optimal choices between complete offshore procurement and domestic purchase. Even if the decision to purchase from abroad is somehow decided, we still want to know the cost of the industrial benefit.[37]

Some studies have also looked at the defence policy for clues on a meaningful industrial strategy. Byers found the early stages of the policy (early 1970s) lacked vision and depth as they made no attempt to link procurement policy with the defence sector.[38] Byers also attempted to link the apparent disinterest in defence procurement to the lack of long-term commitment from Cabinet on the real growth in the defence budget.[39] This omission of the defence sector in the formulation of the procurement policy is remarkable considering defence capital expenditures accounted for 50%-60% of the total federal capital expenditures.

Fergusson looked at the evolution of the policy from its formative years (early 1970-1980), which he believed to be fraught with several shortcomings attributable to the learning process, to the current modified policy that is constrained by conflicting goals of regional development and fostering industrial competitiveness.[40] Although the main theme of their studies was impact of defence spending, Treddenick and the Centre for Studies in Defence Resources Management-CSDRM also provided some analysis on offset contracting.[41] In general, these studies indicated that offsets produce benefits to a very specific industry and region, typically Quebec or Ontario regions and the aerospace sector, while incurring a substantial premium on the contract.

Unfortunately, the value of the "substantial premium" is not quantified. Galigan and Herring analyzed the industrial offset policy of the CF-18 procurement and, consistent with the CSDRM studies of 1984, found the impacts of offsets were primarily concentrated in one or two provinces (Ontario primarily and Quebec) and a limited number of industries (aerospace, electronics and communications, and automotive and military vehicles).[42] Offsets tend to generate higher labour income than defence and other federal procurement; on the other hand, government revenue tends to be higher for other federal and defence procurement due to orders being placed with crown.[43] The study did not elaborate, however, whether offsets generated higher labour income because of the nature (capital intensive, skilled/ scientific labour or a short-term phenomenon dictated by supply-demand constraints). In addition, the I-O methodology employed by the authors did not have an occupational matrix to verify whether offset-related industries disproportionately represent high-skilled labour. Their study also found offsets generated 25-33% less employment impact than alternate government programs like public works, which is not surprising (the latter tend to be labour-intensive).

Most importantly, however, Galigan and Herring pointed out that any further analysis would be inconclusive until a number of questions such as the cost of the premium on the original contract, proportion of orders placed under offset arrangement, and the quality and extent of the technology transfer were answered.

While the authors identified the necessary data and information requirement to fully conduct a cost-benefit analysis on the policy, neither they nor any other attempted to follow up on the collection and analyses of the data. Haglund provided a policy perspective on the Canadian defence industrial base and Bland provides a national and international perspective on defence management issues with implications to the size and composition of the resultant industrial base.[44]

IRB POLICY DESIGN

In 1996, both DND and Industry Canada commissioned a study to evaluate the impact of IRB to date and to seek guidance on the viability of the program.[45] The study, which was conducted from 1996 to 1997 used various interview and focus group information from the relevant groups and stakeholders to formulate findings. In general, the study found important policy gaps that required amendment or further scrutiny. In particular, the following were highlighted:

a.   First, changes in the procurement environment, such as international agreements, limit the application of restrictive trade policies. In addition, the one
area where the policy may apply, defence, is much smaller in size and number
and the overall sector is in decline worldwide.

b.   Second, government interest in policy implementation has flagged as resources devoted to IRBs have decreased steadily. In addition, there is evidence of a
lack of senior-level guidance and vision or long-term strategic thought. Subsequently, monitoring of the results of the policy is poor, and feedback of the
results into the decision-making process is non-existent.

c.   Third, given the small and diversified CDIB, both the government and DND
missed an opportunity to engage in an acquisition strategy where cost and
quality are the main determining factors.

d.   Fourth, IRB evaluations tend to be perfunctory. Penalties have not been imposed when IRB commitments are not met despite the fact that the IRB are
part of the contracts and legally binding. In addition, IRB strategies are vague-
ly worded allowing companies to include activities that supported company
business instead of sectoral strategies that would more likely have created
incremental benefits (note that the Hickling study did not provide specifics
on which projects did not meet an agreed upon IRB commitment). [46]

Looking at Hickling's findings, the policy emphasis on enhancing international competitiveness may be ill-advised considering the small domestic defence market. First, as
a result of a special Defence Production Sharing Arrangement (DPSA) with the US, Canadian defence firms enjoy special access to the lucrative US defence market. Second,
the Canadian defence firms are engaged in dual-use production with as much as 70%
of its production in civilian markets.[47] Given these facts, the emphasis of government
policy for defence firms should be focused on the maintenance and or enhancement
of the special status to the US market and the exploration of administrative efficiencies
and alternatives in government procurement policies.

The Hickling study also attempted to quantify the benefits of the IRB. In particular the study used an input-output simulation model to assess the impacts. Like previous studies on IRB, the Hickling study showed that the policy has a modest impact
on the Canadian industrial landscape with some, albeit marginal, benefits in regions
outside the dominant Quebec-Ontario region (Alberta and the Prairies). However, the
study did not assess whether the offset policy helped expand industrial capabilities or
whether defence/aerospace capabilities were enhanced or created in new regions and
sectors.[48]

In general, the studies on both the significance of the CDIB and the impact of the
IRB policy tend to be limited to the assessment of economic significance without a
careful analysis of the costs and benefits of policies and an assessment of the potential
and challenges of the industrial sector. In particular, the following generalizations on
the policy design are enumerated:

•   The primary objective of procurement is to acquire the goods with the best
value for money. Secondary objectives such as industrial benefits should be

pursued only after identifying the incremental costs and benefits of achieving the additional goal.[49] However, the IRB policy is vague and does not provide a clearly laid-out process on how to achieve this. In reality, most industrial benefit programs include a number of objectives that are often mutually exclusive, and consequently convey conflicting signals.

- The Nielsen Report and the current IRB policies do not stress the fundamental problem: What do you want the policy to accomplish? Once this is clearly stated then one can avoid mutually exclusive objectives such as regional development (in a depressed region) and industrial competitiveness (which benefits from clustering rather than regional dispersion).

- An oversight body instead of cabinet review, which is constrained by ministerial and constituency politics, should have been instituted. If there are vested interests, as the Nielsen report alluded, then the policy should promote gain-sharing as an incentive to cooperate. For example, various departments can be persuaded to co-operate if they are allowed to keep any significant savings from the collaboration. The recommendation to target R&D is unnecessary since Canada already has one of the most generous R&D credits in the OECD.

Given the empirical studies on the economic significance of defence spending, it does not make economic sense to set up a production capability to serve or to expect a number of Canadian firms to compete for a relatively small domestic defence market.[50] International markets are very competitive, and countries with larger demands usually supply their own needs. This problem is growing as the demand for defence equipment drops in response to declining defence budgets around the world. In this highly competitive market, most CEOs feel that Canada needs a clear industrial strategy and a stable defence policy to guide industrial development initiatives. In the opinion of a number of CEOs, government officials need to consider entirely new approaches. One example of the kinds of policies that could be considered is the possibility of concluding strategic deals between nations in which another country might supply an entire weapon system, but would agree to buy a competitive Canadian product such as remote sensing technology or simulators.

Table 6.3 presents a summary of the major studies on the Canadian defence industries and policies. The results of these studies generally indicate that the Canadian defence industrial base is less dependent on domestic defence demand and the economic significance of the defence industrial sector is relatively smaller than other industrial groupings. In terms of defence industrial policy, the surveyed studies show that the effort to develop depressed regions and industrial sectors through procurement policies have not been successful as the targeted regions continue to receive substantially fewer benefits from the policy. The studies surveyed also suggest that the administration of the regional and industrial benefit policies may have added an expensive premium to the overall contract price of defence procurement. General analytical and empirical studies on the CDIB suffer from a lack of consistent and up-to-date databases on the industry, its products, sales, revenue and exports. Most studies cited in the earlier section point to this shortcoming and the following key aspects need to be recognized:

Table 6.3: Major Studies on the CDIB and IRB Policy: A Summary

Article/Author(s)	Issue/Methodology	Results	Gaps/Deficiency
Treddenick (1986) CSDRM (1984) Poole and Wall (1992) Caron (1994)	Assessing the economic significance of the CDIB	Dependent on the export market less so on domestic demand. Different from earlier studies (Rosenbluth, 1967)	Defence Exports not assessed. Data limitation recognized but alternatives are not provided
Poole and Bernard (1992)	Military Production and Productivity	Negative intra-industrial externalities associated with military production	Did not account for positive spill over for downstream industries
Galigan and Herring (1986) Treddenick (1984)	Industrial Offsets, Regional policies	Policy impact concentrated in Ontario and Quebec and selected industries. Labour income higher than other defence production	Cost-benefit analysis was not conducted. Data problems cited but alternatives were not pursued.
Fergusson (1996)	Industrial Regional Benefit Policy	The policy strategy is not clear with conflicting goals.	There were no empirical examinations.
Hickling (1997)	Assessment of Industrial and Regional Policy	Some benefits outside the Canadian main Industrial regions of Ontario and Quebec	The cost of the policy not examined. The I-O model used was an older vintage.

First, Statistics Canada and Industry Canada do maintain a database on the defence and aerospace sectors, however, the databases are not updated regularly. Second, the defence association (Canadian Association of Defence and Security Industries-formerly CDIA) compiles its own data but the methodology associated with employment estimation and industry coverage is not consistent with Industry Canada or Statistics Canada data.

For example, the industry association database estimates indirect employment using a multiplier of 1.75,[51] This multiplier is not derived from an economic or theoretical model but an adaptation of a multiplier generated for the information technology sector by another study.[52] In order to ease administrative burden on industries, the questionnaires designed by the industry association tend to be light on specifics. For example, respondents are asked to provide percentages allocated to defence without any guidelines as to whether they should add dual-use products or whether the distinction between civilian and military is to be determined by customer or other criteria. Details such as these are important because most Canadian firms are sub-contractors and tend to provide sub-systems to companies who in turn may supply to defence customers (see for example, endnote 5).

Third, the studies discussed in previous sections on the economic significance of the CDIB tend to concentrate on the domestic impact and none have estimated both the domestic and export sales due to lack of reliable data on exports. Since the sector is heavily export dependent as discussed in previous sections, any assessment of the CDIB without the export sales is inadequate. Table 6.4 shows the existing variation in export information.

Table 6.4: Revenue and Employment Data

Year	Total Defence Sales/Revenue $B 1997 Dollars		Employment		Exports $B 1997 Dollars	
	CDIA	IC	CDIA	IC	CDIA	IC
1996	5.6	2.9	28701	14238	1.8	2.01
1998	5.1	2.9	25355	12848	1.9	2
2000	6.8	3.2	33058	12842	2.6	2.3

Source: Grover-CDIA (1997), and Solomon (1999) See endnote 4 for full citation..

Fourth, as discussed in Solomon, the use of an I-O market share matrix revealed that the CDIB exhibit a considerable amount of sub-contracting activity especially in the aerospace, electronic components and specialized services sectors. The high level of interdependence in a number of defence industrial sectors may have led to the inconsistent data presented by Industry Canada and the trade associations.[53] Fifth, if the sector is deemed important from an overall economic and strategic perspective, there is a need for an institution- or government-sanctioned regular census of the sector. In addition, I-O based estimation remains a viable option for the inter-census period and for conducting impact and inter-industrial relationship analysis.

INDUSTRIAL OFFSETS: EMPIRICAL ASSESSMENT

Hickling's study, which is the latest on the industrial and regional benefit policy, used I-O based simulations to assess the impact of the policy on regions and the general economy. The I-O model employed in the study was the 1991-92 version of the Canadian industrial structure. In this section, the 1997 version of the I-O tables and matrices are employed to simulate the same input data used by Hickling.[54] In addition, the latest inter-provincial trade data, to assess regional flows, and GDP by industry (at factor cost), to benchmark the results, are also employed.

The results of the new simulations and the trend analysis from the census data are shown in Tables 6.5 and 6.6. First, the re-estimated I-O simulation results show that, as expected, 85% of the benefits from IRBs were spread among 10 industries of which half were the CDIB and the rest were trade and service industries such as wholesale trade and finance and real estate industries. The provincial summary is equally concentrated with Quebec and Ontario accounting for the lion's share and Alberta and BC accounting for the remaining portion. The benefit of the program mirrors the existing Canadian manufacturing distribution. The Atlantic and Prairie provinces, where the IRB's regional focus is centered, received only marginal amounts. This is to be expected, as the region does not have the required infrastructure to exploit the benefits of the IRB policy.

Table 6.5: Industrial Offset Impact of Selected Defence Crown Projects

Industrial Sector	Share %	Provincial Distribution
Communication and Electronics	24.2%	Alberta, Ontario, BC
Aircraft and Parts	21.3%	Quebec, Ontario, Manitoba, Alberta
Other business services industries	7.7%	Ontario
Professional business services	7.0%	Alberta, Ontario, BC
Shipbuilding and repair industry	6.4%	Quebec, New Brunswick
Railroad rolling stock industry	5.2%	Ontario
Air transport and related service	5.0%	Quebec, Ontario, Manitoba, Alberta
Wholesale trade industries	4.0%	Alberta, Ontario, BC,Quebec, New Brunswick, Manitoba
Finance and real estate industries	2.5%	Quebec, Ontario, Manitoba, Alberta
Primary steel industries	1.3%	Ontario
Sub Total	84.6%	
Rest	15.4%	All Provinces

Source: See Endnote 4.

A cursory examination of the time-series between 1985-2001 reveals that the Atlantic region's share of defence and aerospace sector sales increased from about 2.6% in 1985 to a high of 5.9% in 1999 and settling to 5.5% in 2001. Similarly the Prairie region saw its share increase from 1.4% to 5%. As a proportion of their respective regional GDP, the increase is relatively more significant in the Atlantic region than in the Prairies. What is striking during this period is the decline of Ontario's share from a high of 49% in 1984 to the 2001 level of 33%. Quebec on the other hand, saw its share climb from about 40% in 1985 to approximately 47% in 2001. Most of the gain in Quebec was at the expense of Ontario. To a large extent, the consolidation of the aerospace sector explains the change in Quebec and Ontario. Even if this shift from Ontario to other regions is a result of the offsets, this may be counter-productive since it may hinder companies from capturing the synergistic benefits of a clustering approach. In other words, established regional clusters may be hurt by movement of work to other regions, making the sector as a whole less competitive (Table 6.6).

Table 6.6: Distribution of Aerospace and Defence Sector Sales

Fiscal Year	Maritime Provinces	Quebec	Ontario	Manitoba	Prairie Provinces	% of GDP Maritime Provinces	% of GDP Prairie Provinces	British Columbia
1985	2.6%	39.7%	49.0%	5.7%	1.4%	0.3%	0.1%	1.5%
1990	3.0%	42.5%	43.5%	7.2%	1.8%	0.5%	0.1%	2.0%
1995	2.5%	48.9%	37.8%	4.9%	3.2%	0.4%	0.3%	2.7%
1996	2.7%	49.7%	36.8%	4.6%	3.2%	0.5%	0.3%	3.0%
1997	2.7%	49.4%	37.1%	5.2%	3.4%	0.5%	0.4%	2.2%
1998	4.8%	45.5%	35.2%	6.0%	2.8%	0.7%	0.4%	5.7%
1999	5.9%	46.0%	33.0%	5.7%	5.0%	1.0%	0.4%	4.4%
2000	5.6%	46.4%	33.3%	5.4%	4.9%	1.3%	0.4%	4.3%
2001	5.5%	46.6%	33.0%	5.4%	5.0%	1.4%	0.4%	4.5%

Source: Industry Canada-Statistics Canada Survey 1997, 2000 (also see http://strategis.gc.ca/epic/internet/inad-ad.nsf/en/h_ad03628e.html for updated information)

It is interesting to note that one of the findings from the focus group review was that the IRB policy is seen as necessary to the defence industrial base as Canada imports more than it exports.[55] The existing data shows that in the last 15 years the trend towards import dependence has accelerated (Table 6.7). Currently about two thirds of the sector's input requirement is imported.

Similarly, the policy is found to strengthen the transportation and IT sectors in Canada by adding to the Canadian capacity through transfer technology or bringing new technology investments from abroad. Are these regions capable of developing manufacturing sectors without an IRB policy? New Brunswick, one of the Atlantic Provinces, has successfully brought major communication and IT sector activity to its province without the IRB policy but with a combination of tax incentives and well-established infrastructure including a bilingual educated work force. Furthermore,

British Columbia increased its share of defence and aerospace sales without the IRB incentive (Table 6.6).

Table 6.7: Sources of Input

Current Millions $

Fiscal Year	From Canadian Aerospace and Defence Manufacturers	From Other Canadian Sources	Imported from US Suppliers	Imported from Other Foreign Sources	Total	Import Content (%)	Import Content from US (%)
1985	286	466	1012	61	1825	59%	55%
1990	654	940	2093	233	3920	59%	53%
1995	913	976	2561	405	4855	61%	53%
1997	987	1068	2944	852	5851	65%	50%
2000	1408	1360	3609	1797	8174	66%	44%
2001	1448	1391	3758	1823	8420	67%	45%

Source: http://strategis.gc.ca/epic/internet/inad-ad.nsf/en/h_ad03628e.html for updated information.

In general the revised I-O simulations and data from the Industry Canada census show that the IRB has positively affected the regional distribution of defence manufacturing industries. As shown in Table 6.6, the Atlantic and Prairie provinces saw their share of defence production increase by about 3% and 3.5%, respectively during the period 1985 to 2001. Reducing import dependence of the defence sector, another goal of the policy, was ineffective, however, as import dependence has increased from 59% to 67% during the period 1985-2001. Note that dependence on the US market for material and sources of input declined from 55% in 1985 to 45% in 2001.

A focus group employed by the Hickling study observed that while the absolute value of the work flowing to regions was not found to be high, the benefits to firms have been very important. The focus group believed that technology transfers occur as a matter of course even if the IRB does not formally request technology transfer.[56] While this may be true, one could also use other less intrusive policies such as trade missions or subsidized foreign advertisement funds to promote the smaller Canadian firms. In addition, there are competing policy tools such as tax credits to start-up businesses that can provide similar benefits and therefore IRB may not be suitable to some regions or sectors. In particular, the IRB's stated goal of maximizing benefits flowing to a region "facing particularly difficult economic circumstances" may be futile if the community does not have the means to exploit and retain the benefits flowing from a large procurement as a result of an underdeveloped infrastructure or supply chain.

One other crucial facet that remains to be explored is the analysis of the IRB policy is the cost of the program. From an analytical perspective, the ideal data set will reveal the cost with and without the IRB provision as well as what facets of the policy generate the most cost. In the absence of such data one has to look for an indirect method. A price trend analysis based on a defence deflator is one attractive alternative. This method will be employed in the next section after formally introducing the concept of defence specific inflation.

The Cost of Offsets: Empirical Tests

As discussed in previous sections, government policies designed to protect defence industries may be costly and may be one of the reasons for the existence of defence specific inflation. In the previous section the possibility that industrial offset or regional benefit policies may be costly and inflationary was suggested. As discussed earlier, one other crucial facet that remains to be explored in the analysis of the IRB policy is the cost of the program. Previous studies discussed earlier in the chapter indicated that the cost of the IRB provision on the overall project cost is minimal; however, there are no readily available quantitative data to verify the assertion. From an analytical perspective, the ideal data set will reveal the cost with and without the IRB provision as well as what facets of the policy generate the most cost. Specifically, we should be able to determine: the cost of the administration, monitoring and reporting of the policy goals to Canadian public departments and the prime contractor(s); the cost of the regional component of the IRB on both public and private stake-holders, the cost of domestic sourcing as opposed to off-shore or off-the-shelf purchase and other related issues. Without detailed information such as that mentioned above, the review will be incomplete.

In the absence of such information, a price trend analysis of projects with IRB is used as an alternative measure. In this section the DND price index will be used to impute the likely costs of IRBs and to assess the impacts on DND's purchasing power. In particular if one can extract the price trend of the project from other activities in the same class (without IRB) and with the general price trend in defence and the national economy, we can make some general statements about the cost of IRB policy.

The DND historical price trend model, developed in the early 1970s, tracks the price trend of some 500 items that the Department purchases in a given year. In addition, because of general government accountability regulations, Major Crown Projects (MCPs are capital projects in excess or equal to $100 million) are also required to use a "tailored model". A tailored model is part of the Economic Model (EM) and is based on specific contractual factors and cash flow information supplied by the project management office.[57]

Methodology and Results

MCPs are not given their own special expenditure code or GL. Thus, the inflation rate of the GL against which the MCP is coded will be a composite of the price trend of all expenditures coded under the given GL and the MCPs. To illustrate, suppose the GL with the MCP is X and further assume that only one other item is included in X. Then the price index for X can be expressed as:

$$q_0 \, p_1 + (1 - q_0) p_2 = X$$

Equation 1

Note that $0 < q_{01} < 1$. Since X is published annually in the Economic Model and q01 p11 is given in a tailored model analysis to the project office of the MCP, one can easily compute the non-MCP portion for Equation 1. The result of the price trend analysis is shown in Table 6.8. Nine major projects were considered for this exercise as a consequence of data limitation. The New Fighter Aircraft (NFA)-CF18 acquisition project and the Long Range Patrol Aircraft (LRPA) projects were proven platforms and the inflation trend is not expected to be significant. All the remaining projects are expected to have higher inflation rates as shown in the previous section. The fact that these projects include R&D, testing and evaluation, and other contractual factors contributes towards inflationary pressures. Note that the Canadian Patrol Frigate (CPF) and the Canadian Search and Rescue Helicopter (CSH) projects included well-publicized IRB packages but the projects are still ongoing and one cannot draw firm conclusions from these projects. The fourth project, Tactical Command and Control Communication System (TCCCS), included policy with more regional emphasis.

Table 6.8: Price Trends of Selected Projects

	NFA-CF18	Non-MCP	DSP	PGDP
82-83	100.0	100	100.0	100.0
94-95	148.4	194.3	165.8	154.0
	CSH	Non-MCP	DSP	PGDP
94-95	100	100	100	100
00-01	122.32	122.72	116.7	110.5
	CPF	Non-MCP	DSP	PGDP
81-82	100.0	100.0	100.0	100.0
00-01	199.9	198.9	219.2	183.4
	TRUMP	Non-MCP	DSP	PGDP
83-84	100	100	100	100
95-96	145.6	145.0	146.7	139.4
	LRPA	Non-MCP	DSP	PGDP
81-82	100	100	100	100
91-92	127.1	182.8	157.8	148.4
	LAV	Non-MCP	DSP	PGDP
85-86	100	100	100	100
89-90	120.6	107.3	117.4	117.8
	HLVW	Non-MCP	DSP	PGDP
82-83	100	100	100	100
94-95	155.6	133.3	153.8	142.7
	LLAD	Non-MCP	DSP	PGDP
83-84	100	100	100	100
95-96	159.2	167.2	146.7	139.4
83-84	TCCCS	Non-MCP	DSP	PGDP
	100.0	100.0	100.0	100.0
00-01	151.9	131.7	169.5	152.6

Notes: DSP is the price index for total defence procurement; PGDP is the GDP deflator.

The results show that five of the nine projects evaluated had higher inflation rates than similar products with the same material and labour requirements. While detailed information on the administration and premiums would be preferable, the results from the inflation analysis should be considered indicative at this stage. The CSH project inflation rate was virtually identical to the non-MCP rate but considerably higher than the GDP and defence deflators. This is generally true of projects that are in the development stage. The older project such as the CF 18 CPF had an inflation rate over its project life of 48%, which was substantially lower than the non-MCP components (94%) and the defence and GDP deflators (66% and 54%, respectively).

The LRPA project, which commenced in 1981, had an inflation rate of 27% in the project's life span of 10 years. The non-MCP component meanwhile averaged 83% during the same period. The defence inflation during the same period was 58% and the GDP deflator grew by only 48% during the same period. While these early projects may not have produced the desired offsets as they were proven designs, it saved DND about 17% less compared to other defence purchases during the same period. One of the more recent projects that showed a smaller inflation rate than the non-MCP component (but higher than both the defence and GDP deflator) was the LLAD (Low Level Air Defence) platform. Any advantages from fixed-price contracts (some of the projects may have such provisions) will be reflected in a lower inflation rate and may underestimate the IRB related cost pressures. Future research in this area should refine the index to identify fixed-price contracts.

For those projects that had higher inflation rates than their respective non-MSP components, the cost is estimated to range from $11M (TRUMP project) to $380M (TCCCS). The TCCCS project was slated to provide a 33.7% direct industrial benefit. Based on the cost analysis performed here, at least 20% of the benefit will be absorbed by policy-facilitated inflation. This differential excludes costs from exchange rates, price inflation of foreign labour and parts, domestic inflation on labour and parts and policy variables (such as special administrative costs on defence procurement excluding IRB).

The above analysis of projects with IRB provisions show that the strategy to purchase a proven platform may have benefited the Defence Department and by extension the tax payer by reducing the inflationary costs associated with major defence procurements (by as much as 17%). These projects, however, did not realize worthwhile industrial benefits since technology transfer often occurs in projects that are in the design and development stages. The price trend analysis also provides a likely estimate of the costs associated with IRBs. Of the nine projects examined, five had substantial inflationary pressures indicating a cost anywhere from $11M to $380M. Specifically, the TRUMP project offset-related average inflation differential of 0.6% on $1.8B project translates to about $11M while the TCCCS project's inflation rate of about 20% is estimated to cost the Department $380M on a project worth about $1.9B.

The use of the defence deflator to decompose major Crown projects for subsequent analysis of the likely costs of government policies is the main contribution of the exercise. Previous studies did not adequately address the cost of IRB policies due to the lack of cost estimates or data. In the continued absence of such data the methodology proposed and employed here should provide an indirect and preliminary indication.

Future Prospects and Summary

PROSPECTS: SHORT-TERM

The immediate future of the CDIB from a domestic defence budget perspective is tied to the Defence Policy Statement (DPS) of 2005, the Canada First Defence Strategy of the new Conservative Government and the Defence Capability Plan of DND.[58] The Conservative Government plan for defence is predicated on a broad "Canada first" strategy that shares some similarities with its predecessor, the 2005 DPS. For example, the Conservatives re-affirmed the three traditional roles of the Canadian Forces (defence of Canada, defence of North America in cooperation with the US, and contribute to international peace and security), and the need for a multi-role, combat capable military.

The new government, like its predecessor, also plans to increase the size of the Canadian Forces, albeit much more significantly (by 13,000 regulars and 10,000 reserves, compared to 5,000 and 3,000 in the DPS). Once this increase is fully implemented, the Canadian Forces will total 75,000 regular and 35,000 reserve personnel. In addition to the funds provided in Budget 2005, the current government increased defence spending by $5.3 billion over the next five years in Budget 2006. As a result, Defence will see an increase to its 2005 baseline of $1 billion in 2006-2007 and $2.3 billion in 2007-2008.

The new plan puts a stronger emphasis on the defence of Canada and particularly placed a much higher priority on the Arctic, including exploring plans to station naval vessels in Iqaluit, build a deep water docking facility, establish a new Arctic National Sensor System to monitor northern waters, and build an Arctic army training centre. The continental security approach, however, remains consistent with the DPS as it proceeded with the renewal and expansion of the NORAD Agreement, which now includes a maritime warning function. The new government has shown a strong commitment to international operations including the renewal of the Canadian Forces' contribution to operations in Afghanistan until February 2009. Moreover, the government has announced plans to increase the deployability of the Canadian Forces by acquiring strategic and tactical airlift, medium-to-heavy lift helicopters, medium sized logistics trucks and joint support ships.

Specifically, the government has announced plans to replace the Auxiliary Oil Replenishment (AOR) ships with Joint Support Ships at a cost of $2.9B (including $0.8B in service support), purchase of logistics trucks at a cost of $1.2B ($0.1B in service support), acquire strategic and tactical airlift at a cost of $8.3B and medium-to-heavy lift helicopters at a cost of $4.7B. These investments in equipment are reflected in the Defence Capability Plan that provides the long-term plan for Defence, including guidance on the roles and missions of the Canadian Forces and equipment priorities.[59]

The Defence Capability Plan will provide further detail on the CF's transformation process, including enhancing their deployability and mobility. To support this undertaking, DND and the CF are modernizing the force development process and adopting capability based planning as a tool to shape the future force. This new approach permits the Forces to make future force development decisions on the basis of what the Forces need, rather than based on what equipment is merely due for replacement. The ultimate aim is to enhance those capabilities that are most relevant to the projected future security environment.

Prospects: Long Term

While the trans-Atlantic mergers and acquisitions and the impacts and implications of asymmetric warfare are the leading issues of concern for the future form, size and composition of a national DIB, for the CDIB, the most important factor remains the US market. Specifically, two issues dominate. First, what is the policy of the day regarding protectionism? Second, what are the long-term implications of the war on terrorism on defence equipment budgets?

The Joint Strike Fighter (JSF) program, the biggest military program in history, is the model of future acquisition strategy that includes a clearly-designated prime contractor (Lockheed-Martin), work shares based on competitiveness, and a contract with financial incentives and penalties. The US, UK, Canada and six other nations are currently involved in the development of this next-generation fighter project. In theory, such collaboration among allied nations makes sense. There are gains from economies of scale since weapons are likely to be bought from a selected few firms and risks associated with research and development will be jointly shared. Since Canada is unlikely to fight any major wars without its NATO allies, especially the US, inter-operability of equipment and systems is vital.

However, the big concern for the partner nations including Canada is technological transfers including the software codes used to maintain and upgrade the planes. The US seems to have serious concerns about technological "leaks" to non-allied nations. There are always protectionist sentiments in Washington than can easily hide under the guise of national security.

The other concern for the CDIB is the implications of the war on terrorism to the US defence budget. The war on terror may seem to be a boon for defence budgets and by extension for equipment purchases. Unfortunately, finding extra money for operations in Iraq and Afghanistan implies difficult choices between operations and maintenance funding versus equipment purchases. However, the nature of asymmetric threats posed by terrorists requires a different approach. Particularly, it makes little sense to allocate funds for big-ticket items such as war ships or stealth fighters when the current and future threat is expected to occur in the form of an urban guerrilla conflict.

While it may be safe to assume that in the long-term equipment budgets will be directed to personnel protection and power projection (strategic airlift and self-sustained combat units), the political risks of cutting big projects and associated jobs may imply the economically inefficient scaling down of projects as opposed to their elimination.

Another trend in the current security environment with some implications for defence firms is peacekeeping missions and the conspicuous presence of for-profit firms providing logistics and other support to the military and Non-Governmental Organizations (NGO) contingents in theatre. There is scope for further research on the costs and benefits of private provision of peacekeeping whether in the role of logistics support or security provision. For example, it is not clear whether private military companies are large enough to be involved in peacekeeping operations in a significant way. Another question for further research is the feasibility and cost effectiveness of private security provision.

Of course some of the political and administrative constraints, such as the International Convention against the "Recruitment, Use, Financing and Training of Mercenaries", need to be addressed as well. Recent studies such as Fredland use a transactions cost approach to suggest the combat support role of private firms are limited due to the inevitable contractual hazards.[60]

Summary

The CDIB, as the data show, is a small niche player and export dependent. The export-orientation and reduced dependence in domestic defence procurement signals Canadian plants operate efficiently enough to thrive in international markets. Given shrinking defence budgets and competing defence services needs, in the post Cold-War era, this outcome is economically desirable.

An industrial and regional benefit (IRB) policy aimed at defence procurement and the CDIB was also assessed using I-O methodology in this chapter. The analysis of the perceived benefits revealed that the IRB policy has positively impacted the regional distribution of defence sales. Reducing import dependence of the defence sector, another goal of the policy, was ineffective, however, as import dependence has increased from 59% to 67% during the period 1985-2001. In should be acknowledged that another important assessment of the policy's benefits would have been the comparison to other alternative policy prescriptions. This was done only briefly in this chapter. Future assessment of the policy should include this important aspect.

The most important conclusion to draw from this chapter is the need for a defence industrial strategy. A coherent defence industrial policy or white paper is required to provide comprehensive data on the sector and to outline the Canadian government's strategy towards the sector. Specifically, such a document should address issues such as the key industrial capabilities, which should be retained, the challenges and opportunities facing the sector and the socio-economic rationale for the policies to be undertaken.

Endnotes

1.   Hitch, C.J., and McKean, R., *The Economics of Defense in the Nuclear Age* (Cambridge, MA: Harvard University Press 1960).

2.   Hartley, K., and Sandler, T., *Handbook of Defence Economics. Volume 1* (Amsterdam: North Holland 1995). Page 6.

3.   Rosenbluth, G., *The Canadian economy and disarmament* (Toronto: Macmillan of Canada 1967).

4.   See Grover, Bernie, *Canadian Defence Industry: A Statistical Overview of the Canadian Defence Industry* (Ottawa: CDIA, 1997) and Binyam, Solomon, "The Canadian Defence Industrial Base," Paper presented at ASSA/ECAAR, 1999-2000 (http://www.ecaar.org/Articles/Articles.htm).

5.   Grover, Bernie, *Canadian Defence Industry: A Statistical Overview of the Canadian Defence Industry* (Ottawa: CDIA 1999 Page 5-7).

6.   Edgar, Alistair D., and Haglund, David G., *The Canadian Defence Industry in the New Global Environment* (Montreal & Kingston: McGill-Queen's University Press 1995).

7.   See endnote 5, page 10-14.

8.   Aerospace Industries Association of Canada –AIAC 1999 Annual Report-Setting the Standard for Global Competition, (Ottawa: AIAC 1999).

9.   Poole, Erik, and Bernard, Jean-Thomas, "Defence Innovation Stock and Total Factor Productivity", *Canadian Economics Journal* 25 (2) 1992: 438-452.

10.   Solomon, Binyam, "The Canadian Defence Industrial Base," Paper presented at ASSA/ECAAR, 1999-2000, Page 17-18.

11.   *Ibid*, Page 18.

12.   *Ibid*.

13.   Hartley, K., "Industrial Policies in the Defense Sector," in Harley, K., and Sandler, T., eds., *Handbook of Defence Economics Volume 1* (North Holland: Amsterdam 1995) Page 462.

14.   Dunne, J.P., "The Defence Industrial Base," in: Hartley, K., and Sandler, T., ed.; *Handbook of Defense Economics, Volume 1* (North Holland: Amsterdam 1995) Page 410.

15.   Stone, Craig and Solomon, Binyam "Canadian defence policy and spending", *Defence and Peace Economics*, 16, no 3 (2005):145-169.

16.   M. Lebreton, "The Economic Impact of Allied Training in Canada," *ORAE Project Report* 418 (Ottawa: DND 1987).

17.   See, for example, endnote 10, page 12.

18.   *Ibid*. Note also Canadian Defence Industries Association. "Statistical Overview of the Canadian Defence Industry for the Year 2000". (Ottawa: Unpublished

paper CDIA 2002) and Conference of Defence Associations " (Ottawa: CDAI 2001).

19. See endnote 17.

20. Parai, L., and Solomon, B., "Economic and Social Impact of Submarine Acquisition Options," *ORA Project Report* 598 (Ottawa: DND 1992) Page 68-71.

21. Parai, L., Solomon, B. and Wait, T., "Assessing the socio-economic impacts of military installations on their host communities," *Defence and Peace Economics* 7, no. 1 (1996): 7-19.

22. Parai, L., Solomon, B. and Lalonde, D., "The Socio-Economic Impacts of Allied Military Training at CFB Goose Bay On The Canadian Economy," *ORA Project Report* PR9501 (Ottawa: DND 1995).

23. See endnote 21.

24. Solomon, Binyam "The socio-economic assessment of military installations using an integer-programming model," *Defence and Peace Economics* 7, no.1 (1996):21-32.

25. See endnote 3.

26. Treddenick, J., "The Military Keynesianism Debate" *CSDRM Report* No. 8, (Kingston: RMC 1986). Also Poole, E., and Wall, P. "The Economic Impact of Canadian Defence Expenditures FY 1990-91" *CSDRM Report* 22, (Kingston: RMC 1992) and Caron, Serge, "The Economic Impact of Canadian Defence Expenditures" *CSDRM Report 23* (Kingston: DND 1994).

27. See endnote 9.

28. *Ibid.*

29. Dobell, W.M., "Defence Procurement Contracts and Industrial Offsets Packages," *International Perspective* (1981):14-18.

30. For a non-Canadian examples of offsets see Martin, S., and Hartley, Keith, "UK Firms Experience and Perceptions of Defence Offsets: Survey Results," *Defence Economics* 6 (1996): 123-139.

31. See endnote 4.

32. Department of National Defence *Defence Management System (DMS) Manual* (Ottawa: Canada Communication Group 1998).

33. Nielsen, Erik, *Management of Government: Procurement* (Ottawa: Minister of Supply and Services 1985). Also Gray, Herb, *New Fighter Aircraft Industrial Benefits Analysis and Evaluation* (Ottawa: Ministry of Industry, Trade and Commerce 1980).

34. Industrial benefit programs are self-contained in the sense that they are individually negotiated, administered and accounted for. However, they are also included in the account ledgers of the Canada/US defence production sharing agreement in cases where the equipment is purchased from the United States.

35. See endnote 33.

36. *Ibid.*

37. See endnote 10 page 5.

38. Byers, R.B., "Canadian Security and Defence: The Legacy and the Challenges". *Adelphi Papers* 214 (Winter 1986): 31-44.

39. *Ibid.* page 35.

40. Fergusson, James, "In Search of a Strategy: The Evolution of Canadian Defence Industrial and Regional Benefits Policy," in *The Economics of Offsets Defence Procurement and Countertrade* (York: Harwood Academic Publishers, 1996) 107-137.

41. Treddenick, J., "Regional Impacts of Defence Spending" *Discussion Paper,* No.4, (Kingston: RMC 1984) Centre for the Studies of Defence Resources Management "Economic Impact of Industrial Benefit 'Offsets' Contracting" CSDRM *Discussion Paper* (Kingston: Royal Military College 1984).

42. Galigan, C.G., and Herring, P.G., "Defence Industrial Impact: 'Offsets' and Exports" *CSDRM Discussion Paper* 13: (Kingston: RMC 1986).

43. *Ibid.* Page 20-21.

44. Haglund, David A., *Canada's Defence Industrial Base: The Political Economy of Preparedness and Procurement* (Kingston: Ronald P. Frye and Company 1988) and Bland, Douglas L., *Issues in Defence Management*, Kingston: School of Policy Studies, Queen's University 1998).

45. Hickling, Arthurs, Low Consulting, *Industrial and Regional Benefits Policy, Report to Industry Canada* (Ottawa: Hickling Corporation 1997).

46. *Ibid.* Page 18.

47. Industry Canada *Industrial Survey and Analysis* (Ottawa: Industry Canada various years; also available electronically at www.strategis.gc.ca).

48. See endnote 46 Page 21.

49. See endnote 33 for Neilsen's report.

50. Pepall, L. and Shapiro, D.M., "The Military-Industrial Complex in Canada" *Canadian. Public Policy* 1989:265-285.

51. Endnote 5 for Grover citation (Page 9).

52. Endnote 5 Solomon citation (Page 15).

53. *Ibid.*

54. See endnote 45.

55. *Ibid* Page 26.

56. *Ibid* Page 30.

57. Tailored inflation models are based on The Economic Model, an internal DND publication.

58. A new Conservative government was elected on January 23, 2006.

59. At the time of writing it was anticipated that this plan would be finalized before the end of 2007. It now appears that it will be called the Investment Management Framework but this has yet to be approved.

60. Fredland, E., "Outsourcing military force: a transactions cost perspective on the role of military companies," *Defence and Peace Economics*, 15 (2004): 205-219.

Chapter 7

BECOMING AN EMPLOYER OF CHOICE: HUMAN RESOURCE CHALLENGES WITHIN DND AND THE CF

ALAN OKROS

Introduction

Many of the early chapters in this book deal with the material resources associated with the administration and management of defence – budgets, military equipment and the nations' industrial capabilities to support defence. This chapter examines the other side of the administration and management challenge for defence – the people that make up the institution. The chapter provides a broad, conceptual overview of Human Resource (HR) Management as an integral component of ensuring overall organizational effectiveness. It will not, however, provide a practical, step-by-step summary of the actual HR processes used to manage the civilian or military components of Defence.

The first reason for this approach is that, at the time of writing this chapter, the CF HR System was undergoing a number of changes intended to produce an HR/Personnel System that will support CF Transformation objectives. These latest changes started in April 2006 with the renaming of Assistant Deputy Minister Human Resources-Military (ADM (HR-Mil)) as Chief of Military Personnel (CMP) accompanied with reorganization and/or renaming of some Divisions and Directorates. Among other initiatives currently being developed, it is anticipated that additional changes will be made to the CMP organizational structure, that a long range Campaign Plan will be launched and that, for the first time, integrated CF Doctrine for HR will be promulgated. Given the significance of these changes, this chapter has been written to provide a macro, theory-based presentation of HR functions in Defence rather than a description of the current HR System(s).[1]

The second reason for this approach is that for both the novice and the expert it is more important to understand why HR decisions are made rather than how to conduct HR activities. Standard HR Management texts provide excellent information on HR processes and techniques however almost all are focussed on applications in the private sector, corporate domain. In particular, none provide the information needed to understand the unique aspects of HR in a military context. Hence some of the taken-for-granted assumptions underlying the common applications of HR procedures either do not or should not apply when considering HR in the Canadian Forces. Thus, this chapter provides an overview of the key principles, philosophy and objectives to understand why HR could or should be organized, structured and administered so as to fully support the operational requirements of the CF and DND.

The primary purpose of any HR Management System is to ensure that the organization's workforce can accomplish assigned tasks and achieve intended objectives. The simplistic summary of the role of HR is to put the right person in the right job at the right time. This necessarily means that the HR System must address: the job (defining what work is to be done); the person (ensuring incumbents are capable of doing this work; and, the enabling structures (providing requisite system supports such as policies, skill development, enabling tools, etc.). A slightly broader view of HR requirements recognizes that ensuring that individuals are able to perform required tasks is only one component of organizational effectiveness and, in particular, that the HR System must also support individual motivation, commitment and retention and provide policies and programs that contribute to desired workplace behaviours. Together these requirements produce five core HR functions:

a.   Jobs: defining and structuring work requirements;

b.   People: selecting and preparing individuals to do this work;

c.   Careers: managing changes in work requirements and/or personnel;

d.   Sustainment: supporting work motivation and career retention; and,

e.   Conduct: enabling appropriate standards of conduct in the workplace.

This chapter will provide an overview of the key elements of the dominant HR Systems in Defence. Noting that the total Defence workforce is comprised of a civilian component including public service, non-public funds employees and contracted private sector workers and a military component including the Regular Force, Primary Reserve, Supplementary Reserve, Cadet Instructor Cadre and the Rangers, the main focus of this chapter will be on the HR System designed to managed the CF Regular Force (Reg F). Where relevant, comments will be provided on key commonalities and differences with the Primary Reserves (PRes) and the Public Service (PS) elements.

It is important to note that references to the HR System and to HR functions pertain to the broad range of policies, programs, procedures and practices related to personnel. In contrast, the scope of HR Management is often constrained to the HR staff organizations of CMP and the Assistant Deputy Minister (Human Resources – Civilian) (ADM (HR-Civ)) and HR Management in this context spans across the National Defence Headquarters (NDHQ) and extends through Formations and down to the unit level in sections such as Unit Orderly Rooms. While the divisions of responsibilities between line and staff are generally understood, these are not neat dichotomous domains and it must be realized that many elements addressed in this chapter are conducted at the unit level.

Finally, it should also be noted that there exists a wide range of options across various work settings for how HR Systems are defined, organized and operated. Some of these differences are dictated by external factors or characteristics of the sector in which the organization operates, hence elements over which the organization has limited or no control. Others, however, reflect internal decisions regarding how employers have chosen to structure the work to be performed or to discharge their obligations to employees. An obvious example for the CF is that, as a result of government direction, few other organizations require 'employees' to take the life of another human being and no other employer denies individuals the legal right to refuse to perform tasks when they believe their own life is at imminent risk. The implications of military unlimited liability are just one of many factors that differentiate CF HR from the standard models found in business or described in standard textbooks. Therefore, prior to presenting the five HR functions listed above, the next two sections will present the key factors that define current Defence HR System requirements (what is to be achieved) and organization (who does what).

Defining HR System Requirements

While all organizations have to address aspects of the five HR functions, important differences in requirements exist between, first, the private sector and government; second, the Public Service and the Canadian Forces; and, third, the various components of the CF. These differences serve to define what the core HR functions are supposed to achieve and, for the CF in particular, generate requirements for additional functions that are not normally part of a private sector or public service HR System.

PUBLIC VERSUS PRIVATE SECTOR

The primary consideration in this domain is that the government must concurrently meet its obligations as an employer and also serve as the guardian of the social good. In discharging responsibilities to the citizenry for the management of the social good (including the use of their tax dollars), governments must place increased emphasis on accountability, probity and transparency. As with other domains, such as financial administration, equipment purchases and information management, these requirements result in a more formalized and bureaucratic approach to HR management than is the case in the private sector. There is an increased reliance on rules-based procedural controls. Additionally, the Federal Government has undertaken to ensure that the government workforce proportionately represents key Canadian demographics and that workplace practices reflect certain social values. These serve to define certain job requirements (e.g., bilingualism) and to require a broad consideration of personal characteristics in making employment decisions with a resultant increased emphasis on equity and parity. The requirements for accountability are illustrated in key legislation such as the *Financial Administration Act* and the *Public Service Modernization Act* while the objectives of representation are reflected in the *Official Languages Act* and the *Employment Equity Act*.[2]

The net result is that, in comparison to private sector practices, government HR Systems tends to emphasize prudence and equity over risk taking and efficiency. Further, the combination of concerns regarding equitable treatment and a generalized model of service to the public as a profession have produced a relatively closed labour system with individuals normally only entering the workforce in lower level positions and a formal requirement to give priority of employment to existing job incumbents over potentially better qualified external job applicants.

Amongst other implications, those attempting to implement significant changes in public sector HR policies and/or practices must be aware of the consequences of attention paid to accountability and fairness. Over time, these emphases have produced an implicit HR culture that is focussed on rule compliance and the avoidance of establishing precedents that erode existing norms. The efforts in the mid-90s to draw on private sector models in order to reduce HR staff and to create more streamlined HR processes encountered significant difficulties when senior decision makers did not fully consider either the requirements for a more bureaucratic HR model suited to the organization or the implicit HR culture found in the organization.

DND versus CF[3]

The critical factors of importance in differentiating the CF from the public service pertain to the conditions for achieving assigned military objectives. Three issues, in particular, serve to define key requirements of the military HR System. The primary factor is that the obligation for the CF to be able to undertake a wide range of government tasks requires a significant degree of flexibility in order to respond in a timely manner.[4] The second is that the nature of these taskings requires that individuals work in conditions of extreme physical, psychological and ethical demands to the point of both putting one's life at risk or taking another's life with each individual held responsible for his/her personal conduct.

Together, these two factors serve to fundamentally differentiate the nature of the 'work' to be performed with resultant implications for how tasks are conducted and how individuals are prepared to carry out assigned duties. Of importance, the requirements to respond to unscheduled taskings and to conduct activities in extreme conditions serve to sufficiently redefine 'work' such that standard civilian HR practices are often not applicable. Failure to understand these two factors explains why some efforts to transfer external 'best practices' are less than effective. A persistent tension in the military HR System is between optimizing proficiency to perform predetermined tasks versus generating the latent ability to adapt to novel tasks.[5] To balance these requirements, the CF places a greater emphasis on: mutually-dependent teams; professional development and socialization; the behavioural influences arising from leadership, institutional culture and team climate; and, the application of a generalist model emphasizing common obligations and standardized work standards.

These two factors also serve to significantly differentiate the CF from the PS in how work effort and career commitment are generated and sustained. To ensure that individual members respond to the lawful taskings provided by government, the CF incorporates a philosophy of compliance with direction at the expense of individual rights or discretion and therefore assigns significant powers and responsibilities to the organization rather than the member. As a result, the CF HR System tends to be more directive and authoritative than in the PS. While the decision to join the CF is voluntary, members are obliged to accept significant restrictions over rights and freedoms including many aspects of employment decisions. This is very different from the PS and the normal civilian HR practice.

The legal authority given to the CF as the employer to impose employment decisions and restrict rights in order to ensure that the military achieves assigned mission objectives is contained in the concept of Universality of Service.[6] The open-ended nature of this employment contract leads to the third issue that defines HR requirements. The legal, moral and motivational implications of requiring individuals to place themselves in harm's way, to be separated from family for extended periods or to relocate across Canada or abroad generates a requirement to attend to additional factors that are not normally part of a private sector or public service HR System. Amongst others, these special functions include: family support services, extended medical care, religious/spiritual services and maintaining professional identity through unique customs, traditions and ceremonies.

In sum, when comparing either the private or public sector HR approaches to the requirements of the CF HR System, two key points should be recognized. The first is that the nature of the work to be performed is sufficiently unique that certain assumptions underlying standard HR practices do not hold. The second is that the broader obligations arising from military service serve to significantly expand the nature and scope of HR activities. Failure to grasp the conceptual and philosophical implications of these two factors when drawing on external models to amend the CF HR System can result in sub-optimal outcomes.

To complicate matters further, the CF is composed of three specific environmental services commonly referred to as the Army, the Navy and the Airforce. As well, each of the environments has a full time and a part time component traditionally referred to as the Regular Force (Reg F) and the Primary Reserve (PRes). These different components have unique cultures and operational roles and responsibilities that make it challenging to apply one common HR model.

COMPONENTS OF THE CF

The primary differentiation within the CF arises from the two issues of professional status and control over changes in employment conditions. As articulated in *Duty with Honour*, those in the Reg F and the PRes are considered to be members of the profession of arms while those in the Supplementary Reserve, Cadet Instructor Cadre and Rangers are seen as auxiliary. Although the differentiation between Reg F and PRes is often seen as one of full time versus part time service, the true factor pertains to the fact that the individual PRes member exerts greater control over employment changes related to posting, deployments or full versus part time contracts.[7] Together, the requirements to address both professional and auxiliary status and volunteers and the 'voluntold' result in the HR System having to address key differences pertaining to: professional development; employment obligations and expectations; and, CF versus member's control over certain decisions.[8]

Although beyond the scope of this chapter, it should also be noted that there is a range of models for how a nation structures the permanent and occasional components of the military workforce.[9] Some such as Switzerland rely on a very small cadre of permanent members and a large reserve component while other nations take the opposite approach with large standing military forces and smaller reserves. Simplistically, the key decisions pertain to whether the reserve component is seen as the basis for expanding numbers or for maintaining unique expertise. In Canada, the Militia or Army Reserve represent the former as providing a base for mobilization by mirroring their Reg F counterparts in key areas while the Naval Reserve represent the latter by developing certain skills such as de-mining and naval control of shipping that are not a major component of current activities but may be needed under some circumstances.[10]

This initial section has provided a brief overview of the key factors that serve to define the requirements of the civilian and military HR Systems in Defence. These lead to three strategic HR requirements:

a.   Serve the organizational mission: hence deliver core services and achieve key objectives by ensuring the required numbers of skilled, competent, and motivated personnel needed to perform assigned organizational tasks. For Defence HR, accountability is through the Minister and Cabinet and, ultimately, to the Canadian people. For the CF, there is an additional requirement to create the capacity to perform plausible but not predicted functions.

b.   Comply with societal values and statutory obligations: thus, ensure that the organization's outcomes and procedures are consistent with Government policies and statutory obligations that reflect core social values. For Defence HR, accountability is to the Government and its central/regulatory agencies (e.g., Treasury Board, Office of the Auditor General, Canadian Human Rights Commission). For the profession of arms (the Regular Force and Primary Reserve components of the CF), there is a broad requirement to attend to stewardship of the profession including the two facets of ensuring that individual and group conduct reflects values seen as legitimate by Canadian society and discharging the institution's moral obligations to safeguard individual rights and freedoms.

c.   Take care of your people: therefore, maintain motivation and commitment by ensuring that the organization discharges all legal and moral obligations as an employer. Accountability is to the public service employees in DND and members of the CF. For the CF, there are special requirements to manage and honour the implied social contract between the institution and the member including supporting families when they are significantly affected by employment decisions imposed by the CF.

For those with even limited HR knowledge, it is clear that these three macro HR requirements are complex and difficult to optimize. Not surprisingly, the norm, which is incorporated in the CF leadership doctrine, is that key elements are often in tension with each other.[11] For example, ensuring maximum effort to achieve mission success can often be in competition with the need to attend to member wellbeing and commitment and enabling initiative and adaptability in dynamic settings can be in conflict with the requirement for standardization. Thus, in addition to the limitations in transferring private sector HR solutions to the public sector or the CF without considering whether underlying assumptions are valid, it is of equal importance to adopt a systems perspective to examine the secondary and tertiary consequences of amending even one of the HR components.

Finally, to expand on this introductory note on the current organization of HR in the CF, the new draft HR Doctrine provides a slight variation on these three broad responsibilities by grouping the essential HR functions into: generation of personnel, support to personnel and alignment with Canadian Society along with a fourth grouping reflecting the following discussion: integration of the Personnel System.[12]

Organizing the HR System

Given the range of differing requirements that must be addressed by the HR System, it is evident that this requires a coordinated effort involving many individuals. Although the common assumption is that HR management is the responsibility of HR staff, it must be understood as a shared responsibility assumed by: Human Resource staff; Senior Leaders; Unit-level Commanding Officers (CO), managers and supervisors; and, individual employees/members. It is important to recognize the role of the individual not just the CO/supervisor.

There are three key factors that influence the basic organization of the HR System to describe 'who does what'. The first is drawn from the set of obligations and requirements highlighted in the previous section as these serve to define the primary objectives of the system ('what' needs to be done). The second arises from the strategic 'business' decisions as to the most efficient and/or effective manner to allocate resources and responsibilities.[13] As an example, the requirements for standardization and consistency to ensure equity in a number of HR career decisions such as promotions leads to centralized, common decision making rather than a distributed, flexible approach. The third, and most important, pertains to the approach taken to determining how individual tasks and small-group activities are to be performed and integrated. This latter point will be illustrated with reference to the differences between the classic industrial era model versus the information age perspective.

PRODUCTION LABOURERS VS KNOWLEDGE WORKERS

The dominant model of the 20th Century, as illustrated in Henry Ford's assembly line and Fredrick Taylor's time and motion studies,[14] was the application of scientific management techniques to determine the optimum set of procedures to be followed to perform any task in the most efficient manner possible. The underlying philosophy was that there was only one 'best method' such that workers need only be trained to perform the requisite activities and, through rote repetition, would become proficient in maximizing their efforts. The related role for first line supervisors was to prioritize or schedule work activities and provide necessary resources. Interventions by supervisors were needed only when workers failed to perform or when unusual events disrupted the predetermined flow of work. In this static view of work, the domain of original/ creative thinking and complex problem solving was reserved for the small number of senior managers responsible for adaptation of core business processes.

Over the last 20-30 years, there has been broad recognition that this mechanistic, routinized approach did not describe the work conducted by the majority of first line supervisors or even individual employees. The combination of increasingly dynamic, complex and often chaotic work demands; drives to achieve efficiencies by reducing the numbers of middle managers; and improvements in the general level of education among front line personnel led to an increased delegation of authority to the working level to exercise creativity in deciding how to conduct work. The core concept was that workers needed to shift from following predetermined procedures to applying expert judgement to determine the optimum manner to achieve work objectives. The related shift for supervisors is to provide the broad guidance needed to ensure that individual and small work groups' actions are integrated, coordinated and aligned.

Although often simplified in the literature as a logical evolution in business practices with the information age knowledge worker replacing the industrial era production labourer, the reality is that many organizations require elements of both. This requirement is clearly illustrated in the Institutional Effectiveness Framework presented in the CF Doctrine Manual *Leadership in the Canadian Forces: Conceptual Foundations*. As highlighted in the tension between ensuring consistency, efficiency and coordination (labeled Internal Integration) and optimizing flexibility, creativity and growth (External Adaptability), certain aspects of work still require that individuals follow proscriptive, detailed procedures in conducting certain tasks while others require that the same person be able to exercise judgement to respond to novel circumstances. The CF doctrinal principle of mission command is intended to address the requirement to concurrently provide necessary structure while also authorizing adaptability. As will be illustrated throughout, these tensions are evident in many aspects of the core HR functions of defining work, preparing individuals and ensuring motivation.[15]

ASSIGNING RESPONSIBILITY FOR HR FUNCTIONS

In determining "who does what", the typical differentiations involve distributing responsibility or 'ownership' among individual employees, their line managers and the corporate and field HR staff for various HR activities ranging from routine administration to strategic decision making. As illustrated in Figure 7.1 below, Ulrich integrated the 'who' with the 'what' by dividing HR functions into four domains based on two key factors. The first is whether the activities are primarily related to day-to-day functions or to longer term strategic planning while the second pertains to whether the focus is on the process (information, procedures) or on the people (motivation, commitment, competencies, etc.).

Figure 7.1: Responsiblity for HR Functions

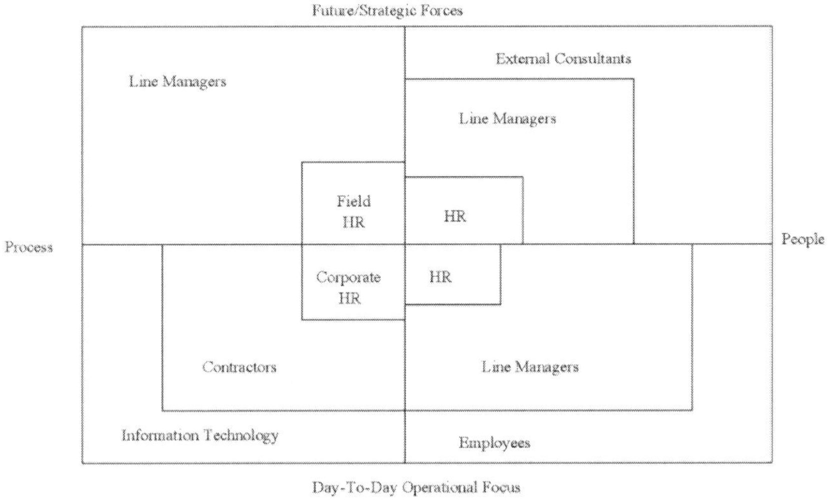

Future/Strategic Forces

Line Managers

External Consultants

Line Managers

Field
HR

HR

Process

People

Corporate
HR

HR

Contractors

Line Managers

Information Technology

Employees

Day-To-Day Operational Focus

Source: Ulrich

Included in Ulrich's consideration are the roles filled by the employees, managers, HR staffs, contractors and Human Resource information systems with the proportion of activity conducted or 'owned' by each shown in the relative amount of space allocated each. For example, the norm is for line managers and HR staff (aided by consultants) to develop the long term strategies to adjust and reskill the workforce for anticipated future requirement while it is up to the employees and their line managers (aided by HR) to develop the short-term plans for individual learning and development. In the day-to-day administration, it has become common for organizations to rely on contractors and automated information systems to carry out functions such as managing pay and benefits with the corporate HR staff providing a monitoring role to ensure that the functions are carried out appropriately and that the data generated is accurate.

In applying Ulrich's model within the Public Service there is an implicit assumption that the line managers and the individual employees are responsible for many aspects of HR. This approach describes the de facto HR System implemented across the Federal Government following the workforce reductions that were imposed during the mid-90s as part of the deficit fighting activities discussed in Chapter 3. During this period there was a shift from the industrial era model to the information age model with consequent adjustments in the roles and responsibilities of workers, supervisors and managers. Concurrently, there was also a shift from a focus on employment, with the implied job security, career ladders, career managers, etc. associated with that concept, to a focus on employability thereby allowing supervisors and employees to co-manage changes in work requirements and career advancement.

Importantly, neither the Central HR Agencies nor the Assistant Deputy Minister Human Resources – Civilians are responsible for ensuring that DND has the civilian workforce needed to achieve their assigned components of the Defence mission.[16] Within the Federal Government, the Central "Corporate HR" staff, specifically Treasury Board and the new Public Service Human Resource Management Agency, are primarily responsible for developing the broad policies, procedural rules and managerial tools to support those at the directorate/work unit level. The department or "Field HR" staff (the ADM (HR-Civ) organization) are responsible for translating these policies, rules and tools into a format that meets the unique requirements of the department and in assisting managers and employees in their co-management of changes.

Beyond achieving a simple reduction in the number of individuals on employment status and attempting to improve the efficiency of the existing system through 'business process re-engineering', the last decade has seen a concerted effort by the Federal Government to fundamentally alter who does what in HR.[17] Although this initiative, referred to as the Universal Classification Standard (UCS) project, was neither well understood nor well managed, the objective was to facilitate the process of allowing employees to control their careers, or at least remain employed when work requirements changed by opening up the internal labour market.[18]

The model depicted at Figure 7.1 needs minor modifications in order to be relevant to the CF. Unlike the civilian public service model, the CF HR System reflects a significantly different division of responsibilities and implied philosophy of who controls which HR functions. Emanating primarily from the nature and obligations of military service highlighted earlier, the CF has retained a highly controlled and controlling HR System with significant centralization of many HR functions. The relative role accorded the Central HR staff in this context is shown at Figure 7.2. It should be noted that the issue of centralized versus decentralized HR pertains to whether decisions are made at the level of those doing the work (managers/ COs and individuals) or by those at higher levels in the organization.

The main difference between the two approaches deals with the implications of a decentralized versus a centralized system. A decentralized system places both responsibility and control at the level at which the work is performed with a fully devolved system passing much of the ownership to the employee. This is the model shown at Figure 7.1 and applicable to the civilian workforce within DND and the broader Federal Government. The centralized approach shown at Figure 7.2 is applicable to the CF and its military members. Thus, while the Regular Force individual is absent from this diagram and the member of the Primary Reserve would be allocated a very small component in the lower right quadrant regarding the choice to accept full time contracts, the significant difference in comparing the military and civilian HR systems pertains to the confused role at the level of line manager/Commanding Officer.[19] When supervising civilian employees, the manager is responsible for a significant proportion of the HR business (defining work requirements, selecting and skilling the employee, managing rewards, etc) while, conversely, having very little control over key aspects for their military personnel.

Figure 7.2: Responsiblity for CF HR Functions

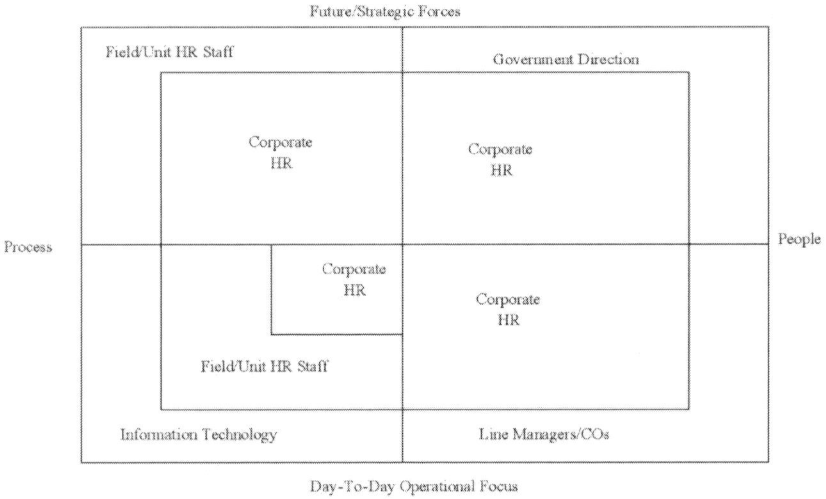

Future/Strategic Forces

Field/Unit HR Staff

Government Direction

Corporate
HR

Corporate
HR

Process

People

Corporate
HR

Corporate
HR

Field/Unit HR Staff

Information Technology

Line Managers/COs

Day-To-Day Operational Focus

Source: Ulrich

Both external factors and internal choices determine the basic model adopted by any organization to structure and organize the HR System. For a similar function such as defining work requirements or selecting individuals to fill vacancies, significant differences exist across organizations in terms of both what gets done and who makes the key decisions. This section has highlighted aspects of the dominant civilian and military HR Systems to illustrate the divergent philosophies and approaches applied for each. It should be noted that there are also very different models in use across allied militaries. The United States Services, for example, operate more decentralized HR Systems including using elements of a free-market economy to enable both COs and individuals to apply cost-benefit analyses in making choices concerning postings, course selection and other career decisions.

Although beyond the scope of this chapter, there are a number of organizing principles that guide decisions regarding how a centralized HR System is structured and how 'corporate' HR is integrated with other strategic functions. Key in these considerations are the subsequent decisions regarding the amount of effort to be devoted to any or all of the HR functions. The principles of effective administration suggest that, when deciding on the type of HR structure to create, it is more important to pay attention to the quality rather than the quantity of HR staff.[20] The CF Transformation activities underway in 2006-2007 represent the latest initiatives in an almost continuous search since Unification in the 1960s for an optimal CF model.

Having provided an overview of both key factors that define what HR is to achieve and who is to do what, the following sections will present the essential elements for the five core HR functions. As stated, the emphasis will be on the dominant Regular Force HR System with references to the Public Service and Primary Reserve approaches where relevant.

Jobs: Defining and Structuring Work Requirements

Virtually all aspects on any HR System are derived from the nature of work to be per-formed. Whether described at the level of specific positions, the small work unit/team, a larger section or element (covering: a ship to a task force, battalion to brigade group or a directorate to a division) or a major component of the defence team (the land force, special operations force, an ADM-level Group), the basis for defining and structuring overall workforce requirements is typically to start with describing work at the discrete position level through the process of job analysis.[21] The information generated is then commonly used to: link jobs into logical groupings; develop all of the procedures to put the 'right person' in the respective job, and create administrative procedures to ensure optimum work productivity.[22] This section will describe the overall approaches used by the CF and PS to define work requirements (what needs to be accomplished) while the subsequent section will then address workforce composition (the people who do the work). As with all HR functions, organizations may select from a wide range of models to define and structure work requirements.

JOB ANALYSIS

The fundamental purpose of any job analysis is to provide a systematic approach to understanding and defining the work requirements at the individual level. The two primary approaches to examining work are generally referred to as task-based and worker-based job analysis.[23] Although the two have significant differences, both are used to collect information on the nature of the work, which leads to a determination of the capabilities that incumbents must possess and the conditions under which the work must be performed. Decisions on the conditions of work lead to the establish-ment of a range of physical/physiological job requirements such as vision, mobility, strength, etc.

The focus of task-based techniques is to describe the activities or procedures that are typically performed by compiling the frequency and importance of key tasks or activities that the job incumbent normally performs (e.g., fires small arms, prepares memos, communicates via radio, manages a budget, etc.) Consistent with the indus-trial era philosophy upon which they are based, task-based job analyses are normally selected when the work to be performed is: predictable, structured and routinized; requires precision and/or synchronization; carries significant consequences when pro-cedural errors occur; and/or must be performed in high demand circumstances where proceduralization can overcome fatigue, stress or panic. The primary results from these analyses are output-focussed work descriptions that are useful for developing standard operating procedures, creating managerial control mechanisms and defining work productivity. These, in turn, lead to objective, performance-oriented criteria for selecting new personnel, creating declarative knowledge training programs or measur-ing the job performance of incumbents. A typical example would be 'types letters at 30 words per minute' or 'strips and re-assembles their weapon in 3 minutes.

The alternate to the task-based approach is the group of worker-based job analyses that identify the capacities that the job incumbent must possess in order to determine how to perform the needed work. Rather than assessing the tasks to be performed, worker-based techniques focus on the intellectual and interpersonal abilities of individuals to exercise independent thinking and apply acquired expertise in deciding when and how to achieve the overall outcomes assigned to the position or, more often, the team. Consistent with the Information Age 'knowledge worker' philosophy, worker-based job analyses are normally applied when the work performed involves: constant work adjustments to meet conflicting or competing work demands; adaptation, creativity and anticipatory thinking to respond to complex, dynamic or novel conditions; inter-dependencies amongst individuals or across teams; expert judgement or reasoning; and/or significant consequences from errors in moral or ethical decision making. The primary results from worker-based job analyses are outcome-focussed individual and team work descriptions that are useful for: creating generic work descriptions, developing accountability frameworks in order to delegate decision making authority and defining overall work objectives. These, in turn, lead to normative, behavioural-oriented criteria for selecting new personnel, creating broad intellectual learning programs or measuring the job performance of incumbents. Typical examples would be: to make effective decisions under pressure, apply professional knowledge to solve complex problems, and adapt communication style to the needs of the audience.

Although most organizations opt for one or the other approach, the reality is that most jobs contain some elements of standardized, procedural tasks and of unstructured, novel reasoning.[24] A generalized model found across many organizations including in the public service and CF HR Systems is to emphasize the task-related declarative and procedural knowledge to define the criteria to be used in selecting/placing the person in the job and then emphasize the worker-related reasoning and behaviours in assessing subsequent performance on the job.

The CF Approach. The approach applied by the CF to conduct systematic analyses of work requirements is derived from task-based job analytic techniques. Originating in the Second World War and developed by the US Air Force, the Task Inventory – Comprehensive Occupational Analysis Programs (properly TI-CODAP although usually referred to as CODAP) provides a powerful tool for conducting task analyses on a workforce wide basis. The results of Occupational Analyses (OAs) provide the basis for what is referred to as the Military Occupational Structures (MOS). The recent Military Occupation Structure Analysis, Redesign and Tailoring (MOSART) work along with the previous Trade Advancement for Skill and Knowledge (TASK) represent attempts to redefine how the overall military workforce is structured.[25]

The core of the MOS is a complex grouping of individual positions with similar task requirements into broader 'job families' that, in turn, are used to structure long term career patterns. Statistical analyses of the amount of commonality or difference in the tasks performed across jobs are used to generate three outputs of importance. The first is the identification of commonalities to create broader grouping of 'jobs' and job families into occupations and of occupations into career fields. As the CF is currently not able to adopt a 'clean slate' to structure occupations,[26] the more accurate description is that the results are used to make decisions to amend the existing groupings of jobs and occupations.[27] The second output is the use of differences in types of tasks and/or level of complexity to split occupations into different learning stages or Developmental Periods. The third output is to identify significant commonalities across either the same DP/rank or across a broad number of jobs found in the larger sectors or elements of employment (typically those in the land, sea or air operational environment) to split job requirements into CF common, environmental common or occupation specific.

The net result is that the CF applies a cyclical approach to systematically collect task-based data and conduct statistical analyses in order to make decisions to amend the existing groupings of positions into jobs, jobs into occupations and occupations into career fields and/or to amend the established CF common, environmental or occupation specifications.[28] The results generated are then used to make subsequent changes in key HR functions particularly in defining job qualifications, training requirements, and informing career management and professional development requirements.

Occupational Analysis results also inform decisions in other key HR Functions including amending elements of compensation and establishing medical/fitness standards as well as providing input to decisions in other supporting activities such as the acquisition of equipment and clothing or the design of work stations, work places or offices. In particular, the CF HR System incorporates a complex approach to address physical work requirements. Reflecting the tensions between capability to perform current tasks versus capacity to perform a range of plausible future tasks, and noting that there is a direct relationship between the type of equipment available and physical standards, the CF has placed an emphasis on the ability to perform a group of common physical activities that are used as an indicator of capacity to perform a range of plausible demanding tasks. [29]

One of the significant weaknesses of the current approach to Occupational Analyses is that CF requirements change much more rapidly than the periodic OAs and resultant amendments to specifications.[30] Both formal and informal strategies are used to address this issue. One approach is to 'reverse engineer' the workforce structure and based on the implicit generic/generalist model that all individuals of the same rank and MOC have met the same qualification (hence possess the same job-relevant capabilities), new organizations can be created through the use of expert judgement. As an example, those responsible for creating a new section may decide that one position requires the capabilities assigned to the Captain level in the Intelligence occupation while another requires the capabilities possessed by all CF LCols etc. Thus, rather than defining the job requirements and amending the MOS, the existing MOS is used to define the job requirements. A second approach is to allow units/Formations to amend key aspects of specific positions (assigned ranks or occupation, or certain occupations qualifications) with centralized controls exercised to manage the overall impact on the force structure. A third approach is to conduct specific OAs when major new equipment/platforms are introduced.[31] The primary informal strategy employed is to implicitly allow experienced practitioners to modify their interpretation of job requirements particularly in the areas of professional development and career management when they know that the published specifications have been overcome by events.

One of the reasons for the use of reverse engineering to fit the existing structure is that OA's contribute to defining the personnel structure, which includes the specification of duties, responsibilities and qualifications related to performing tasks. However, the personnel structure is embedded within the overall force structure that is used to create the military capabilities needed to discharge CF obligations and achieve mission objectives.[32] Thus, amendments to the personnel structure are constrained in two key dimensions. First, the nature of the roles and responsibilities assigned to a unit necessarily define the sum total of all work to be performed while the type of equipment and infrastructure allocated often set limits in how this work may be performed. Second, the numbers of positions allocated restrict the latitude in assigning specific tasks to specific positions. Simplistically, force structure decisions drive key elements of assigning who does what with which knowledge and what type of enabling technologies. Thus, it must be recognized that efforts to adjust or 'transform' the personnel structure (such as the TASK and MOSART initiatives) cannot overcome problems inherent in the force structure.

The PS Approach. As already stated, over the last ten years, the Federal Government has adopted the opposite model of focussing on worker characteristics and delegating the general responsibility for defining work requirements down to the manager. In theory, individual managers create new position-specific work descriptions or, more often, amend existing work descriptions to reflect changing worker requirements. The worker elements that reflect intellectual effort, level of responsibility etc contained in the work description are evaluated by reviewers with knowledge of worker-based job analysis to assign the appropriate classification and level based on existing norms applied across the Public Service.[33] The 'classified' work description is then used to establish hiring/selection standards or on-job performance requirements including identifying requisite new learning/training for the job incumbent.

Similar to the CF and reflected in the previously mentioned UCS exercise, the Public Service HR System is also based on long-standing, well-established approaches to organizing and managing the overall workforce. As with the submission of a change in a specific CF position, managers are constrained by working with an existing broad framework of classifications and levels. As a result, the overall PS HR System is heavily based on reverse engineering which can include the manager picking a predetermined, already classified 'generic' work description rather than writing one tailored to the real position requirements or in applying a predetermined evaluation of generic knowledge, skills or abilities rather than selecting a new employee based on a position-specific selection procedure. Thus, while the PS system is advertised as embracing the philosophy of decentralizing ownership of the job to the manager and employee, there remain significant centralizing control mechanisms that serve to ensure the comparability, equity and parity across work units. This remains a key difference between the public service and private sector HR Systems.

Administration And Organizational Structure

Although the establishment of work requirements through some form of job analysis is considered to be the core of any system to organize and structure the work to be done, organizations also create complex administration to integrate, coordinate and align individual and team activities. Given the bureaucratic requirements of government, both the CF and PS rely on administrative systems and organizational structures to control/ guide the work to be performed. The four administrative areas that are most commonly addressed pertain to: specifying the outcomes or outputs to be generated; allocating requisite resources; providing principles, rules or procedures to be followed; and, defining the authorities vested in specific positions to make decisions affecting work outcomes or procedures. The primary organizational function applied is the creation of 'organization charts' to structure who works with whom under which supervision.

More importantly, the core Federal Government approach that is applied to all aspects of Defence is the use of business planning techniques to: assign broad responsibilities; define the 'lines of business' with specified outcomes and/or outputs to be achieved; and, allocate key resources to do so.[34] As discussed in the earlier chapters on the defence management system and budgeting, business plans are typically created at differing levels of organizational responsibility starting with the single overall (L0) plan for Defence as a whole and often breaking down to the unit or sub-unit level (L4 or L5). As the next level down is the individual position, the final component is the individual position job description. Thus, the integration of a job description for the specific position with an organizational chart showing who reports to whom, along with a business plan describing the upcoming year's objectives to be achieved, provide the basis for structuring the workforce and ensuring that key outcomes are achieved. This entire process is connected to a performance measurement system that is intended to provide the feedback and strategic oversight to ensure that planned outcomes were, in fact, attained.

While this approach generally describes 'who does what with which resources', two additional components are used to provide the administrative framework that controls what is achieved and the means used to do so. The first is the application of a top-down departmental organizational and accountability framework that specifies ongoing responsibilities and authorities for key positions.[35] It is through the assigned authorities that the wide range of bureaucratic policies, rules, and procedural controls are applied to regulate how work is to be conducted. For example, the integrated DND and CF, Departmental Administrative Orders and Directives (DAODs) represent a key element in the regulatory systems used to define how work may be conducted.

The second component is the use of a broad framework of reporting and measurement to provide the complementary bottom-up feedback on how well delegated responsibilities were met. Again, reflecting the bureaucratic nature of government functioning, Defence uses a complex set of programmed reports to routinely capture key outputs and outcomes and to provide both Departmental authorities and Central Agencies with selected information on individual and team performance. For public service executives, personal assessments are generated based on individual Performance

Management Agreements. In theory, these are used to allocate annual work objectives including selected key objectives for which financial bonuses may be awarded.[36]

Although there is a well recognized set of principles to be applied in creating the organizational structures linking jobs together (e.g., span of control, commonality of work, etc.),[37] there are two issues of note in their application within Defence. First, the combinations of tradition and implicit norms (the way it has always been done) and 'turf war' conflicts created by formally delegating responsibility to the line manager yet retaining centralized control over many facets that dictate work structures (e.g., limits on available salary wage envelopes (SWE)) have resulted in organizational structures that appear to be sub-optimal.[38] One key indicator is the type of work being conducted through private sector contractors. While the concept of the boundary-less organization and the use of 'outsourcing' can be an effective way to get work done the administrative procedures related to business planning, accountability frameworks, etc., provide surprisingly little information to manage, coordinate or measure these activities.[39]

Second, while organizational charts remain common in the private sector as well, those businesses that rely heavily on flexibility in highly dynamic markets have shifted from a focus on individual jobs to the concept of self-organizing teams. As a result, they have abandoned the static organization chart approach and instead map out broader, team-based functions with the idea that the composition of the team can grow or shrink based on the expertise needed at the time. A good example is a hospital operating room where the exact composition of any one surgical team is determined based on the patient's condition and the requirements of the surgical team. Thus a particular medical practitioner can lead one team in the morning and serve as an assistant in another team in the afternoon. Although seniors in NDHQ have been referring to a matrix management approach for over 20 years now, there are persistent indicators that the staff functions in Defence continue to be managed in a classical, hierarchical control manner.[40]

Unique Aspects in the CF. Although the overall approach of organizing and structuring work based on business planning, accountability frameworks, and org charts is applied equally to the CF and the PS, the reality is that these mechanisms are neither fully effective nor, in some cases, appropriate. The fundamental problem created through the application of these approaches is that these are overly rigid/static and do not permit the flexibility that the CF, in particular, requires to respond in a timely manner to plausible but not planned taskings. As a result the CF has developed (or, more accurately, retained based on decades of experience) unique additional elements that serve to augment or replace the standard government approach to organizing who does what.

First, is the focus on capabilities which, in turn, allows the CF to organize using the force structure and, implicitly, incorporates elements of the self-organizing team presented above. Whether at the level of a Brigade Group or Naval Task Force or, more discretely, a Military Police Platoon or a Helicopter Air Detachment, the core concept is to rely on units/teams rather than individual positions as the fundamental building blocks to ensure the CF can achieve a wide range of mission objectives. Within this structure, the capacities and responsibilities of the individual are represented by the allocation of rank, occupation and any specific qualifications (rather than relying on a job description). This allows Commanding Officers and their subordinate supervisors considerable flexibility in assigning people to tasks within the Unit.

Second, the use of doctrine to articulate the principles to guide what is to be done and, as part of that doctrine, the application of mission command through which those in responsibility provide sufficient direction to ensure that mission objectives are understood without unduly constraining the latitude, flexibility or creativity of subordinates to determine how to do so. Third, the application of a professional model that, amongst other purposes, serves to replace the use of job descriptions and Defence Administrative Orders and Directives (DAODs) to dictate work activities with articulation of the philosophy, obligations and values that allow individuals to exercise judgement in determining how to operate within the mission command concept. Together, these three elements serve to shift the dominant managerial model from the control of individual work outputs to the coordination of collective effort. This emphasis on collective effort is one of the key factors that limit the direct transferability of private sector HR practices to the CF.

This section has provided a brief overview of the core issues and approaches used to organize and structure the work requirements of the Defence workforce. In defining the work requirements, the two HR Systems differ in two key aspects. The first is that the CF uses a task-based approach to analyze work requirements while the Public Service has shifted to a worker-based model. The second is that the CF has retained a centralized approach with 'corporate' HR Staff responsible for many aspects of defining work requirements and establishing work-related standards while the PS has delegated a significant degree of discretion and responsibility for these functions to the line manager. Given the size and complexity of the Defence workforce and the generalized requirements of the HR System, both rely on a complex system of administration to establish the parameters within which COs/managers and individuals must operate in determining both what needs to be accomplished and how to do so. The key difference between the two systems is that the CF augments or replaces the standardized government bureaucratic approach with unique ways to organize the force structure and guide individual and group activities. As will be presented starting with the following section, the way in which core work requirements are defined and controlled has direct consequences on the 'people' requirements – who does this work based on which individual capacities, motivation and values.

People: Workforce Composition

Regardless of how work is measured, organized or administered, it is the people who fill the various positions that are the essential element in 'getting work done'. As indicated in the basic description of HR, putting the right person in the right job, the definition of work requirements provides the basis to ensure that job incumbents are able to achieve assigned work objectives. Thus, a key facet of filling the workforce with the right people is that work requirements must be translated into the personal qualifications that individuals must possess.

As neither the work requirements nor the workforce are static, the two principle activities that the HR System must address regarding workforce composition are to select new individuals to fill vacant positions or to prepare current members/employees for changing job duties. In filling vacant jobs, analyses have to be conducted to determine whether it will be possible to simply select the ideal person from a pool of job-ready (qualified) candidates or whether it will be necessary to provide extensive job preparation for those with the potential to learn how to perform this work. As both the PS and CF operate a primarily closed labour system, the third critical element, involving a combination of both, is to develop a system for succession management to ensure that individuals are prepared for and selected to fill positions with greater responsibilities. All three components rely on the criteria derived from job analyses to establish the essential characteristics or qualifications that individuals must possess to carry out their duties. Thus, this section will discuss the approaches used to translate job requirements into personnel qualification and then apply these to define the selection and training/ development functions.

JOB QUALIFICATIONS: COMPETENCIES VS KSAOS

In managing workforce composition, the core element to be defined pertains to the requisite job-relevant capacities that incumbents must possess. The traditional Industrial Era approach, derived from task-based job analyses, was to identify the position-specific knowledge, skills, abilities and other attributes (KSAOs) that the individual needs to possess to perform key functions or tasks. The lists developed tended to focus on factual/declarative knowledge, physical skills and the abilities needed to follow proscribed procedures in order to perform the tasks to a set minimum standard of proficiency. The shift to information era work demands and the related use of worker-based job analyses expanded the domain of KSAOs to include broader theory-based knowledge, reasoning, communication and inter-personal skills and the ability to apply judgement and creativity to ensure optimum or exceptional job performance. Over time, this expanded approach to defining KSAOs has become labeled competencies and many organizations (including the Public Service) have shifted to what are referred to as competency-based systems to manage workforce composition.

While there is still some debate about the two,[41] competencies and KSAOs are generally similar with most definitions of both terms reflecting that they: describe the essential individual characteristics that underlie effective job performance; must be measurable or observable; and, must distinguish superior performers from others.[42] The differences between competencies and KSAOs are primarily in the amount of emphasis given to the capability of the person to work effectively in the specific position versus their capacity to adapt to new requirements either due to a change in their current job duties or moving to a new position. Thus, an HR System built on position-specific KSAOs is designed to ensure that individuals can perform their specific duties effectively but may need assistance (often through preparatory training/education) in learning to transfer their expertise when they change jobs. Conversely, a system based on broader career-focused competencies is intended to identify those who can be transferred from one job to the next recognizing that they may need some assistance (often through supervision/ on-job-training) in learning how to apply their broad expertise to the specific requirements of the new job.[43]

To integrate the previous discussion of task-based versus worker-based job analyses with the use of broad transferable competencies versus position-specific KSAOs, virtually all HR Systems have to manage two requirements. The first is to balance the relative emphasis given to individuals' abilities to follow proscribed procedures to perform predicted tasks efficiently versus the ability to apply independent reasoning to perform novel tasks effectively. Too much of a focus on procedural efficiency can result in individuals being paralyzed when faced with novel tasks while the opposite focus can result in very creative individuals who lack the ability to perform key tasks to the required standard. The second is the emphasis on the short-term optimization of performance in a single position versus the capacity to transfer previous learning through a series of positions following a career path. An exclusive focus on the current position can leave the individual and/or organization with little information as to other jobs they could perform while an over-reliance on broad career capabilities may make it very difficult to identify the specific position for which a person is ideally suited.

Job Qualifications: CF Approach. As stated in the summary of job-analyses, the CF collects workforce-wide data on job requirements using position-specific task-based job analysis and then aggregates these results into broader groupings of 'job', occupations and career fields with identification of CF-common, employment environment-common and occupation-specific requirements. This approach provides the CF with a basis to balance the two demands presented above. Based more on acquired wisdom rather than theory-based logic, the process of extracting CF 'qualifications' implicitly applies two key criteria. The first is to identify the critical tasks/procedures that must be performed with maximum efficiency (e.g., emergency drills, safety procedures, etc.) to generate (task-based) performance-oriented qualifications versus identifying those types of tasks that require flexibility and judgement (e.g., leadership, command, strategic planning etc.) to generate (worker-based) reasoning-focussed qualifications.[44] The second is to apply a generalized model of professionals as developing over 10-12 years from being an apprentice through journeyman to mastery of their profession. Implicit in the concept of 'learn to walk before you run', this model emphasizes job-specific capabilities in a narrow range of the professional domain in junior positions with an expansion of the range of job requirements as one develops their expertise and understanding of the profession.

As a result, the CF HR System operates with a shifting focus across the successive stages of a professional career. Entry-level job qualifications tend to focus more on procedure-based, within occupation, output requirements (what tasks do I as an individual have to perform today) while the most advanced level (senior officer/NCM) job qualifications focus almost exclusively on reasoning-based, profession-wide, outcome requirements (what net effects do I as a leader have to ensure the broader team achieves in the future).

To very much simplify the 50 year evolution that occurred from the beginning to the end of the Cold War era, the primary change in how CF job qualifications are defined has been to compress the time allotted for transition from novice to competent to mastery. For example, junior officers are now expected to enter the real workforce (operational units) at the journeyman/competent stage rather than allowing the Lieutenant and junior Captain level positions to be merely extended apprentice/learning phases and senior NCMs are expected to reach the mastery level rather than peaking at the journeyman/technical expert level. As will be highlighted in the subsequent discussion of training, the primary consequence of this shift to have CF members fully competent within the profession at an earlier stage is the requirement to change the nature of preparatory learning (i.e., the professional development system).

Job Qualifications: PS Approach. Following the shift to decentralized management of the workforce, the PS has addressed the requirements to balance the two dimensions of procedure-based efficiency versus reasoning-based flexibility and position-specific capability vs capacity to transfer expertise to other jobs by adopting a broad competency approach for overall workforce planning while delegating responsibility for job performance to the individual manager. Thus, the Central and DND HR Staffs draw on the worker-based, judgement, reasoning and inter-personal competencies that are highlighted in standardized work descriptions to ensure that the existing workforce is both capable of making appropriate decisions to get current work done and, collectively, has the capacity to assume positions of greater responsibility when promoted. HR Staff also assume that the individual manager will address the requirements to optimize work productivity in the current position by providing appropriate supervision, guidance, SOPs and position-specific training.

In comparing the CF and PS approaches, it is important to recognize that one of the assumed outcomes of the mid-90s "Program Review" process was that the breadth of the managerial work to be performed in the Public Service would be reduced with increased commonality across departments. It was the assumption that the Federal Government Public Service component of the workforce need only address a relatively narrow domain of senior/executive functions that is underlying the PS HR System's emphasis on using broad competency frameworks to define job qualifications. The related assumption that there are significant commonalities in core job requirements across all positions in all departments also explains the model of a single generalist career path leading to becoming a Public Service Executive. The application of this model in those departments that have retained multiple lines of operations and extensive service delivery functions that are quite unique, such as that found in DND, has led to mixed results to date.

LABOUR POOL ANALYSES

Regardless of whether using the CF detailed, differentiated model to define job qualifications or the PS generic competency approach, once job qualifications are defined, it is then necessary to consider who might be interested and available to fill these positions. Whether evaluating the existing labour force to assess candidates for internal advancement or the broader, external labour market to assess applicants to join the CF or the Public Service, the conclusions reached have significant consequences for the two core functions of selecting and preparing people. The key assumption applied for PS staffing is that there will be a suitable pool of job-ready candidates to enter the PS and that subsequent experience augmented by employee directed self-development should also provide an acceptable number of job-ready candidates to move up to higher positions. The CF, on the other hand, recognizes that there is no pool of already qualified job candidates ready to join and that experience and self-directed learning are not sufficient to generate the required number of candidates for advancement within. Thus, for the CF, the core assumption made is that there should be a suitable pool of individuals interested in joining or advancing who possess the potential to complete the intermediate stage of job preparation (i.e., able to pass entry level courses).

The combination of these assumptions regarding the labour pool and the differences between the CF centralized versus PS decentralized HR Systems result in the CF expending considerable effort to deliver the selection, development/training and career management functions while the PS concentrates on simply providing the policies and tools to allow the manager and individual to carry these out. In this context, the CF applicant pool is an important factor in the CF approach to selection and development.

CF Applicant Pool Analyses. A key consideration for the CF (and the PS) in assessing who is interested in joining is the question of why they are interested in joining. The dominant assumption in most HR Systems is that people are looking for jobs that pay well. Thus, the typical private sector labour pool analyses is conducted by applying cost-benefit models to determine the salary level for any job that will ensure a suitable number of candidates without paying more for their services than is necessary.[45] An alternate (and rather idealistic) assumption is that individuals join professions such as law, medicine, the profession of arms or the public service because they are motivated to serve society. Noting that the concept of a 'calling' likely only applies to the clergy and both the CF and PS would like to attract individuals with a vocational rather than an occupational ethic,[46] the reality is that the analyses of who is interested in working in any organization is based on a complex set of factors. The three that are most relevant for Defence are:

a.   the current labour market conditions - the availability of alternate jobs for which the person is qualified, the number of others interested in the same job, the relative benefits offered by one employer compared to another;

b.   the potential applicant's perceptions of the fit between their personal career and life objectives and the opportunities presented by an employer; and

c.   the general image, reputation, and visibility of the employer or chosen career.

Simplistically, any combination of: high unemployment amongst one's labour market peers; a perceived good fit between personal goals and job characteristics; and, a positive image/known reputation of the employer will likely lead to a large pool of applicants while low unemployment, a poor fit or a negative image/lack of awareness will result in a smaller group of individuals applying.[47]

Of importance, while remuneration is a factor, both internal CF and external labour market analyses have demonstrated considerable 'elasticity' whereby individuals have to be offered considerably higher rates of pay before they will choose an unattractive job over one that is of greater interest to them.[48] Conversely, while many military members may stay in uniform to serve society, the evidence suggests that this is an acquired orientation not the motive for joining in the first place.[49] Instead the characteristics of many applicants to the CF are that they represent groups that are seeking alternatives for employment, personal growth, and/or social advancement that are not readily available or accessible to them due to a combination of level of education, geographic location and/or discrimination based on group identity. Thus, those joining tend to over-represent rural or smaller communities, lower income families and/or those who have not had success in school or initial employment. Two additional characteristics are that those who have had contact with the military (either through family members who served or cadets) tend to be over-represented while members of several culturally distinct groups, particularly first generation visible minority communities, express a strong interest in joining however those who actually join tend to opt for service in the Reserves rather than in the Regular Force.[50]

The net result is that the CF continues to operate somewhere between the preferred status of 'employer of choice' selecting from amongst 'the best and the brightest' and the pessimistic 'employer of last resort' forced to choose the best of the desperate. There are two primary indicators of the depth and breadth of the potential number of CF applicants. The first is that the number of job applicants relative to the number of positions to be filled tends to be smaller than is the case for quasi-comparable other organizations such as the Royal Canadian Mounted Police (RCMP) or allied militaries such as in the United States, the United Kingdom or Australia. Although there are significant differences across nations that explain what is usually referred to as youth propensity to join, the CF has traditionally attracted about one-half the number of applicants per vacancy than has been the case for similar allied nations and only about one-third the ratio of those who have completed high school (for NCMs) or a baccalaureate degree (for officers). The second indicator is the concern that the CF has regarding the management of retention, particularly for occupations with comparable civilian careers (doctors and pilots tend to lead the parade followed by engineers and technicians). The overall indicators are that those who have a range of job choices either after completing their education or once qualified in a skilled area tend to choose an employer other than the CF.

ATTRACTION AND TRAINING

In assessing the implications of the traditional demographics of the CF applicant pool, it is important to recognize the links among the four functions of: attraction, selection, placement and professional development. When the ratio of the number applying to the number of job vacancies is large, it is possible to raise the normative selection standard, to optimize the placement of individuals into the most appropriate occupation/career stream and, finally, to minimize the professional development needed to close the gap between applicants' competencies and CF job requirements. Conversely, when the ratio is low, it is necessary to reduce the normative selection standard, to place individuals into occupations for which they may not be best suited and to increase the developmental investment to make them job ready. In this regard, the normative standard refers to the qualifications of the majority of those enrolled not the minimum standards to be considered eligible to join. Most involved in the CF Professional Development System would recognize that there would be significant consequences if every enrollee met only the minimum standards for each of: education, physical health, fitness, work experience, life success, maturity and work motivation.

In managing the tensions between quality of enrollees and investment in subsequent training, the CF tends to focus on two key 'success' indicators: the total numbers enrolled and the proportion who pass the training to become occupation qualified. These generally reflect the dominant 'sufficiency' model in the CF personnel generation system. The intent is to ensure that those enrolled possess sufficient potential (i.e., meet the minimum recruiting standards) to be able to achieve the course standard (i.e., the minimum required to pass) and can, therefore, perform their job adequately (again, meet the minimum standard required). As expressed in the MOS principle of cost-effectiveness, the rationale is to minimize the initial HR recruiting and training costs by concentrating on threshold competencies.[51]

The alternate would be a mastery model that is focused on selecting and developing those who will have the highest level of job performance. The key underlying difference is the metric used for measuring cost effectiveness. The current model uses the numbers 'produced' (enrolled or trained) divided by the resources invested (hence average cost per enrollee and cost per course serial) to measure effectiveness.[52] Conversely, a mastery model would use the level of subsequent individual job performance to optimize return on investment per person. The assumptions for focussing on ROI (utility analysis) include the notion that teams/Units with more top performers will be more effective in operations (the ultimate criterion) and the understanding that top performers will more likely (and more quickly) be able to assume increased responsibilities. In comparison to the CF, the US and UK militaries tend to put more emphasis (and invest more resources) in attracting college and university graduates based on their assessment that these individuals are much more likely to attain top marks on courses and to demonstrate outstanding performance on the job. Thus, in comparison to measuring numbers enrolled and proportion who completed training, an alternate model based on emphasizing performance effectiveness would assess the accuracy of selection decisions through the quality of subsequent on-job performance appraisals and the accuracy of job placements through the assessment of retention in occupation rather than early release or occupation transfer.

Training And Development

Based on the clearly opposite assumptions of PS hiring (entry-level candidates will be job ready) and CF recruiting (all need significant additional development), the two HR Systems take a very different approach to providing job-related development. As indicated earlier, the PS provides relatively little job-specific preparatory training however does provide short courses in a range of skill areas that managers and/or employees can choose to use to upgrade skills. As with the private sector, the PS offers very selected career advancement training through accelerated mid- or senior-level executive development programs such as the Policy Internship program for preparing Master's level graduates to become policy officers or the Career Assignment Program to rapidly move middle managers up to the executive (EX) level.[53]

The key factor underlying the majority of PS professional development is the general assumption that the 'half-life' of factual knowledge is about four years hence individuals must constantly update their knowledge just to remain productive in their current job.[54] Thus, much of what is offered in the PS is what the CF would refer to as refresher training. Consistent with the general PS model of employability, the onus is clearly on the individual to develop their own career/learning plan and to access the limited career development opportunities.

In contrast, the CF Professional Development System assumes that the onus for keeping individuals qualified or in preparing them for the next rank lies with the CF and not the member. The CF, therefore, operates an extensive professional development system comprised of both individual and team development. The CF Individual Training and Education System (CFITES) consists of sequential, pre-determined and standardized courses designed to prepare individuals for effective employment in their first operational unit and to subsequently either retain skills or to prepare them for increased levels of responsibility. Complementing this individual learning is the critical Force Generation function of engaging in team/collective training to similarly prepare units for operational employment and to subsequently either retain unit level capacities or to prepare the unit for unique missions. Within the overall CF management framework, the domain of "professional development" is usually constrained to the individual preparation component however it should be noted that it is the collective, cyclical, operational and/or pre-deployment unit level training that is of the greatest importance (and greater cost in terms of person-years, equipment and operating budgets).[55]

Over the last decade, the Professional Development System has been shifting in two important ways to provide more effective, longer term learning that is, in fact, based on the development of professionals.[56] The first is the recognition that the expertise that members of professions apply to provide their unique service to society is based on a theory-based body of knowledge. True professional development, therefore, requires an understanding of the theories and concepts that underpin professional practice. Guided by the objectives of *Officership 2020 and NCM Corps 2020*, the CF Professional Development System has been giving greater emphasis to providing the broad framework, models and theories that inform the tactical, technical procedures that are emphasized in entry-level training and initial operational employment.[57] Often seen as a shift from skills training to academic education, both Junior Officers and, increasingly, mid-level NCMs are exposed to coverage of broader, conceptual subject matter that informs the role of the military. In doing so, individuals are being assisted in developing intellectual skills in independent and critical analyses through logical thinking and inductive and deductive reasoning which, in turn, facilitate the life-long, adult learning that is critical to maintaining professional competence.

The second shift in developing professionals is the concurrent recognition of the role of professional identity and the requirement for members to internalize the profession's orientation, values, expectations and obligations in order to exercise personal judgement when faced with complex or ambiguous settings. Although implicitly included in traditional individual and collective training, the CF has gradually recognized that the formal, industrial era CFITES emphasis on performance-oriented skill acquisition did not fully address the formation of the 'whole person' as it lacked the complementary requirement to instill a professional identity.

Reflecting the tensions between developing the ability to perform predicted tasks versus the capacity to adapt to meet novel demands, the most significant shift in the CF PD System has been to expand development to address the 'slow growth' attributes related to internalizing the military ethos and acquiring the unique perspective needed to exercise judgement in applying military capabilities to achieve assigned mission objectives. Together, the increased emphasis on providing broader, theory-based learning and in shaping professional identity have altered the focus of CF PD from training the individual on how to perform tasks to educating them as to why the task is required.

This section has provided an overview of the key factors that define the core HR function of selecting and preparing individuals to be able to carry out required job activities. Drawing from the initial discussion of the unique nature of military service and, in particular, the requirement for the CF to prepare unqualified civilians for a range of plausible tasks versus the PS assumption that individuals will be job ready, the two apply significantly different approaches. The CF has maintained a planned, structured and centralized Professional Development System while the PS has adopted the opposite philosophy of delegating to the manager (and employee) the responsibilities to both select the right person and provide them with necessary job-relevant training. Given forecast Canadian demographics including age profiles, education levels, rate of urbanization and segmented identity,[58] both will likely have to continually evaluate the effectiveness of their respective attraction strategies and may have to alter elements of the HR production system. Within the CF individual professional development component, changes have been implemented to provide a broader foundation of professional knowledge and orientation with, in particular, significant shifts occurring for Junior Officers and mid-to senior NCMs.

Careers: Workforce Management

Of equal importance to the entry-level activities of selecting and preparing new hires for their initial job, all HR Systems have to address the subsequent management of the overall workforce including advancing those who are able to assume increased responsibilities, laterally transferring those who would be better employed in alternate areas or terminating the contracts for those whose services are no longer required. As with virtually all HR Functions, workforce management practices have to balance organizational requirements with individuals' expectations. Given large workforces that rely on a closed labour market and promotion from within, the PS and CF are faced with significant planned and unforecast 'churn' as individuals move from one position to another or exit the organization.[59] The CF engages in much more detailed and planned workforce management under the general label of career management while the PS provides HR services that generally respond to individual manager/position requirements. This reflects the core difference between the centralized, controlled CF HR System and the decentralized, supporting PS HR System.

Also, the CF works very hard at things like succession planning or management. When considering overall workforce management issues, it is important to differentiate between succession management and vacancy management. Succession management (also referred to as talent management) reflects a proactive, intentional process of identifying those individuals with potential to make a significant contribution by assuming more senior responsibilities. It is usually conducted in the context of analyses of the job demands of the more senior executive and forecasts of likely vacancies. On the other hand, vacancy management generally reflects a more passive, reactive approach of developing policies and procedures to fill vacant positions if and as these arise. As employees may be absent due to personal circumstances or leave their current position on relatively short notice, all large organizations have to engage in some amount of vacancy management including deciding where and/or when managers are going to be faced with an imbalance between the amount of work assigned and capabilities of available employees. Reflecting the underlying philosophies of each, the CF emphasizes a comprehensive succession management program while the PS tends to follow the private sector model of applying a vacancy management approach for entry-level and more junior positions with the selected use of succession management strategies for more senior positions.[60]

Forecasting and HR Information Systems. Whether referred to as succession planning or vacancy management, all HR Systems have to conduct some form of analyses and projections of the workforce in order to anticipate future requirements. Linking together the two previous sections on work requirements and workforce composition, these assessments must consider likely changes in both the nature of the work to be performed including the creation or deletion of individual positions, workgroups/teams or larger organizational structures and changes in job incumbents including potential promotions, postings, vacancies, retirements or other separations. HR information systems such as the PeopleSoft application in Defence are intended to provide the essential information to conduct these forecasts by collecting both job- and person-related information.

Although both use the same system, there are four significant differences between the PS and CF approaches. The first two arise from the fact that the PS use reflects the PS philosophy of employee-directed careers that PeopleSoft is intended to support. As a result, the PS is closer to the private sector model of allowing the individual and the manager to access, use and amend information within the system whereas the CF tends to restrict the use of PeopleSoft data to more senior levels or to HR staff. Further, the PS relies on the overall outputs from PeopleSoft as the primary basis to conduct forecasting while the CF uses PeopleSoft data as one input and incorporates other information sources to conduct forecasting. The third factor is that the focus of the PS workforce management is on large groupings of jobs or employees (most typically the EX community and the EX –1 feeder group) while the CF individually manages each position and each individual. Finally, reflecting the meso-level responsibilities of the civilian HR (HR-Civ) organization within DND, overall PS workforce forecasting is conducted within the Treasury Board Secretariat (TBS) while individual vacancy management occurs at the local level with the HR-Civ organization primarily extrapolating from the TBS analyses to examine emerging issues for DND or, on occasion, identifying potential requirements within a specific sector of the DND workforce.

CF Forecasting. The significantly greater emphasis given to workforce forecasting and anticipatory planning in the CF is due to the four related factors. The first is the almost exclusive use of internal mobility to advance individuals from entry level position through successive stages of employment. The second is the fact that, given the demands of military service, the CF would, ideally, like to have a generally younger workforce than most employers and, therefore, has to pay greater attention to moving people out of the organization. The third is the requirement to offset frequent operational employment with more static non-operational postings leading to increased numbers of job changes. The final factor is the use of job rotation and lengthy career courses to prepare individuals for future employment. Given the resultant inter-connections where one job change influences many others, the CF conducts succession planning at each rank for each occupation.

Occupation forecasting is conducted using a range of inputs with most based on a combination of historical trend analyses to predict attrition and policy/program input to forecast significant changes in numbers or levels of positions. Typically integrated into an Annual Military Occupation Review (AMOR), the results of modelling projections and subject matter expert inputs are used to forecast rates for overall attrition leading to predicted promotions which, in turn, tend to drive key course loadings, job changes to prepare individuals for the next rank and, finally, new recruiting intakes. Since all CF members serve on a specified length contract, predictions can also be compared to preferred long range planning models (the ideal profiles of years of service for each MOC) to establish parameters for exercising decisions to retain or release members. These decisions are typically made when members are nearing the completion of their current engagement or are subject to a career review for reasons such as a change in medical category that would restrict their subsequent employment.

While results vary significantly by rank and MOC, in normal circumstances, between 25-30% of all Regular Force members are forecast to change jobs each year with approximately 7% predicted to leave the CF annually.[61] In understanding the implications of an average attrition rate of 7%, consideration must be given to the typically elevated loss rates during the first 2-3 years of service resulting from training failures, medical problems and individuals' realizing that they really do not want a military career.[62] The net result is that the CF planning models assume that those who make it to 3 years of service will complete an average of 22 years of service or past the initial point where they are eligible to draw a pension. It should, however, be noted that, the combination of workforce structure decisions taken in the mid-90s combined with current efforts to expand the Regular Force have resulted in the CF recently opting to retain more individuals for a longer period of service hence accepting an older workforce in order to reduce attrition and decrease the strain on the recruiting and initial training components. Figure 7.3 below is an example of the Years of Service Profile for the Regular Force prepared by Directorate of Strategic Military Personnel Research and Analysis (DSMPRA).

Figure 7.3: Example Years of Service Profile - Reg F 1 Apr 08

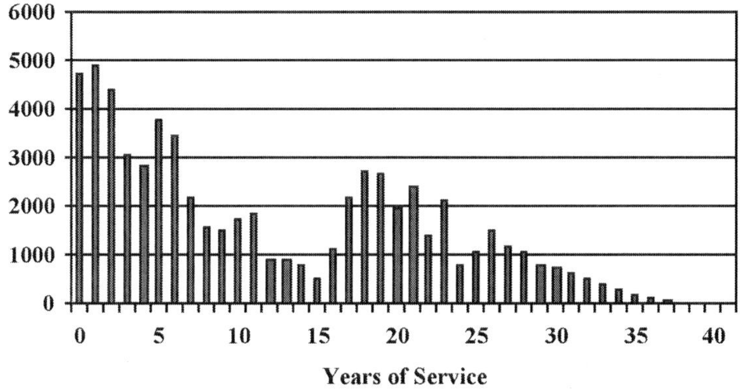

Source: Directorate of Strategic Military Personnel Research and Analysis (DSMPRA)

PS Vacancy management. Although the PS does apply some elements of succession management to address the EX level and certain hard to attract/retain classifications, the overall workforce management is generally addressed using a vacancy management approach. The core of this system is the use of job competitions to fill positions when the job incumbent leaves. In the past, competitions were conducted by the manager for each position with HR staff assisting in preparing the statement of qualifications and the assessment criteria to be applied. Over the last decade, the PS has engaged in a gradual shift towards employee directed careers with the development or increased use of certain policies to support this philosophy. For example, recent changes implemented under the Public Service Modernization Act are intended to shift from the time and labour intensive process of position-specific competitions and enhance the transparency of competitions by moving to the use of generic job competitions to fill a number of generally related positions by producing a list of eligible candidates rank ordered by merit.[63] The PS has also increased the emphasis given to temporary changes in job status through deployments, acting appointments and secondments as these are intended to facilitate personal growth/learning for employees and allow for short term replacements due to a temporary absence of the incumbent.

As with most reactive vacancy management systems, the PS approach can produce difficulties especially when compared to the proactive succession management system run by the CF. The increased emphasis on employee directed careers can produce negative consequences for the manager. For example, managers could be placed in the difficult position of having to choose between allowing an employee to take a deployment that may advance their career but leave the manager's team with an unfilled vacancy. It is also possible that some positions are seen by employees as valuable 'stepping stones' to gain the experience needed to move up the (implicit) career ladder with the result that some managers can be caught up in an almost continuous process of hiring, training and then losing employee after employee. When combined with the time taken by HR Staff to ensure that the earlier identified increased emphasis in the

Federal Government for fairness, equity and transparency is obtained, an indirect consequence of the current PS HR vacancy management system is that managers are more likely to resort to alternate means to have work conducted. This would include alternatives such as the use of casual employees, call ups under standing offers with firms that specialize in providing non-public service employees or having work conducted under personal/professional service contracts.

CF Succession Management. Although generally viewed by most CF members as a single function labelled career management, the CF system is actually comprised of three, interconnected activities. The first is to identify and select individuals for advancement in rank through placement on career courses, promotion and/or commissioning. The second is to optimize the placement of CF members into specific positions in order to meet CF requirements and address individuals' expectations regarding their long term employment. The third activity is to manage changes in the status of individuals either in response to a voluntary request to terminate their contract or change their occupation or in response to a significant change in their employability due to reasons such as reduced medical categories, personal conduct or failure to complete required 'career' courses.

All three functions involve decisions that are intended to balance multiple and often competing priorities. Amongst others, factors of consideration typically include:

- ensuring CF effectiveness by giving priority to filling operational positions (hence assigning known vacancies to non-operational positions);

- minimizing the financial costs to the CF and potential personal impact on members and their families that arise due to physically relocating individuals;

- providing members with logical, sequential employment that builds on previous development and experience and serves to help prepare individuals for advancement;

- complying with federal government legislative requirements including meeting objectives for bilingual representation in specific positions, occupations and/or ranks;

- honouring the implied Social Contract between the CF and the member for equitable treatment, personal growth/career advancement, reasonable workplace accommodation particularly if injured as a result of military service and attending to members' interests in balancing career and personal life goals;

- managing terms of service policies so as to maximize the trained effective strength of the CF and approximate preferred years of service profiles; and

- ensuring that career decisions are based on the merit principle and ensure equity and fair treatment.

In order to balance these requirements, career decisions are intended to be based on assessments of the individual's capabilities (and interests) and the CF's immediate and longer term requirements. Formal inputs typically include annual performance appraisals, CF qualifications reflecting training and education, assigned medical categories, recommendations by supervisors/Commanding Officers, advice from MOC or Branch Advisors and the expressed interests of the member.[64]

Particularly with regard to the core function of military postings or assigning individuals to specific positions, HR theory suggests that the overall intent is to optimize the 'person-job fit'. Three factors influence how these decisions are made. The first is that the CF HR System lacks the person- or job-specific information to actually make decisions at the individual level. As highlighted in the earlier discussion of position-specific KSAOs versus broader, transferable competencies, much of the formal information available for career decision making is of the latter type. For example, the performance appraisal system applies a standardized set of items across the CF with common 'word pictures' for each rank level rather than providing either position or occupation specific evaluations of actual performance. As identified earlier, the second is that job placements or promotion decisions have to be based on an estimate of both ability to perform predicted tasks and capacity to perform plausible but not planned activities. The third is that the application of existing HR career policies and, in particular, the balancing of competing requirements is conducted using a complex set of acquired or implicit norms.

The net result of these three factors is that a significant amount of the CF career management system is based on the concept of appointment to level rather than position-specific criteria. Specifically, those making career decisions apply a broad, generalized understanding of the typical duties associated with a particular rank and, for larger occupations, sub-groupings of jobs and then rely on individual career managers' familiarity with the nature of employment within this broad domain to, where necessary, interpret or infer position-relevant requirements and individual differences.[65]

The methods used to manage the overall workforce and to ensure that the right person is placed in middle and senior level positions have direct consequences for both the organization and the individual. Failure to identify or develop good candidates for positions can result in sub-optimal work unit performance; delays in filling vacancies reduces productivity and increases the burden on others; and, perceived inequities in selecting one candidate for advancement over another can result in individual dissatisfaction leading to attrition, grievances or poor performance. As highlighted throughout, the PS and CF apply very different models and methods to manage the overall workforce. Emanating from the unique nature of military employment, the CF uses a broad model of developing individuals to the level of professional mastery through a closely interconnected system of sequential learning, job rotation and advancement based on potential to adapt to a range of responsibilities at the next rank. This model requires that the CF engages in continuous workforce modelling to forecast requirements and results in the development of a complex set of employment policies including terms of service, medical standards and career reviews that are intended to optimize the CF's operationally-capable, trained effective strength.

Consistent with a professional career focus, the implicit 'talent management' model assumes that the vast majority of military members have the interest and potential to assume the responsibilities of higher rank. In contrast and consistent with the employee-directed employment model, the PS operates a more passive vacancy management approach relying on individual motivation and manager's support in identifying and preparing those interested and able to move up.

Sustainment: Supporting Motivation and Commitment

As stated in the introduction, in addition to ensuring that the right person is placed in the right job with the right skills to be able to perform required tasks, the overall HR System must support the efforts of Commanders/supervisors to ensure that individuals actually complete assigned tasks and also contribute to ensuring that individuals possess the motivation and commitment to continue serving.[66] Across organizations, highly different models are used to create the conditions that will influence individuals to exert intellectual or physical effort to achieve assigned objectives and/or to create the conditions that will lead to long term commitment and retention.

Most often, these two elements are seen as split between the operational/line responsibilities to generate task motivation and the supporting/staff responsibilities to attend to long term retention. These two are, however, inter-related. Key elements that influence task motivation such as the quality of leadership, the challenges inherent in the assigned work and the satisfaction derived from accomplishing difficult meaningful tasks have a direct link to long term career satisfaction, organizational commitment and reduced turnover.[67] Conversely, the presence (or more often, absence) of effective long term career sustainment programs can enhance (or erode) task motivation.[68]

Virtually all approaches rely on some combination of extrinsic and intrinsic motivators. The dominant model in the private sector is to use the extrinsic 'carrots and sticks' of potential financial rewards for outstanding performance and possible firing for unsatisfactory work.[69] To a large extent, employment practices in the Federal Government preclude the use of either significant bonuses or rapid dismissal as the primary enablers of workplace motivation and career commitment. As a result, the public sector tends to rely more on intrinsic, internalized motivation (self-satisfaction, personal pride, public recognition/praise, etc.) supported by potential extrinsic rewards through future advancement based on job performance.

Particularly given the unique nature of the 'work requirements' in operational settings, the military relies heavily on conditions in the workplace rather than broad HR programs to provide the primary motivators for performance under extreme circumstances. Simply stated, a few centuries of lessons learned about why soldiers fight has consistently demonstrated that the dominant reasons arise from loyalties and perceived obligations to the immediate group, not promises of financial rewards, medals or promotions.[70] As a result, the CF emphasizes the role of social systems and the behavioural influences arising from leadership, institutional culture and team climate as the primary means to generate motivation and sustain commitment. This emphasis, combined with the recognition that the use of individual financial rewards such as performance bonuses erode the core professional ethic of service before self, result in the HR System providing a reduced, supporting role in generating effort.

The net result is that, in contrast to the significant role that the HR System plays in managing the core reward systems in the private sector, the primary concern in the CF has been to ensure that the methods used to address compensation, promotions, dismissal or recognition programs do not inadvertently erode the core military motivation system that operates at the working/unit level. To return to the introductory discussion of the differentiated HR System requirements in the CF and the PS, the emphasis given to fiscal prudence and accountability in government results in what is labeled a commercial morale syndrome. This has the HR staff controlling the keys to the vault rather than that found with a guardian morale syndrome where the Commanding Officers dispense largesse when earned or as needed.[71]

Ps Reward And Recognition Systems

In comparison to either the private sector use of significant extrinsic rewards (or punishments) or the CF reliance on a professional culture and small unit cohesion, the Public Service appears to be still attempting to develop a new motivational system to replace the previous approach of offering job security and the probability of promotion provided one did not demonstrate egregiously poor performance. Elements of this implicit reward system are still evident in the concept of employee-directed careers combined with the well recognized difficulties of firing members of the public service. One aspect of the set of intrinsic motivators that has been given somewhat increased prominence is the use of (internal) public recognition programs allowing managers (or peers) to nominate individuals for a number of 'outstanding employee' awards.

In the absence of published research to examine the issue, it appears that the PS operates a rather weak system to generate work effort and sustain commitment. The retention of symbols such as long service certificates, lack of a formal system to effectively address poor performers and a standardized pay structure combine to minimize the ability of either the HR System or managers to really reward outstanding performers or punish the incompetent. Of importance, the implicit reliance on PS supervisors to generate work effort without some attention to professional culture and social systems can produce two difficulties. The first is that this approach tends to result in the use of transactional influence techniques which can result in a focus on ensuring minimal performance standards are maintained but is of limited benefit in generating additional effort. The second is that the essential transactions leading to retention that can be (implicitly) negotiated, particularly promotion for the best and the assignment of unsatisfactory tasks for the worst, can easily lead to perceptions of favouritism and/or discrimination.

Sustainment: Motivation and Commitment in the CF. As already stated, the HR System plays a supporting role in generating motivation and sustaining commitment in the CF. The primary sources arise from the development of a professional ideology, the use of transformational leadership influence techniques and the application of a formal system of discipline that serves to regulate professional conduct (not just work performance).[72] Drawing on the models of differentiated commitment, the CF relies on the internalized perception that one should perform to a certain standard rather than on the use of external forces that signal that one has to do so.[73] Under the generalized professional model, several elements of the typical HR-based reward system are given a different interpretation. One example is that promotions are intended to be seen more as an increase in obligations and responsibilities (a challenge to be met) rather than a reward for past service. Similarly, honours and medals are intended to be a formal symbol of 'answering the call' and a measure of professional credibility rather than a claim to 'bragging rights'. Although the CF is constantly concerned about the emergence of careerism and/or an occupational orientation, there is evidence of a strong professional culture with an attendant vocational orientation.[74]

The CF HR System does contribute to overall sustainment through a range of activities including elements of professional development and career management presented in the previous sections. The three components that are conducted primarily through the centralized HR System pertain to: compensation and benefits programs; the use of administrative procedures to release individuals; and, the set of special obligations and services that arise from the implied social contract between the profession and the military member and family.

Compensation. Consistent with the vocational, service model, the CF compensation system is based on the egalitarian approach that all at the same rank share the same set of professional responsibilities and obligations and, therefore, perform work deserving of the same level of basic compensation and benefits. For this reason, the CF generally negotiates salaries and benefits with Treasury Board using a grouping of jobs across rank levels rather than attempting to establish pay levels for each individual occupation. In addition, given an overall compensation envelope, the CF provides additional compensation to recognize the significant demands imposed through employment in extreme settings and/or lengthy absences from home/family. For specific occupations, the combination of recognizing specialized skills sets (and labour market competition) have led to some deviations from the 'all one team' approach to compensation with additional specialist pay for certain NCM occupations and/or unique pay scales for Officer occupations such as pilots, medical officers and lawyers. As part of the distribution of the overall compensation package, the CF also provides a generous pension plan that is intended to both encourage continued military service up to the pension eligibility point (twenty years) and, then, contribute to achieving preferred years of service profiles for the overall CF workforce through significant attrition past this point.[75]

Termination of Employment. In contrast to the PS, the CF does use a range of administrative procedures to complement the military justice system in regulating performance and, in particular, in compulsorily releasing members who are either unable or unwilling to perform to required standards. Although often still a lengthy process, in part due to the desire to follow the principles of natural justice,[76] Commanding Officers can apply an escalating system of administrative sanctions and procedures that can lead to release, particularly when individuals fail to complete required career courses; are unable to rectify significant performance deficiencies despite formal notification and supervision; or, through their personal conduct, violate core principles of professional conduct. As identified in the following comments on the Social Contract, although also handled using similar administrative decision making structures, release due to medical conditions beyond the member's control are recognized as a philosophically different issue with policies for medical release intended to honour the contract between the member and the CF through appropriate career transition support.

As already stated, a key component of military workforce management pertains to efforts to encourage some individuals to leave at a relatively early age or stage in their employment career. In order to facilitate this process, a number of services are offered to facilitate an effective transition from military service to civilian employment including information on financial planning, job search and labour market conditions. Depending on the reason for release, additional benefits can include reimbursement of re-training or education programs and preferential consideration over external candidates in applying for PS positions. Although these career transition services are occasionally seen as encouraging individuals to leave prematurely, research has, in fact, demonstrated that these programs can lead to increased retention as individuals have increased confidence of finding viable employment at a later stage (e.g., at 20 or 28 years of service) rather than taking a sub-optimal job earlier.[77]

The Social Contract and Special HR Functions. The core idea underlying the concept of a social or psychological contract is that, in addition to tangible, personal motivators, individuals will continue their employment as long as they perceive that the organization is honouring a set of implicit assumptions regarding the respective obligations of the member and the employer. Perceived violations of this contract can erode motivation, resulting in significant dissatisfaction, poor performance, distrust and cynicism and, often, attrition. Over the last twenty years, the CF has produced a number of HR principles that represent aspects of articulation of the implied contract and elements are contained in both *Duty with Honour* and *Leadership: Conceptual Foundations.* Although not specifically articulated in this manner, there appear to be three broad principles that members expect that the CF will honour.

First is the need to provide the member and their family a standard of living and/or quality of life that approximates the norm for those of similar professional/work status in Canadian society. Beyond the implications for the overall level of compensation provided, this expectation leads to the CF undertaking additional services/functions in two areas:

a. the need to ensure that families are afforded a relatively consistent level of community functions (access to schools, recreation facilities, quality of accommodations, etc) when required to relocate or, appropriate additional support (compensation, leave to be with family, etc.) when required or opting to be separated.

b. the need to provide a reasonable level of member care and support if injured or extended financial compensation and community support to the family if the member dies.

The second principle is to facilitate personal growth and self development during ones career. Although rarely articulated in this manner, it can be recognized that a military career is a demanding commitment that can consume a significant amount of an individuals' time, effort and focus possibly to the detriment of other aspects of their life.

In particular, members have some expectations that the CF will provide support to allow people to attend to both their professional development as a military member and their personal growth as an individual, citizen and family member. Traditionally, this expectation has had implications for the provision of religious/spiritual services and opportunities for non-career related, academic learning. More recently, this has been expanded to include recognizing the need to support involvement in activities of importance to retain one's unique ethnic or cultural identity.

The third principle is that the CF will maintain professional cohesion and status. Complementary with the CF's expectation that individuals will internalize a set of professional expectations, obligations and values, members also expect the institution to maintain the reputation and functioning of the profession. At a generalized level, this expectation leads to a number of functions to maintain customs, traditions and, in particular, to honour the sacrifice of those who have given their lives in service to the nation. At a more specific level, there is also an expectation that the CF will engage in active regulation of professional conduct and will project an effective professional image to the Canadian people. It is of concern that from time to time there are per-ceptions of double standards within the profession and issues related to the actions of senior leaders such as abusing the privileges of senior rank or publicly criticizing subordinates.

Based on the unique nature of military service and the implicit Social Contract, the CF HR System supports member motivation and commitment through a number of functions that are not normally part of HR. These include:

-   Religious/Spiritual. In addition to providing religious services, activities or support for practicing members of faith, members of the Chaplain Branch also provide advice for those seeking to reconcile ethical demands and coun-sel for those seeking a neutral opinion regarding organizational decisions that impact on their personal life.

-   Health Services. Beyond the requirements to provide job-specific medical services, the CF undertakes to ensure that members can receive a standard of health care comparable to that available to other Canadian citizens, thus providing a broader range of services designed to support healthy lifestyles and well-being including elective procedures. Over the last decade, the CF has paid increased attention to issues related to the care of those who sustain physical and/or psychological injuries on duty with, in particular, a more integrated transition program involving both DND and Veteran's Affairs.

-   Personal growth/Self improvement. Again, beyond the provision of job-relat-ed intellectual and physical development; the CF endeavours to ensure that members (and families) have access to a range of leisure, recreational, learn-ing and fitness activities to support healthy lifestyles and overall well-being. Included under this broad label are the services provided by Military Family Resource Centres; opportunities for members and families to engage in social activities such as mess functions, sports days and local activities; and, active support for charitable causes and community involvement.

- Managing professional identity. The profession of arms and organized religion are likely the two traditional professions that recognize the importance of customs, traditions and symbols in conveying aspects of identity and giving meaning to ones life. As a strong and positive identity can directly support motivation and commitment, a number of activities have been assigned to the HR System including: managing changes in military uniforms, dress and ceremonial activities; preserving military history through the generation of official histories, managing historical archives and supporting the preservation and display of artifacts; and, managing changes in military customs, rites and symbols.

In any organization the HR System can play an important role in the generation and sustainment of motivation, commitment and effort resulting in increased workplace performance and improved longer-term retention. Consistent with the previous sections in this chapter, the PS and CF operate under very different philosophies however neither case reflects the dominant model used in the private sector. The PS is presented as having a relatively weak system relying on immediate workplace practices to influence levels of performance and a balance of some opportunities for advancement complemented by a low likelihood of dismissal to ensure long term retention. In contrast, the CF engages in much more proactive approaches to ensure both maximum effort, persistence and dedication when performing in extreme circumstances and attending to longer term career and personal expectations to sustain motivation, commitment and retention.

Both aspects are based on elements of professions and professional practice with 'workplace' motivation arising from immediate social systems and the behavioural influences of leadership, culture and climate while longer term commitment is linked to an egalitarian approach to financial and career rewards augmented by policies, programs and activities that are seen to honour the implied contract between the member and the profession. In linking this discussion to current CF HR activities, two comments are offered. First, noting again that the current HR organization is continuing to evolve, it appears that many of the activities presented in this section are currently being related to the maintenance of a high state of morale. Second, following from the late 1990s work by the Parliamentary Standing Committee on National Defence and Veterans Affairs (SCONDVA) and augmented by several reports by the CF Ombudsman, a large number of policies and programs involving aspects of compensation and benefits, as well as some of the Social Contract activities, have been grouped together under the general heading of Quality of Life (QOL) initiatives. References to both maintaining morale and to QOL are seen as alternate ways to link HR functions to the broad domain of sustainment.

Conduct: Workplace Practices

As the final major domain that is related to HR Management, the requirement to develop policies and programs to influence how people conduct themselves is drawn from three requirements. The first is the general recognition that it is best to have work conducted in a positive, supporting environment where individuals feel welcome, included and respected. As stated in the introduction, a more specific requirement for the Federal Government is to ensure that workplace practices reflect specific societal values and government objectives to have a workforce that represents the Canadian population. This objective is reinforced through various legislative acts that are monitored by Central Agencies thus leading to a requirement to comply with statutory obligations and legislation.[78] Particularly for the CF, the third requirement is directly related to the focus on small unit morale and cohesion as a critical component of combat effectiveness. Fundamentally, units with high levels of mutual trust and respect will outperform those lacking these characteristics. Underlying all three requirements is a basic recognition that, as the vast majority of 'work activities' occur in a setting involving interactions amongst individuals and small teams, productivity and beneficial worker relations (often referred to as organizational citizenship behaviours) will be enhanced through the establishment of a positive work environment and, conversely, that it is not possible to create the conditions for high performance teams if people feel that they are being subject to marginalization, discrimination, harassment or abusive leadership.[79]

While the broad objectives of ensuring that Defence has effective, cohesive teams comprised of individuals who trust and respect each other is a relatively easy goal to endorse, the fundamental issues at play tend to revolve around the relative priority given to individual rights and organizational obligations versus individual obligations and organizational rights. Although consideration of individual rights (or personal sensitivities) are occasionally trivialized over discussions of the use of 'politically correct' terminology, it is important to recall that the Canadian Human Rights Tribunal that ordered the full integration of women in the CF based its decision on the conclusion that the CF needed to give greater emphasis to the rights of women to participate in the military and less emphasis to the importance that the CF placed on its obligations to ensure combat effectiveness.[80] Thus, the relative weights of which rights and which obligations can have significant consequences.[81]

Reflecting the differing philosophies of workforce management presented throughout this chapter, the PS tends to address personal conduct solely as an issue of workplace practices while the CF adopts a broader professional approach whereby policies and procedures are intended to also influence conduct off hours or outside of the workplace.[82] Further, the PS approach is almost exclusively informed by the need to comply with statutory obligations while the CF expands the domain to also include the requirement to shape professional conduct. As with the discussion of effort and motivation, both the PS and CF rely heavily on COs/managers/supervisors as the primary agents to ensure appropriate workplace practices with central HR organizations providing a supporting role in the four areas to be presented below. An additional factor of consideration in the PS approach is the implications of regulating conduct with a unionized workforce. Although beyond the scope of this chapter, when compared to private sector unions it is considered that the relative power of the Federal Government as both legislator and employer results in PS unions placing a greater emphasis on issues of regulating workplace practices (where they can exert some influence) and less on negotiating hours of work or remuneration (where they can be subject to legislated imperatives).

INTER-PERSONAL RELATIONS

The first of the domains under workplace practices pertains to the broad group of policies to ensure that individuals treat each other in an open, supportive and respectful manner. In particular, formal policies have been developed to articulate rights and obligations to prevent harassment, discrimination and marginalization in the workplace. Applying a preventative rather than punitive model, the policies and established procedures for investigating incidents and taking corrective action are supplemented by education/professional development programs to ensure that all are aware of standards and expectations as well as the reliance on effective leadership to provide role models, establish the appropriate workplace climate and ensure that early interventions are made when potential problems arise.

While a clear requirement to address inter-personal relations is related to managerial concerns over formal complaints, the overarching philosophy is intended to reflect the idea that a positive harmonious workplace results in increased productivity, lower rates of absenteeism and reduced turnover. Although often the source on some confusion, the application of policies also recognizes that some individuals may require guidance or corrective direction in order to avoid offending others. As a result, the general approach in applying regulations is one of striving from zero incidents (as a goal) rather than one of zero tolerance (that implies automatic punishment for any deviation from the proscribed behavioural norms).

VOICE

The second element recognizes that employers must ensure that individuals have the means to speak up when they perceive that they are not being treated properly or when they believe others are acting in an inappropriate (or illegal) manner. The need to address 'mechanisms of voice' is a concern in the public sector where the government acts as both employer and neutral arbitrator of legislative violations. This issue is magnified in the CF given specific policy restrictions on rights and freedoms and the operant culture of not by-passing the chain of command.

Both the PS and the CF continue to update policies and procedures to provide an appropriate balance between addressing issues through the hierarchical supervisory chain versus through alternate routes. The preference for the former is based on the philosophy that it is most often the immediate supervisor or CO who can address the issue, that these individuals should be aware of problems that may impair unit effectiveness and that they are accountable to their supervisors hence must be aware of issues. The counter perspective is that individuals are less likely to bring problems to the attention of immediate supervisors if part of the complaint involves the supervisor; if they do not expect the concern will be given fair consideration; when they believe that the supervisor may be unwilling or unable to address the problem; or, if they do not perceive that confidentiality and privacy will be respected. It is most often under one or more of these conditions that unionized PS employees will seek the assistance of their bargaining unit to mediate complaints. CF members, on the other hand, must utilize a formal grievance procedure.

The balancing of the chain of command versus independent mechanisms of voice has resulted in five developments within the CF HR System. The first pertains to the grievance system with attention to both streamlining the process by having grievances go directly to the office that can actually provide the requested redress and impartiality in the process by establishing an external board to address issues with potentially significant career consequences. The second has been the expansion of the principles of natural justice, specifically by ensuring that individuals are provided with disclosure packages that are intended to contain all information that will be used in making significant decisions and allowing the member the opportunity to review, comment and re-present relevant information. The third has been the creation at various bases of offices to provide principle-based dispute resolution. The fourth was the establishment of the office of the CF Ombudsman and the fifth development was the linking of diversity with the establishment of Defence Advisory Groups for the four employment equity designated groups along with the appointment of four senior leaders as Departmental Champions.

DIVERSITY

The third area pertains to policies and programs to address a number of areas under the broad label of diversity. A key element is to ensure that Defence is discharging its responsibilities under the Employment Equity Act to increase the representation of those from the four designated groups of women, Aboriginal Peoples, visible minorities and persons with disabilities. Of importance in contrasting the Employment Equity Act with the Human Rights Act, while Human Rights legislation is intended to remove discriminatory barriers, Employment Equity represents a more proactive philosophy of requiring employers to put in place proactive measures to accommodate the needs to Designated Group Members and, in doing so, facilitate career success and redress historical marginalization.

A significant amount of the effort invested in Employment Equity programs has been concentrated on increasing numerical representation with both the PS and CF conducting self-identification census and employment systems reviews to determine declared representation and potential barriers, respectively. The extent to which senior officials and/or COs/supervisors express concerns that a self-identification census likely leads to an under-estimate of the real representation of Designated Group Members should be seen as an indicator that Defence, as a whole, has yet to recognize that a fundamental goal of the Employment Equity Act is to create a workforce culture and workplace climate in which individuals feel comfortable in providing their group identity, if relevant. It is this philosophy that links compliance with the Employment Equity Act and numerical representation into the broader policy domain of multiculturalism and diversity. Both the PS and CF continue to develop and refine policies designed to provide reasonable accommodations to those who have difficulty retaining important elements of their identity within the dominant Defence culture. Recalling earlier observations that the Federal Government HR Systems tend to focus on rules-based decision making with a concern over establishing new precedents, efforts continue to develop and interpret policies regarding the balancing of elements of organizational effectiveness and the development of a unifying professional identity, on the one hand, and ensuring reasonable accommodations for unique religious practices, family obligations and ethnic/cultural/community engagement, on the other.

The more fundamental issue regarding diversity pertains to the requirement to balance the need for commonality of purpose amongst all members of a team while ensuring that differing opinions, perspectives and ideas are presented for all to consider. Particularly in the context of addressing complex, dynamic or ambiguous settings, the establishment of workplace practices that encourage creativity, debate and critical thinking can be highly useful yet challenging to the status quo and existing authority.

WORKPLACE HEALTH AND SAFETY

The final domain pertains to the aspects of ensuring that workplace practices protect individuals from unnecessary or unwarranted physical risks. Reflected in the long-standing professional discussions about mission accomplishment versus force protection, the CF, in particular, has developed a set of policies covering topics ranging from equipment safety through exposure to hazardous materials to requiring individuals to take preventative vaccinations. As with many other topics presented, the CF relies on COs to draw on the advice of specialist staff in exercising judgement concerning the appropriate and reasonable risk to which they should expose themselves and their subordinates. Importantly, as articulated in *Duty with Honour*, while the advice of specialists is to be given full consideration, the CF places the responsibility for final decisions in the hands of the CO not the specialist.

This section has examined two related issues regarding workplace practices. The first is the role of HR policies and programs designed to ensure that individuals are able to perform their duties in a positive, accepting workplace with appropriate consideration and accommodation of individual's rights and identities. Although the issue of achieving appropriate numerical representation of Employment Equity designated group members tends to dominant much of the PS and CF HR policies in this area, the second, broader issue presented pertains to the relative weight given to rights versus obligations. While the CF has, on occasion, signaled that the focus on operational effectiveness should trump all other considerations, both Central Agencies and engaged external audiences have clearly stated that individual and collective rights must be fully considered.

Particularly for the CF the fundamental challenge in determining how to reasonably accommodate differences will be to mirror the evolution in Canadian society over the last 50 years by shifting from a homogenous "tight" culture to a pluralistic "loose" culture.[83] Tight cultures are typically characterized by a number of factors. They emphasize homogeneity with clear boundaries as to who is a member of the culture (and who is excluded) and a strong single identity for all members. They have explicit social norms and associated standards of appropriate behaviour with severe sanctions applied to those who deviate from these norms. There are clearly differentiated and stratified role requirements (father versus mother, manager versus supervisor versus labourer, etc) with a high level of role obligation (social pressure to fulfill role requirements and to do so in a way that is consistent with the role and social norms). Tight cultures put an emphasis on the subordination of one's own interests (or perspectives) to the good of the overall group often incorporated in a common prototype of the 'good citizen' as one makes personal sacrifices to contribute to an overarching goal.[84] There is also a concern for clarity in language, rules and social regulation with limits on the articulation of contrary viewpoints or acts of disobedience.[85] Finally, there is a reliance on history, customs and traditions to reinforce key themes and to ensure cultural continuity and stability over time.

Loose cultures, on the other hand, are seen as very much the opposite in many of the key areas. They tend to be characterized by heterogeneity with a general philosophy that it is the individual who determines whether they are part of the larger group and acceptance that individuals may have multiple or poly-morphic identities. They allow flexible social norms and standards of behaviour shaped by the idea that one does not impose their own norms, values or standards on others (thus, an acceptance of diversity in various forms). There is a lack of emphasis on roles and role requirements with few status distinctions or role-specific obligations with, conversely, an emphasis in citizenship and ones' obligations to others on maximizing the benefits to all hence the concept of 'good citizen' as one who voluntarily makes a contribution to other's well-being, quality of life or community initiatives. There is an acceptance of ambiguity and the likelihood of miscommunication and misunderstanding with the obligation of each to understand the other's perspective. Finally, they are characterized by an expectation that societies and social norms will evolve hence an orientation towards the future as something to be created rather than a past to be preserved.

Not only do the characteristics of a tight culture describe most military organizations, the rationale for the development of a tight culture further serves to demonstrate the relevance. These cultures are likely to arise under conditions when the society or nation as a whole is threatened by external forces with the belief that is it only when all members of the society contribute that preservation can be achieved. The general philosophy communicated is one of conformity within a clearly defined social hierarchy and a system of strong socialization mechanisms. Thus, tight cultures not only strive to ensure commitment to the important overarching goal of survival but attempt to perpetuate this focus through customs, traditions and norms as this level of national will cannot easily be generated if allowed to erode.

Given this logic, it is not surprising that militaries practice many of the characteristics of a tight culture. In fact, the content, tone and purpose of *Duty with Honour* is intended to articulate the military role, purpose and ethos in a manner so as to create or reinforce a tight culture. Further, this objective is predicated on exactly the conditions that lead to tight cultures – the requirement for a collective contribution of all to overcome significant threats to actual survival. It is this taken-for-granted assumption that the military must be a tight culture in order to succeed in the most extreme of endeavours that is at the root of the Combat Male Warrior prototype and the concerns of military leaders about the consequences of introducing the pluralistic, post-modern perspective which is called for under the EE Act in order to accommodate diversity and individual differences.[86]

While the characteristics of a loose culture have been seen by some military leaders as the recipe for confusion and disorder which would significantly erode the essentials of combat power (cohesion, discipline, obedience, etc.), others have recognized that these would clearly accommodate individuals who do not share the same characteristics of the current military culture. By authorizing pluralism, permitting contradictory behaviours, tolerating ambiguity and seeking consensus through understanding rather than the use of power to enforce rules, militaries could, in fact, authorize a range of role definitions, norms and behaviours. The net result is that the prototype 'ideal' soldier could evolve to encompass a number of perspectives of 'effective soldiers' and, importantly, align the military culture with that of Canadian society. A logical extension would be to recognize that each member of the CF will acquire a professional identity (shaped and supported by a tight professional culture) and a personal identity (shaped by a loose socio-political cultural). One of the ongoing challenges for the HR System is to develop policies and programs to enable individuals to inhabit both spaces simultaneously. Even more challenging is how the system can manage all of the various rules, regulations and procedures while at the same time allowing individual's choice in their career paths.

Endnotes

1. In, particular, it should be read in conjunction with CF HR Doctrine (B-GJ-100/FP-001) and Procedural Doctrine for the Management of the CF HR System (B-GJ-005/FP-010) (when released), Military HR 2020 (and subsequent updates), the CMP Campaign Plan (when published) and the current year Military Personnel Functional Planning Guidance issued in conjunction with annual Defence Planning Guidance.

2. Federal legislation may be broadly grouped in three domains: those laws that apply to all Canadians (the *Charter of Rights and Freedoms, Criminal Code, Canadian Human Rights Act*), the four presented here that apply to all components of the Federal Government, and those that contain specific provisions for the Canadian Forces (the *National Defence Act*).

3. A more complete discussion of the key factors is presented in the CF doctrine manual *Duty with Honour: The Profession of Arms in Canada*.

4. Potential government tasks include the spectrum of activities such as combat, stability, emergency/disaster response and nation-building activities. A significant degree of flexibility in order to respond in a timely manner to these plausible contingencies but not necessarily planned taskings.

5. These competing requirements are manifest in the representation of training as providing a well practiced response to a predicted situation versus education as allowing a reasoned response to an unpredicted situation.

6.   See, in particular, DAOD 5023-0 "University of Service" with the linkage of the broad authority and latitude afforded the CF in utilizing CF members and their skills to the principle of university of service under which "CF members must at all times and under any circumstances perform any function that they may be required to perform."

7.   Noting that Reg F members can be on part time service (particularly due to accommodations for medical conditions) and that Reserves do serve on a full time basis including in the core role of deployments. One of the persistent challenges for the CF has been to move beyond well-established Cold War models of 'regular' status as only full time service.

8.   These differences also explain why members of the Primary Reserve are awarded less compensation when not employed on operations.

9.   As with many aspects of decision-making regarding the Canadian Forces, it is important to recall that the concept of civil control of the military means that the 'people' (through their elected representatives) get to decide what kind of military they want to have and what they want to do with it. See Okros, A.C., Hill, S.A. & Pinch, F.C., *Between 9/11 and Kandahar: Attitudes of Canadian Forces Officers in Transition* (Kingston: Queen's University School of Policy Studies, 2007) for a recent review of CF Officers' attitudes and opinions in this domain.

10.   For a number of reasons including the fact that the CF has, de facto, been operating at Stage 2 mobilization since the end of the Cold War, there has been a growing trend of increased commonality in HR policies, programs and standards for the Regular Force and Primary Reserve and, conversely, increased differentiation for those in the auxiliary role. A discussion of the different stages of mobilization can be found in DND, *CF Joint Doctrine For Mobilization* (Ottawa: DND, 2004). However, it is important to note that the use of the 4 stage mobilization model was articulated in the 1994 Defence White Paper and is not part of the recent 2005 International Policy Statement nor the Conservative Governments' Stand Up For Canada Election Platform.

11.   See in particular the Institutional Effectiveness Framework and Quinn's Competing Values Model as presented in *Conceptual Foundations* Chapter Two.

12.   The use of the terms Personnel and Human Resources continues to evolve in the CF. The current draft doctrine links personnel management primary to the workplace activities involving supervisors and subordinates (Leading People) and HR management to the organizational activities of developing and managing the people-related policies, programs and functions that enable supervisors and individuals to support broad Defence objectives (Leading the Institution).

13.   Although clearly related, an emphasis on efficiency normally results in decisions to minimize costs while a focus on effectiveness results in a focus on maximizing the outputs or outcomes achieved. These differences often come in conflict when allocating resources for complex deployed missions as the

CF tends to focus on effectiveness while public service resource managers emphasize efficiency.

14. For a brief introduction, see Cardy & Selvarajan's article in Anderson, N., Ones, D.S., Sinangil, H.K, & Viswesvarn, C. (eds) (2002) *Handbook of Industrial, Work and Organizational Psychology* (Volume two). Sage: New York.

15. These tensions also surface in discussions of how to achieve the objectives of mission command.

16. A fact noted in the Defence Plan and related Departmental Responsibility and Accountability frameworks however are often not understood by many CF 'line managers'.

17. Noting that hard data on numbers are difficult to find, it may be argued that the overall size of the DND workforce remained much the same, the primary difference is that more are now performing work via commercial contract – with a consequential increase in the proportion motivated primarily by economic return rather than service to the nation.

18. In particular, the intent was to create a common standard across all departments, all jobs and all levels for describing work so that all employees could be assessed on a common set of requisite job skills/ competencies and also to establish broader, generic groupings of positions so that individuals had a wider range of possible jobs that they could apply/compete for and, conversely, a large pool of potential applicants for managers to select from. Additional information on the current initiatives for classification reform are currently available at: http://www.hrma-agrh.gc.ca/Classification/AboutUs/ClassReform_e.asp

19. In reality, individual members have little control over key career decisions such as postings or terms of service (even those these are structured to accommodate member choice) nor do they have the power to decide what type of learning/development they wish to pursue to align their skills with evolving work requirements.

20. As the military has learned in combat but has not successfully applied to HR, a small group of highly qualified experts can outperform a large band of enthusiastic amateurs.

21. In reality, this process is a bit more of 'chicken and egg': job analyses of work requirements can be used to create org charts to then structure the work to be done but the org chart defines who does what hence dictating which work is assigned to which positions.

22. Although the term administration is often interpreted as pertaining to documenting work decisions, it is better understood as describing the broader domain of the controls (hence the policies, programs, procedures, information and monitoring) that ensure the smooth functioning of the organization. In particular, the reference here to administration includes those controls put in place to facilitate motivation and ensure appropriate workplace practices.

23. For a recent presentation of the various approaches to job analysis, see Brannick, M. T. & Levine, E.L. (2002) *Job Analysis: Methods, Research and Applications for Human Resource Management in the New Millennium.* Sage: New York.

24. The reality is that very few organizations can afford the costs associated of doing both.

25. As with the Public Service UCS and pre-cursor GE projects, it should be noted that both the PS and CF have attempted to significantly restructure the workforce about once a decade however, after significant investment of time, have ended up adopting only minor/superficial changes. The fact that all four initiatives were conducted by tactical-level practioners rather than HR professionals with an appropriate understanding of the underlying theories and concepts is telling. The second fact that both GE and TASK resurfaced as UCS and MOSART and neither second attempt achieved the strategic objectives would also suggest that a third attempt will likely be tried under a different umbrella at some time in the future.

26. The almost decade long MOSART project is acknowledged to be based on two significant limitations. The first is that it was an effort to restructure the macro levels of occupations into career fields and never considered scrapping all existing occupations and starting from scratch to create a new CF. The second, and the greatest limitation of CODAP, is that the analyses conducted were based on independent slices of data using different task inventories for different occupations and, given the time taken to collect and analyze these data, taken at significantly different points in time. Some of the data used to inform MOSART decisions was collected in the 1980s.

27. With the caveat that the results produced are then subject to amendment through a review process that takes into account anticipated future requirements, historical/traditional patterns and the implications on the current CF if career structures are significantly altered – all filtered through the expectations and desires of Branch Advisors, senior officers and informal councils. Depending on the perspective offered, one or more of these factors have lead to decisions to: amalgamate occupations that, statistically, should have remained separate, to retain separate occupations that should have been combined into one and/or conversely to retain a single occupation that should have been split into several or to split an occupation into two that should have remained as one.

28. The length of this cycle is not clear. While some occupations have undergone several OAs, some have only been done once in the 40+ years since integration. Much of the current common, environmental and individual occupation specifications are based on data generated 6-12 years ago.

29. Equipment does exist that would significantly reduce or eliminate the requirements for several of the current Universality of Service physical fitness standards. It is assumed that it has been determined that it is neither practical nor efficient to ensure that this equipment would be available if/when needed. The relationship between strategic resource allocation decisions and

consequential effects on individuals will resurface in subsequent discussion of workplace practices and the concept of accommodation under the *Employment Equity Act*.

30. Along with the fact that the CF is either unable or unwilling to consider another approach, the current system is a clear reflection of the generalized bureaucratic preference for accuracy over efficiency. Considerable time is invested in developing exhaustive task lists (OAs often include hundreds if not thousands of items) and then collecting data from the entire population rather than a stratified sample. Another of the weaknesses in the OA process is that it is assumed that all job incumbents possess sufficient understanding of their individual position requirements to provide accurate responses. Reflective of the taken-for-granted assumption that work is objective, standardized and static, errors can result if the job incumbent is a novice or has not performed the full range of tasks that may be associated with the position.

31. One of the obvious implications of relying on task-based versus worker-based analyses is that it is difficult to forecast future task requirements without having key elements of the job requirements defined. Thus, it is possible to conduct OAs when new platforms or major equipment systems are introduced but difficult (if not impossible) to do so when new concepts, ideas or doctrine are introduced. The reliance on working from a defined, predictable future has been one of the stumbling blocks in recent efforts to overhaul the workforce structure.

32. Force structure is the integrated allocation of positions, equipment, and facilities that are used to create military capabilities; military capabilities are the actual units and formations that conduct operations for the government when so assigned.

33. Classification and level in the PS are conceptual equivalents of occupation and rank in the CF. Although beyond the scope of this chapter to explain, all aspects of job analyses or job evaluation involve considerable elements of subjective judgement. Thus, while, in theory the classification process involves awarding points based on applying an objective scale to score the work elements presented in the work descriptions, there tends to be a strong tendency to 'situate the estimate'. For example, if the prevailing norm is that Directorates have an Admin Officer position classified at the Administrative Services (AS) 02 level, significant additional documentation may be required to convince the reviewing office to classify a position as AS 04 or to create a second AS 02.

34. Consistent with the delegation of responsibilities to the line manager, the Public Service manages the people through the salary wage envelope (SWE) rather than the number of positions, thus, the primary resource allocated in business planning is money. As the CF manages people through the force structure, the key business plan allocations are O&M dollars and military positions (or Person Years – PYs).

35. The Departmental Organization and Accountability guidance is currently available within DND at http://www.forces.gc.ca/site/minister/eng/authority/OATOC_e.htm.

36. The use of financial bonuses to motivate individuals will resurface in the section on workplace practices. For those interested in the real reason for the implementation of performance pay, see the reports by the Independent Advisory Committee on Senior Level Retention and Compensation chaired by Lawrence Strong currently available at http://www.tbs-sct.gc.ca/media/nr-cp/2001/0110_e.asp:

37. For a thorough discussion of organizational theory in the public context, see Rainey, H. (1997) *Understanding and Managing Public Organizations*. Jossey Bass: San Francisco.

38. Although the general principle is that line managers should be able to organize work in an effective manner, there are a number of formal and hidden obstacles that restrict flexibility at the local/work level thus creating less efficient work structures.

39. For a discussion of emerging concepts, see Verdon, J. (2005) *Transformation in the CF: Concepts toward a theory of Human Network-Enabled Operations*. Directorate of Strategic Human Resources: Ottawa.

40. The central concept of matrix management is to enable flexibility and support initiative when staff are working on complex issues that implicate numerous offices allowing staff officers to liaise, exchange and collaborate with their peers across organizational boundaries without having to seek permission from their supervisors.

41. See in particular, Newsome, S., Catano, V.M., & Day, A.L. (2003). *Leader competencies: Proposing a research framework*. Canadian Forces Leadership Institute: Kingston, ON.

42. As will be developed, the CF has not fully adopted the requirement to distinguish superior performers from 'just good enough to get by'.

43. To link to the CF Institutional Effectiveness model presented in Conceptual Foundation, one could argue that KSAOs are most applicable in the domain of Internal Integration while Competencies for best for External Adaptability.

44. Critical tasks/procedures that must be performed with maximum efficiency are those that apply when the work performed involves: constant work adjustments to meet conflicting or competing work demands; adaptation, creativity and anticipatory thinking to respond to complex, dynamic or novel conditions; inter-dependencies amongst individuals or across teams; expert judgement or reasoning; and/or significant consequences from errors in moral or ethical decision making. Task-based activities are those that pertain to tasks that are: predictable, structured and routine; requires precision and/or synchronization; carries significant consequences from procedural errors; and/or must be performed in high demand circumstances where proceduralization can overcome fatigue, stress or panic.

45. This rationale is often cited in references to the CF approach to compensation and benefits.

46. See, in particular, Cotton, C.A. (1979) *Military Attitudes and Values of the Army in Canada*. Canadian Forces Personnel Applied Research Unit: Toronto.

47. Note also that all three positive conditions need to be present to have the optimum condition. When the size and/or quality of the applicant pool is less than desired, it is necessary to examine all potential factors that may be generating this result rather than concentrating on one aspect with the assumption that this will overcome the others. The 2007 CF recruiting ads were illustrative.

48. As a good illustration, see Bradley, J.P. (1989) *The Determinants of Medical Officer's Intentions to leave the Canadian Forces*. Canadian Forces Personnel Applied Research Unit: Toronto.

49. For a discussion, see Boswell, R.A. & Chevrier, R. (1991) *Socio-demographic Profile of the Successful Enrollee*. Canadian Forces Personnel Applied Research Unit: Toronto.

50. For additional comments, see Chevrier, R. (1990) *Canadian Forces Applicant Profile: Phase II Why do they apply?* Canadian Forces Personnel Applied Research Unit: Toronto.

51. Rather than a just-in-time philosophy, this approach really emphasizes just-enough as the operant principle.

52. Dividing the cost per serial by number of students does not yield the cost of training each individual – this can only be determined through adopting a learner-centric approach, tailoring the training to the person and then measuring the cost for each.

53. This program is operating within ADM (Pol) to develop Defence Policy Analysts and Policy Officers, there is no equivalent for the development of HR Policy Analysts or HR Policy Officers.

54. For information management, it is closer to two years – somebody attempting to operate in an office setting based on knowledge acquired 6-8 years ago would likely be assessed as functionally incompetent.

55. As noted earlier, the CF individual PD System incorporates a shift in emphasis from a focus on factual, performance oriented skill development for entry-level courses to the reasoning-based, profession-wide, outcome-oriented learning in more advanced courses. Entry-level training is generally based on the industrial work production model: assign each individual to a unique position with a specific set of responsibilities and tasks to be performed, conduct a task analysis to determine the factual knowledge and standard operating procedures for each task and then provide people with sufficient practical training to perform the tasks to a threshold level of effectiveness. The CF has developed an extensive set of procedures to assist practitioners in translating the job requirement information from Occupational Analyses (the CF, envi-

ronmental or occupation specifications) into structured learning programs with a declared 'just in time' philosophy to deliver this training to individuals when required.

56. It is important to differentiate between the common usage of the word professional to imply a level of competence as per professional hairdresser versus membership in an established profession such as law, medicine, the clergy or the profession of arms. See *Duty with Honour* Chapter One for additional discussion.

57. Following the publication of the Department wide Defence Strategy 2020, a senior committee originally led by LGen Romeo Dallaire produced two long term analyses of the future Professional Development requirement of the Officer Corps and the Non-Commissioned Member Corps.

58. For a detailed review, see Wait, T. (2002) *Organizational, social and demographic change in the Canadian Forces: 1976 to 2001*. Directorate of Strategic Human Resource Coordination: Ottawa.

59. External replacement for mid-level vacancies means that nobody at a lower level changes jobs. Particularly when vacancies occur at senior levels, the government approach of internal replacements involves a chain reaction of job changes as the first replacement creates a new vacancy etc.

60. Given the time required to develop successors for mid- to senior-level jobs, internal workforce management has to be conducted with a long range perspective and anticipatory planning. Thus, in addition to developing appropriate policies and procedures to manage employee changes, the workforce management function is dependent on forecasting future requirements.

61. Noting that some change jobs but remain in the same geographic locations.

62. It should be noted that early loss rates vary significantly across MOCs. The Combat Arms and certain 'hard sea' Naval Occupations tend to have the highest rates due to a combination of learning, performance and environmental factors that are accentuated in these MOCs. The fact that these tend to be larger occupations with higher rates of mid-career attrition (retirement at 20 years of service) can mask the fact that other MOCs actually have surprisingly low losses during the first 2-3 years of service. As well, to return to a previous comment on the accuracy of placement decisions, the attrition that occurs when individuals realize they are stuck in the wrong occupation.

63. An additional difficulty with individual competitions conducted by the manager was the conflict of interest that occurred when employees in that work unit competed with others. In particular, the Office of the Auditor General has criticized the PS system as susceptible to favouritism and /or discrimination. See Chapter 9 "Streamlining the Human Resource Management Regime: A Study of Changing Roles and Responsibilities" in the April 2000 Report of the Office of the Auditor General.

64. The list of potential informal inputs can be rather lengthy ranging from informal interventions by family members, military colleagues, seniors acting

on behalf of Branch or other sub-group interests, specialist case managers working with individuals through queries coming from third parties such as the CF Ombudsman, Human Rights Commission etc. to formal representation on behalf of the member by civilian lawyers or Members of Parliament. During a process in 1999 of mapping decision making for HR functions, the author was presented with a case study where the Career Management staff had documented 46 different people who had attempted to influence the decision regarding the status of a single CF member.

65. Of note, there are two Public Service classifications that are found only in DND: University Teachers (UT) and Defence Science (DS). Both are managed using an approach that is much closer to the CF succession management system than to the rest of the PS vacancy management model.

66. The seminal work on differentiated commitment (affective, normative and continuous) was Meyer, J. P., & Allen, N. J. (1991). A three-component conceptualization of organizational commitment. *Human Resource Management Review*, 1, 61-89.

67. There is extensive literature on the motivational aspects that may be derived from the characteristics of work. The original research in this domain was Hackman, J.R & Oldham, G.R. (1976) Motivation through the design of work: Test for a theory. *Organizational Behavior and Human Performance*, 16, 250-279. As well, these links were clearly demonstrated in research conducted with senior officers attending the three advanced PD courses conducted at CFC. When asked to identify reasons why they might leave the military, the overwhelming response selected by 74% was if the challenge and sense of fulfillment they derived from military service was reduced. Only 21% selected pay and benefits and a mere 10% endorsed reduced chances of promotion. See again the Okros et al *Between 9/11 and Kandahar.*

68. As with job characteristics, there is also extensive literature on the role of maintenance or hygiene factors that, if absent or reduced, can erode commitment and retention. For the original work here, see Hertzberg, F. (1959) *The Motivation to Work.*, Wiley: New York.

69. A well recognized and successful business person in the Vancouver area built a chain of car dealerships, in part, through the process of every month firing the sales person with lowest sales.

70. For a recent update, See Wong, L., Kolditz, T.A., Millen, R.A. and Potter, T.M. (2003) *Why They Fight: Combat Motivation in the Iraq War.* Carlisle, P.A.: Strategic Studies Institute for analyses in Iraq that will link back to the Samuel Stouffer and S.L.A. Marshall work from the Second World War see Stouffer, S.A., Lumsdaine, A.A., Lumsdaine, M.H,. Williams, R.M., Smith, M. B., Janis, I.L., Star, S.A. and Cottrell, L.S. (1949) *The American Soldier: Combat and Its Aftermath*, (Volume II), Princeton, NJ: Princeton University Press and Marshall, S. L. A. (1942) *Men Against Fire*, New York: William Morrow and Company.

71. For a discussion of the guardian morale syndrome, see Jacobs, J. (1992). *Systems of Survival*. Random House: Toronto.

72. For a complete discussion see both *Duty with Honour* and *Conceptual Foundations* .

73. Again, see the Meyers & Allen work on affective, normative and continuance commitment.

74. Amongst others, see the Director General Land Capability Development (2005) *Canada's Soldiers: Military Ethos and Canadian Values in the 21st Century* and the Okros et al *Between 9/11 and Kandahar.*

75. There are, of course, potential negative consequences of relying on 'economic conscription' to convince people to stay in uniform. While an early, immediate pension at 20 years clearly encourages those at the 12-16 years of service to stay in, doing so because they can't afford to quit (continuance commitment) does not lead to optimal performance.

76. The concept of natural justice is that there are certain principles that should be followed in all cases to ensure that legal proceedings are fair and impartial (even if not specified in law).

77. For an analysis of CF member's perspectives, see Campbell, D. & Wilson, F.P. (1988) *Final Assessment of the Two Needs Assessment Surveys.* Seneca College: Toronto.

78. Amongst others, key central agencies include the Office of the Auditor General, Treasury Board, the Public Service Human Resources Management Agency and the Canadian Human Rights Commission with the CF Ombudsman as an internal/external oversight office.

79. The general literature here pertains to Organizational Citizenship Behaviours (OCBs), for the original work that drew on the military context, see Baterman, T. S. & Organ, D. W., (1983). Job Satisfaction and the Good Soldier: The Relationship Between Affect and Employee Citizenship. *Academy of Management Journal*, 11(4), 587-595.

80. See *Isabelle Gauthier, Joseph G. Houlden, Marie-Claude Gauthier, Georgina Ann Brown* and *Canadian Armed Forces* Ottawa: (Canadian Human Rights) Tribunal Decision 3/89 (20 February 1989).

81. And recalling as Feaver (1996) points out, ultimately the "people" have the right to decide.

82. The boundaries here remain a source of friction most typically with younger individuals/newer members seeking more autonomy over their out of uniform, personal lives.

83. Noting that there are alternate ways to view this issue depending on one's discipline it is important to note that the following is based on the cross-cultural psychology literature. The original author here was P.J. Pelto (1968) The differences between "tight" and "loose" societies. *Trans-actions*, pp 37-40. For a broader coverage of the topic see Berry, J.W., Poortinga, Y.H., Segall, M.H.

& Dasen, P.R. (1992) Cross-cultural psychology: Research and Applications. Cambridge: Cambridge University Press.

84. As per JFK's (only) inaugural speech: "Ask not what your country can do for you but what you can do for your country".

85. The custom of Japanese labour unions negotiating with management which days are authorized or unauthorized, wildcat strikes is an interesting example of the latter point.

86. See Davis, K.D. and McKee, B. (2004) "Women in the military: Facing the Warrior Framework" in F.P. Pinch et al (eds) *Challenge and Change in the Military Gender and Diversity Issues* for a discussion in the Canadian military context.

CHAPTER 8

CANADIAN DEFENCE KNOWLEDGE MANAGEMENT

JOHN GIRARD

Knowledge will be the ammunition of choice for Canada's future military forces. Armed with the powerful weapon of knowledge, Defence leaders will be well positioned to operate in the complex, near chaotic, environment we anticipate dominating the 21st century. Throughout history, disruptive equipments, doctrines and ideologies have shaped defence forces around the globe. Much as the advancements in artillery changed the battlefields of the First World War, or air power changed the battlescape of the Second World War, or as mutual assured destruction provided détente throughout the Cold War, knowledge will be the disruptive force of the new world.

Transformation is the catalyst sparking the revolutionary changes in technology, leadership and culture necessary to create the knowledge environment. The achievement of the knowledge edge will permit Defence leaders to span seamlessly internal boundaries to harvest the invaluable knowledge assets of the entire Defence Team. Heretofore such an idea was nothing more than a dream and yet today we are on cusp of reaping the benefits of this powerful force multiplier.

Charting a course toward the knowledge environment is underway, but requires clarification and refinement. The Canadian Forces' doctrine of manoeuvre warfare, supported by the tenets of mission command, provides a springboard from which we will launch our knowledge initiatives. The next step is to coordinate the trilogy of technology, leadership and culture with a view to creating an environment conducive to knowledge sharing and transfer.

Key to the achievement of the knowledge edge is a radical cultural shift from a need-to-know paradigm to one of need-to-share. Though simple to articulate, this essential move will be difficult for some to accept. Few beliefs are as ingrained in the fabric of Defence as is the need-to-know principle. Though this time tested standard has served us well, the time is right to transition to a new level of trust.

Modern Defence leaders are well versed on the merits of exploiting knowledge. For centuries, military commanders have desired to know what was on the other side of the hill. For the first time leaders will not only know what is on the other side of the hill but also whether we (or our allies) have been here before, and what we did to succeed or fail last time. Armed with knowledge leaders will be much better prepared to make decisions or take actions in complex operations.

The aim of this chapter is to consider how Defence leaders may achieve knowledge supremacy. The journey begins with a consideration of what exactly is Defence Knowledge and Defence Knowledge Management. With this foundation in place the expedition continues by exploring why would leaders wish to implement knowledge management and more specifically why now. The last section of this chapter examines how leaders may put knowledge management into action by reviewing tools, techniques, and processes that enable knowledge supremacy.

What is Defence Knowledge?

The majority of academics and knowledge management authorities make a distinction between the three related, but discrete terms of data, information, and knowledge. The three terms are hierarchical in nature with data being the foundation upon which information builds to a pinnacle of knowledge. Occasionally scholars use the collective noun 'knowledge' to group together the three blocks of the knowledge pyramid. For example, in War and Anti-War, the futurist authors Alvin and Heidi Toffler use the term knowledge as "defined broadly to include information, data, communication and culture"[1]. The outcome of such an unfortunate assemblage is the fallacy that practices such as data processing, information management, and knowledge management are synonymous.

Today several cognitive theories exist that take into account the pyramid of data, information, and knowledge. Some research suggests the hierarchy should extend beyond these three basic building blocks. For example, systems theorist and professor of organizational change Russell Ackoff sees a hierarchy that extends the pyramid to five by adding understanding and wisdom.[2] Verna Allee's Knowledge Archetypes enlarges the original three to seven by adding meaning, philosophy, wisdom, and union.[3]

At present, the Canadian Forces (CF) views this cognitive hierarchy somewhat differently than scholars. Current CF doctrine suggests that there are four elements: data, information, knowledge and understanding. At the low end are individual sensor observations or data. This data may be processed to develop a common relevant situational awareness or information. Through cognition, one may determine the desired end state, including the commander's intent and concept of operations – this is knowledge. At this point, the commander uses judgement to decide what should be done, this is 'understanding' and at this point he or she may take action.

The first three components of this cogitative hierarchy are identical in each of the models and collectively become the knowledge creation process. Typically, these are the steps completed by the staff to assist the commander. The next step or level of the hierarchy, understanding, is ultimately the domain of the commander. The commander uses his or her judgement to decide on the appropriate action. Unlike the very mechanical knowledge creation steps, this step tends to be more of an art than a science. The jump from knowledge to understanding builds on the knowledge already created. However, most commanders rely heavily on experience and intuition, in other words more tacit knowledge than explicit knowledge.

Doctrinally, the CF hierarchy culminates at the level of understanding; however, there may be merit in exploring Ackoff's final level of wisdom. This almost Utopian level presupposes a near perfect understanding of the environment and tends to be a stage achieved by those few commanders who have extensive experience and finely honed intuition. Those military commanders who mastered the art of warfare truly achieved the "knowledge edge" and were feared by their opponents and heralded by historians. The notion of achieving the knowledge edge in operations is a relatively new concept driven by today's innovative leaders. The knowledge edge was designed primarily with operations in mind; however, it applies equally to other areas of Defence.

Figure 8.1: The Knowledge Edge

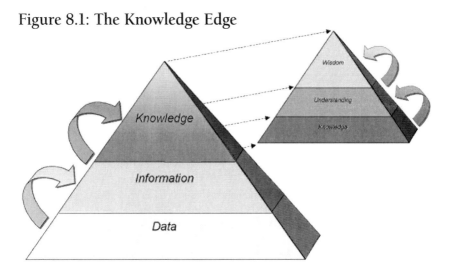

Source: John Girard, "Defence Knowledge Management – A Passing Fad?" Canadian Military Journal 5, no. 2 (2002):18.

What is Defence Knowledge Management?

An agreed definition of knowledge management has eluded scholars and practitioners alike since the term first entered our lexicon. Virtually every paper penned on the subject includes a re-worked definition; nevertheless, the debate continues. In the end, it is not the definition that is important but rather the outputs and outcomes of the process. That said, there appears to be a need for a definition within Defence.

In a 2002 joint letter entitled Future Directions for Information Management in DND/CF, the Chief of the Defence Staff (CDS) and the Deputy Minister of National Defence stated that knowledge management was "An environment that facilitates knowledge discovery, creation and innovation, and which fosters the development of a learning organization."[4] This description encapsulates the vision of what they expected to see in the future.

According to the Defence Terminology Bank, the draft definition of knowledge management is:

> An integrated systematic approach which when applied to an organization enables the optimal use of timely, accurate and relevant information; it also facilitates knowledge discovery and innovation, fosters the development of a learning organization and enhances understanding by integrating all sources of information, as well as individual and collective knowledge and experience.[5]

Like many other knowledge management definitions, this definition is rather complex. A concise phrase is desirable, one that immediately communicates the meaning and yet is not constraining. Perhaps a better definition for Defence would be simply: knowledge management is the creation and sharing of knowledge within Defence with a view to achieving operational advantage. At the end of the day, it is up to individual leaders to decide how to create and share knowledge within their organizations.

Why Knowledge Management?

The focus thus far in this paper has been to define the components and concepts of knowledge management. Using an analogy of the knowledge pyramid, the concentration has been on the data foundation or facts about knowledge management. The next part builds on this important foundation by adding relevance or purpose, in other words, layer two of the pyramid, analogous to information.

Having defined the components of the knowledge pyramid and reviewed knowledge creation and transfer concepts within Defence, it is now possible to focus on the question: Why manage knowledge? Academic and business leaders alike agree that, "In an economy where the only certainty is uncertainty, the only sure source of lasting competitive advantage is knowledge."[6] Experts suggest countless reasons for knowledge management within enterprises, such as globalization, deregulation, technology, downsizing, and information overload.[7]

Though interesting from a professional development point of view, the fact that academia or Corporate Canada apply something called knowledge management may only be of passing interest to Defence. All too often, the public sector has tended to jump on the bandwagon of the newest hype spawned by business schools across the land. Blind faith in seemingly promising quick fix solutions can and frequently does lead to unfortunate, though all too predictable, failures. The newest management magic formula has often required significant investment without any benefits, either real or perceived.

So why is it that Defence would wish to consider knowledge management? Surely, this is just another overrated and underdeveloped business process looking for a home, which will unquestionably go the way of the dodo bird. Perhaps, but this seems highly improbable once given the facts. For at the same time Aristotle was considering the categorization of knowledge, Sun Tzu wrote, "If you know your enemy and know yourself, you need not fear the results of a hundred battles."[8] And at the same time knowledge management gurus were selling their wares to business leaders across North America, we heard General Tommy Franks, Commander-in-Chief (CINC) US Central Command, saying "… as has been the case since Sun Tzu said it, precise knowledge of self and precise knowledge of the threat leads to victory."[9] It is clear that for centuries, enlightened defence leaders, like academics and business leaders, have appreciated the value of knowledge.

In fact, there is little need to venture to Iraq in 2003 or Asia in 400 B.C.E. to establish that Canadian military leaders understand the need for knowledge. Embedded in the CF Strategy 2020 vision statement is:

> The Defence Team will generate, employ and sustain high-quality, combat-capable, inter-operable and rapidly deployable task-tailored forces. We will exploit leading-edge doctrine and technologies to accomplish our domestic and international roles in the battlespace of the 21st century and be recognized, both at home and abroad, as an innovative, **relevant knowledge-based institution**. With transformational leadership and coherent management, we will build upon our proud heritage in pursuit of clear strategic objectives (emphasis added).[10]

Similarly, a recent Army Commander's Vision, which served as a basis for the Army Strategy, includes the following statement:

> Using progressive doctrine, realistic training and leading-edge technologies, the Army will be a knowledge-based and command-centric institution capable of continuous adaptation and task tailoring across the spectrum of conflict.[11] (emphasis added)

Such passages are not penned without considerable debate. These vision statements are a true reflection of where commanders expect their organizations to be in the future. However, one need not look very far to see excellent examples of knowledge management in action. Arguably, DND/CF is one of the most experienced knowledge organizations in Canada and for good reason, given that many knowledge management processes are already commonplace in Defence. For example, DND/CF has a proven ability to externalize knowledge through the application of lessons learned and after-action review processes. Equally notable are the numerous ways DND/CF ensures that tacit knowledge is preserved and transferred within the organization, through mechanisms such as battlefield studies and on-the-job training programs.

The point is that knowledge management is nothing new for Defence. In fact, we trace the origins of knowledge management back to October 20, 1871. On that day, officers of the first Canadian Regular Force units met in messes in both Kingston and Quebec.[12] Their meeting spaces are reminiscent of the ba concept, a revolutionary knowledge concept being imported from Japan. A ba "can be thought of as a shared space for emerging relationships. This space can be physical (e.g., office, dispersed business space), virtual (e.g., e-mail, teleconference), mental (e.g., shared experiences, ideas, ideals), or any combination of them. What differentiates ba from ordinary human interaction is the concept of knowledge creation."[13] A ba is simply a social space where Japanese executives meet to share knowledge. Such a novel concept is exactly what our forefathers expected of the military mess – a trusted environment where one could share experiences and perhaps tell war stories, but more on that later.

Why Knowledge Management Now?

Perhaps the real question is 'why now'? If DND/CF is already a recognized knowledge organization, why then invest in a knowledge strategy? There are three major reasons why this is the time to institutionalize knowledge management within Defence: times have changed; technology; and transformation, each of which are described below.

Times have Changed

Building on the old cliché that "things just aren't the way the used to be," it is critical that DND/CF acknowledge that much of what we do has changed dramatically in the past decade or so. Since the fall of the Berlin Wall, almost everything we do has changed, the tempo of operations is higher, the level of certainty is lower, and there are new and emerging threats. As part of the peace dividend Defence is much leaner than it was in 1989. Add to that a new doctrine of manoeuvre warfare and it becomes apparent that we are operating in a new environment. In short, the world of Defence is very different than it was only a few years ago.

From a knowledge management perspective, this new world order demands new ways to ensure we create and transfer our collective knowledge. In the old world, we had the luxury of deliberate redundancy, that is, many positions had understudies or assistants who were invaluable in capturing and retaining our organizational memory. In the 1990s, the financial realities of the new world forced us to adopt a leaner, more efficient organization. Though more economical, these new structures are thinner, more brittle and less conducive to tacit knowledge sharing. A second example surrounds the social spaces that were once an extremely important part of the military fabric. Ironically, as we downplay the value of our messes, many other non-military organizations are introducing the concept we abandoned into their organizations with the hope of improving knowledge sharing – witness the ba.

These examples and others should not be construed as criticisms or failures. The reality is that organizations change over time and we must develop processes and techniques that work in the current and future versions of the organization. There is little value in lamenting days gone by, other than to learn from our experiences. Rather we should look for creative solutions to ensure that our knowledge creation and sharing is at least as good as it was before. In many cases we should be able to exceed the standards of yesteryear as times were never as good as we remember them.

Transformation

In A Time for Transformation, the 2002-2003 Annual Report by the Chief of the Defence Staff, General Henault stated "For Canada, the question is not whether to transform the Canadian Forces, it is how best to achieve the required transformation."[14] The important message from a knowledge management perspective is that the evolutionary change that we have lived though in the past decade will be replaced by revolutionary transformation in the future.

General Henault advised that "we must transform the way we perceive and think" and that "we are moving from an industrial, hierarchical mode of thinking to a world powered by collaborative human networks."[15] This is the essence of knowledge management, connecting people with people to foster an environment where we can create and share knowledge. General Henault continued by stating:

> We must learn to think, behave, and act as a node in a collaborative network that includes our warfighters, all three military environments, our civilian colleagues in the department and broader public security portfolio, as well as our allies. If the defining feature of the Industrial Age was linear, vertical thinking, then the defining feature of the information age is lateral, horizontal thinking.[16]

Knowledge management will be one of the prime enablers of transformation.

Technology

Technology has changed the way we do many things. In most cases, it has improved our lot, though there remain some areas where one might argue that technology, or at least our management of technology, has not added value. On the positive side, we see an ability to fuse reconnaissance, surveillance and intelligence in ways simply unimaginable only a few years ago. Soon commanders will have immediate access to vast stores of processed, timely and relevant knowledge with which they may make decisions.

However, there are a handful of examples where more work is needed. Fifteen years ago, DND/CF had a robust and ordered staff duties system that demanded the highest standards of writing and administration. We had highly regimented filing systems, which permitted the rapid retrieval of documents and extremely efficient ways to "Put Away" or "Bring Forward" all codified knowledge. We knew how long to keep each type document and had systems for pruning unnecessary or obsolete correspondence.

Today, most non-operational correspondence is by e-mail, and few organizations can boast of an electronic "filing" system as robust as the paper management system that it replaced. Many would undoubtedly argue that technology is the culprit. In hindsight, we now know that technology alone does not solve these sorts of problems and that technology, like all other resources, must be managed to be effective. The same will also hold true in the future as we consider technological approaches to knowledge management.

Enabling Defence Knowledge

The final section of this paper considers how one may more fully enable Defence knowledge management. Returning to the knowledge pyramid analogy, this section represents the knowledge level of the pyramid and focuses on preparing commanders to make decisions and then take action. Specifically, this section describes a model for defence knowledge management that will aid leaders in implementing knowledge programs within their sphere of influence.

At present, a number of models exist that attempt to describe the enablers of knowledge management. To develop a model for defence knowledge management, several well-known models were reviewed, including the Enablers of Transfer; Knowledge Management the Architecture of Enterprise Engineering; European Network for Knowledge Management; and the US Department of Navy's Balanced Knowledge Management model.[17] These four models provide a comprehensive overview of current thinking, both from an academic and from a practitioner's view. Equally, these provide a brilliant balance between profit and not-for-profit organizations, as well as North American and European ideas.

Five enablers – Technology, Leadership, Culture, Measurement, and Process – are common in three of the five models. A detailed review of the remaining four enablers – Organization, Infrastructure, Learning, and Content – reveals that the essence of this latter cluster is in fact embedded within the former.

Having determined the five enablers, the next step was to find an icon with which the Defence Team would associate. The new model is based on an Inuit structure called the Inukshuk. The Virtual Museum of Canada describes an inukshuk as:

> "Like a person". An arrangement of stones, often resembling the shape of a human. The inukshuk is used as a navigational aid, as a marker for hunting grounds and caches of food or supplies, in hunting to lure geese and corral caribou, and as a way to mark sacred ground. These stone cairns embody strong spiritual and ancestral connections and have been erected by Inuit on the Arctic tundra for many generations.[18]

The inukshuk, as shown in Figure 8.2, is an excellent model of Defence knowledge for a variety of reasons. First, inuksuit (the plural of inukshuk) are well-known symbols in Canada and play an important role in our history and tradition. Second, most inuksuit resemble people, to remind us that it is people who play the most important role in knowledge management. Unlike its distant cousin Information Management, knowledge management is simply not possible without people. Finally, while most inuksuit are similar they are nonetheless distinct from one another, much as each knowledge management implementation will be unique.

The inukshuk is built on a foundation of technology, leadership and culture – the TLC of Defence knowledge management. Like a real inukshuk, the model requires an appropriate balance of each or the structure will tumble. If a particular knowledge management implementation has strong leadership support and robust technological basis but fails to consider the cultural implications then it is almost certainly doomed to failure.

TECHNOLOGY

Technology is an enabler of knowledge management; however, it is not synonymous with it. From a Defence perspective, technology is a double-edged sword and we must ensure that technology is an enabler for knowledge management, not an impediment. At present, some would argue that technology causes more problems than it solves. Many will argue that desktop video conferencing, streaming video and instant messaging are more effective ways to share than more conventional means such as e-mail. However, today our infrastructure does not support such enabling technologies.

Figure 8.2. Inukshuk: Defence Knowledge Management Model

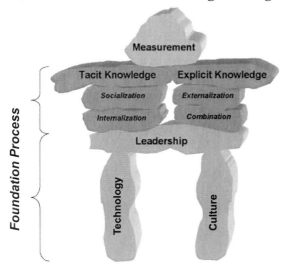

Source: John Girard, "Defence Knowledge Management – A Passing Fad?" Canadian Military Journal 5, no. 2 (2002): 21.

LEADERSHIP

Our current military doctrine of manoeuvre warfare complemented by a mission command style leadership is the ideal environment for knowledge management. We must ensure we "walk the talk" and provide resources, including time, to grass roots knowledge initiatives. Some of the most effective knowledge tools and processes are driven from the grass roots but they require time to become truly effective. A good example of this is a community of practice, which is inexpensive in terms of cost but which must be cultivated through the support of leaders.

CULTURE

Culture is an oft-misunderstood concept in knowledge management circles. Clearly there are many dimensions to culture; however, one of the most significant challenges, from a knowledge management perspective, is the culture of Defence security. Moving from a "need-to-know" culture and a "need-to-share" culture is not a trivial task. Many leaders have commented on the need for organizations to share information and knowledge in the post 9/11 era. Whilst appearing before the Standing Senate Committee on National Security and Defence, Lieutenant-General Macdonald, former Vice Chief of the Defence Staff stated:

> During the 14 months of its [the Canada-US Bi-National Planning Group] existence, its accomplishments and current projects include: . . . and perhaps most importantly, working to transform information sharing between our two nations from a need-to-know to a need-to-share paradigm.[19] (emphasis added)

Such a profound statement clearly demonstrates the understanding of our senior leaders of the importance of supporting a shift to a need-to-share culture.

PROCESS

Once there is a robust, balanced foundation of technology, leadership, and culture in place, one must apply one or more processes to create and share knowledge. A successful knowledge environment encompasses both tacit and explicit knowledge. Most western cultures tend to emphasize the explicit component. We like to write doctrine, tactics and procedures and then assume that all will have the knowledge to complete the necessary tasks. Alternatively, those from the East rely more on the tacit dimension – we must strive for a balance between the two. The inukshuk model helps to establish this relationship in a practical way as the stones represent the four ways in which one may create or transfer knowledge as illustrated in Figure 8.3.

Figure 8.3: Process: Knowledge Creation and Transfer Examples

Socialization

- •Sharing experiences
- •On-the-job training
- •Battlefield studies

Externalization

- •After action review
- •Lessons learned
- •War diaries

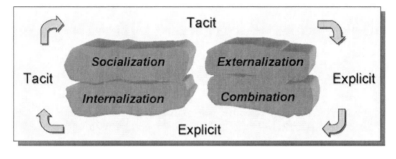

Internalization

- •Learning by doing
- •Experience
- •Values/Ethos

Combination

- •Strategy
- •Doctrine
- •Tactics/SOPs

Source: John Girard, "Defence Knowledge Management – A Passing Fad?" Canadian Military Journal 5, no. 2 (2002):23.

Socialization – Tacit to Tacit. Through social interaction, people may gain knowledge, which is highly personal and difficult to formalize. One of the best examples is the sharing of experiences through war stories. Properly prepared, these stories are a very powerful way of transferring tacit knowledge from one person to another. When a more experienced soldier, sailor, airman, or airwomen recounts a real-life experience to a younger colleague they share more than just the simple facts of the story. Frequently, we witness significant emotions as the veteran shares the difficult and trying conditions lived. The listeners can feel as if they were present at the event. This process of socialization is an important part of our military heritage but could be improved. Imagine if all Majors and Master Warrant Officers were trained to tell stories effectively and we used this tool regularly.

Externalization – Tacit to Explicit. Externalization as a concept of knowledge transfer or creation is foreign to most Western thinkers, with the exception of the military. Within the military construct, we strive to create or transfer tacit knowledge to the explicit form. Our lessons learned and after-action review processes are good examples of how we try to codify tacit knowledge.

Combination – Explicit to Explicit. Through the process of codification, one person may document specific knowledge into some form of repository so that many others may access that knowledge. An organization developing and formalizing best practices is a classic example of the transfer of explicit knowledge. In a Defence setting, this is what we try to achieve using strategy, doctrine and standard operating procedures.

Internalization – Explicit to Tacit. The premise of internalization is knowledge created through an amalgamation of codified explicit knowledge and fuzzy tacit knowledge. An example of this is DND's relatively new value based ethics program. We have articulated a series of principles and obligations with the hope that all Defence team members will internalize these important notions and know at an almost instinctive level how to react when confronted with a difficult situation. Over time, the aim is to get most people to base their actions not on a specific obligation, but rather, through the internalization of what they will know is right and wrong.

This brief review of the knowledge creation and transfer processes highlights that all of the above processes are used within Defence, at least to some extent. The most important point is that we must carefully consider the best way to create and transfer knowledge within our organizations.

Measurement

A sound Defence knowledge management plan must be driven by Defence strategy and based on results. The measurement of the impact of knowledge management programs is often troublesome in that many of the benefits are intangible. How for example can the real impact of war stories be measured? Sometimes commanders intuitively know something is working well; however, it is often necessary to demonstrate the more tangible benefits of a program, especially when funding is required. To this end, each knowledge management program should include a statement of expected results from which we may gauge success.

Defence Knowledge Management Today

Before describing the status of Defence Knowledge Management today, a review of the recent history may be beneficial. Prior to 2003 the Assistant Deputy Minister (Information Management) (ADM(IM)) was responsible for knowledge management within the Department of National Defence. The Director General Knowledge Management Innovations (DGKMI) executed this charge for ADM(IM). Subordinate to DGKMI were the Director Knowledge and Information Management (DKIM) and a Senior Knowledge Management Officer, the senior military person in the KM chain.

In 2001, the Associate Deputy Minister conducted an extensive review entitled the Information Management Strategic Review (IMSR). One of the IMSR recommendation was that the responsibility for knowledge management be moved from ADM(IM) to the VCDS. The rationale for the reorganization was that knowledge management was different from information management and therefore should reside in a more central location – the VCDS organization. In 2003, this change occurred and a new directorate was established within the Director General Strategic Change (DGSC) division. The Directorate of Knowledge Management (DKM) was to be lead by a civilian executive and would include a single military officer (Lieutenant-Colonel level). Unfortunately, the DKM position was never staffed nor were most of the positions in DKM.

In 2006, the DGSC division was dismantled and the responsibility for knowledge management was moved yet again, this time to the Chief of Programme (C Prog) whose mission and vision are shown below.[20]

Chief of Program Mission. To assist the VCDS by providing objective analysis and sound advice on strategic planning options and resource allocations, coordinating the management of the Defence Services Program and measuring and reporting on Departmental performance in executing the overall Defence mission.

Chief of Program Vision. C Prog will optimize Defence capability and force structure across the defence scenarios and the 4, 10 and 20-year planning horizons. We will act as a competent central staff crossroads to facilitate operational effectiveness and to ensure value for money across the Defence enterprise. Credibility is our center of gravity. Thoroughly networked with other Defence, allied and government corporate management organizations, we will provide clear planning direction to Level 1 organizations. We will lead in developing and implementing modern management solutions to meet Defence needs. We will attract and continue to develop talented knowledge workers producing a valued contribution.

Current priority issues within C Prog include:

- Defence Policy Review;
- Performance measurement;
- Transformational capabilities such as C4ISR and Strategic Lift;
- Horizon 2 capability development plan;
- J8 network reinforcement, both departmental and allied; and
- Integration of business, **knowledge and information management** (emphasis added).

Within the C Prog organization, the Director Defence Strategy Management (DDSM) is accountable for knowledge management. DDSM's mission is: *To foster effective management practices to enable Defence strategy execution.* DDSM's vision is: *To be renowned as the key constituents that enabled the DND/CF to become a Best Practice Organization in Integrated Defence Management at home and abroad.* DDSM 7 – Knowledge Management/ Lessons Learned is the section directly responsible for knowledge management.

DDSM 7 strategic framework is based on the balanced scorecard performance management framework and methodology.[21] DDSM 7 is the OPI for the design and implementation of the above "integrated systematic approach" for DND/CF organizational learning and knowledge transfer. We do this by:

a. Fostering an Integrated Knowledge Environment through strategic Level One (L1) partners: the intent is to achieve a more horizontal DND/CF knowledge-sharing culture of organizational learning through continuous improvement;

b. Supporting the maximization of organizational and operational efficiency and effectiveness for DND/CF (L2 and L3 focus) through improved decision-making and knowledge transfer strategies: the intent is to promote better situational awareness and understanding through knowledge transfer (lessons learned and best practices) - a knowledge advantage;

c. Providing practical KM advice and support as the DND/CF "Knowledge-Transfer Service Broker" for a wide range of KM services that vary from knowledge transfer strategy development to actual knowledge-transfer and capture methodologies: the intent is to facilitate collaborative connections (people to people, people to process, people to technology) between those in DND/CF requiring help in becoming true learning organizations; and

d. Acting as a help desk for those in need of "knowledge mobilization" advice: the intent is for our small team to balance the efforts of PEOPLE, Process and technology.

The Future Defence Knowledge Environment

The CDS/DM's view of the future, that being an environment that facilitates knowledge discovery, creation and innovation, and which fosters the development of a learning organization, provides a foundation on which we may build a knowledge strategy. In previous papers we have examined what knowledge management is in a Defence context. Now we turn to what the future may look like. When one gazes into the crystal ball it is easy to see a Utopian environment that will always be out of reach. Care has been taken not to describe a milieu that is unreachable.

Only a decade ago, few members of the Defence team were able to access the Internet from work and a DND/CF-wide e-mail system did not exist. If one looks back five years, wireless technology was virtually nonexistent and yet today we are beginning to see members of the Defence team carrying mobile hand held e-mail and Internet appliances. In short, it is difficult to say with any certainly exactly what the future will hold. Two views of the future environment follow. The first is what Defence leaders should demand and the second is what most team members should expect. Clearly, this vision spans many boundaries and will require a coordinated way ahead.

LEADERS VIEW

- Processes in place to share knowledge, capture lessons learned, thus ensuring we do not relearn the same lessons or reinvent the wheel.
- A single customizable "box," from which s/he enters a recognized knowledge-escape.
- Seamless access to classified and designated material necessary for mission, includes e-mail, chat, video-conference.
- Staff have the ability to prioritize knowledge needs of the commander or executive.
- Single click to knowledge assets: DND/CF lessons learned knowledge warehouse, virtual libraries, expertise locator system.

KNOWLEDGE WORKERS VIEW

- A knowledge environment that encourages and rewards sharing, promotes mentoring, provides the time for detailed handovers, respects and acknowledges the value of people and knowledge.
- With a single logon to a single work station, s/he may access all necessary applications they need to perform their tasks (HRMS, FMAS, Internet, Intranet etc) – depending on needs, this will include read and/or write capabilities.
- Ability to quickly discover career advancement opportunities, includes ability to compete for new positions, participate in virtual training and education.
- Single data entry – never repeat the same form again!

Guiding Principles

Rather than articulate exactly how we move from today toward the future knowledge environment, a set of guiding principles will guide the way. Working within these principles Defence leaders will be able to chart the best course for their organization.

DRIVEN BY STRATEGY – BASED ON RESULTS

In order to increase the chances of success, knowledge management programs and processes must be tied to strategy and based on results. In practice, this requires Defence leaders to identify problems requiring solutions, rather than trying to find a place to apply knowledge management. The latter, often referred to as flirting with KM, is seldom successful.

The most successful knowledge management implementations are often not identified as knowledge management. Take for example the Chief of Air Staff's (CAS) very successful Flight Safety program. This is clearly one of Defence's most successful knowledge management programs and yet it was developed and implemented long before the first guru coined the phase the KM. Even today few members of the Air staff would associate Flight Safety with the notion of knowledge management – that is a very positive statement. In short, we must not do KM for KM's sake, but rather to solve a real challenge.

Some leaders will wish to articulate the importance of knowledge to their organizations. Clearly, this will vary from group to group and is very culture dependant. A good example of this idea is the Army Commander's Vision, which serves as a basis for the Army Strategy, and includes the following statement:

> Using progressive doctrine, realistic training and leading-edge technologies, the Army will be a knowledge-based and command-centric institution capable of continuous adaptation and task tailoring across the spectrum of conflict.[22] (Emphasis added)

DECENTRALIZED

The responsibility for knowledge management will remain decentralized with leaders who are best placed to decide the needs and resources of their organizations. At this point, there seems to be little evidence to support the centralization of knowledge management within DND/CF. This is not suggest that there will not be horizontal collaboration. The principle of decentralization will permit functional groups to decide the best way ahead. A good example is the pioneering work of the C4ISR team; this entire project is knowledge management in action and is best lead by the experts in the operation domain.

COORDINATED

Today many Defence organizations have some sort of lessons learned group, but each takes a different form. CLS has opted to establish the Army Lesson Learned Centre, which collates lessons into a database. One way that CAS promulgates lesson learned is through Flight Comment, which is produced by the Director of Flight Safety. Both of these examples work well in their organization but may not work well in the other culture. Rather than suggest that one or both change a time tested and proven system, it may be wiser to establish a community of practice for those interested in lesson learned. Almost certainly, both groups could learn from each other; however, more importantly those who do not have a lesson-learned process would have the opportunity to learn from two (or more) experts.

Summary

The sharing of knowledge with the defence community is certainly not new. In this chapter, we have seen many great examples of knowledge sharing in action in Defence: the use of social spaces, after action reviews, lessons learned, storytelling, war diaries, on-the-job training, and mentoring, to name a few. Together these examples highlight that Defence in Canada is one of the most knowledge-empowered organizations in the country. However, there are also many examples where improvement is needed. Missing codified knowledge, as was the case during the Somalia Inquiry, or commanders not knowing the number and location of types of equipment can be very embarrassing for Defence leaders. Clearly more work is required.

The tenets of the current Defence Knowledge Management model – leadership, technology, and culture – are sound and provide an excellent foundation from which one may develop processes to share knowledge in a secure and timely manner. To ensure that the value of knowledge sharing is understood and appreciated, a series of measures should be established. The process of creating and sharing knowledge is central to achieving the goal of an environment that facilitates knowledge discovery, creation and innovation, and which fosters the development of a learning organization. To achieve this desired end state, leaders must chart a course toward the knowledge environment. This plan should be driven by Defence strategy and based on results; it should be decentralized; and it should be coordinated.

Endnotes

1. Toffler, Alvin and Toffler, Heidi, War and Anti-War : *Survival at the Dawn of the 21st Century*, 1st ed. (Boston: Little, Brown, 1993), xiii.

2. Ackoff, Russell Lincoln, *The Democratic Corporation: A Radical Prescription for Recreating Corporate America and Rediscovering Success* (New York : Oxford University Press, 1994).

3. Allee, Verna, *The Knowledge Evolution : Expanding Organizational Intelligence* (Boston, Mass: Butterworth-Heinemann, 1997).

4. Henault, R.R. and Judd, J., *Future Direction for Information Management in DND/CF* (Ottawa: Department of National Defence, 2002).

5. Blodgett, Chris, "Mobilizing Knowledge: Status of KM in Defence," *Bravo Defence* (Summer 2005).

6. Nonaka, Ikujiro, "The Knowledge-Creating Company," *Harvard Business Review* 69, no. 6 (1991): 96.

7. Johne, Marjo, "What Do You Know?" *CMA Management* 75, no. 1 (2001): 20. See also, Prusak, L., "Where Did Knowledge Management Come From?" *IBM Systems Journal* 40, no. 1 (2001):1002; Wilson, T. D., "Information Overload: Implications for Healthcare Services," *Health Informatics Journal* 7, no. 2 (2001): 112; and Hanka, Rudolf and Fuka, Karel, "Information Overload And "Just-in-Time" Knowledge," *The Electronic Library* 18, no. 4 (2000): 279.

8. Tzu, Sun and Clavell, James, *The Art of War* (New York: Delacorte Press, 1983), 82.

9. Rumsfeld, D. and Franks, T., "DoD News Briefing - Secretary Rumsfeld and Gen. Franks," United States Department of Defense, Editor. 2001.

10. Department of National Defence, *Shaping the Future of the Canadian Forces: A Strategy for 2020* (Ottawa: DND, 1999), 7.

11. Department of National Defence, *Advancing with Purpose: The Army Strategy* (Ottawa: DND, 2002), 13.

12. Nicholson, Gerald W. L., *The Gunners of Canada; the History of the Royal Regiment of Canadian Artillery.* (Toronto, Montreal,: McClelland and Stewart, 1967), v.

13. Nonaka, Ikujiro and Konno, Noboru, "The Concept of `Ba': Building a Foundation for Knowledge Creation," *California Management Review* 40, no. 3 (1998): 40-54.

14. Henault, R.R., *A Time for Transformation: The 2002-2003 Annual Report by the CDS* (Ottawa: DND, 2003), II.

15. *Ibid.*

16. *Ibid.,II-III.*

17. For a description of these models see O'Dell, Carla, Grayson, C. Jackson, and Essaides, Nilly, *If Only We Knew What We Know : The Transfer of Internal Knowledge and Best Practice* (New York: Free Press, 1998); Calabrese, Francesco Antonio, *A Suggested Framework of Key Elements Defining Effective Enterprise Knowledge Management Programs* (Washington, D.C: The George Washington University, 2000); Weber, Frithjof, et al., "Standardisation in Knowledge Management – Towards a Common KM Framework in Europe," in UNICOM Seminar (London: UNICOM, 2002); and Bennet, Alex and Kantner, James, "Navigating the KM Dimension," in *Next-Generation Knowledge Management: Enabling Business Process* (Houston: APQC, 2001).

18. *Glossary: Inukshuk.* 2002 [cited 2006 10 October]; Available from: http://www. virtualmuseum.ca/Exhibitions/Holman/english/glossary.php3.

19. Macdonald, Lieutenant-General George, "Proceedings of the Standing Senate Committee on National Security and Defence," 23 February 2004, afternoon session (Ottawa: The Senate, 2004).

20. *Chief of Programme (C Prog).* 2007 12 June 2007 [cited 27 December 2007]; Available from: http://www.vcds.forces.gc.ca/dgsp/pubs/org/dgsp_e.asp.

21. *Director Defence Strategy Management (DDSM).* 11 December 2006 [cited 27 December 2007]; Available from: http://www.vcds.forces.gc.ca/dgsp/pubs/ org/ddm_e.asp.

22. Department of National Defence, *Shaping the Future of the Canadian Forces: A Strategy for 2020* (Ottawa: DND, 1999), 7.

Chapter 9

MANAGING CHANGE WITHIN DND

Lieutenant-colonel Michael Rostek

> Change is inevitable. Change is constant.
> Benjamin Disraeli

Introduction

There are many 'forces of change' in today's global environment. Many of these pressures force organizations to become leaner, more productive, more transparent, or more quality oriented. Change is with us and organizations, both private and public sector, must learn to deal with flexibility, spontaneity and most importunately, uncertainty. As a result, the 21st Century presents us with an environment of continuous change. The prominent trends that signal forces of change for a defence organization include: globalization, rapid scientific and technological innovation, shifting power balances, demographic shifts, resource scarcities, weak and failed states, growing significance of non-state actors, prominence of identity based conflict and changing nature of conflict. These trends create forces that drive organizational change, sometimes but not always for the better.

Globalization and rapid scientific and technological innovation are by far the most significant trends driving change; however, the consequences of the remaining trends listed above can also have a dramatic impact on state military structures. Although many of these trends offer greater promise they also convey a more pervasive sense of insecurity demanding careful observance. To a large degree, DND and the CF have already begun to experience the impacts of many of these trends and there have been several change initiatives undertaken in order to deal with the fast paced changes of the international landscape.

It has been argued that DND and the CF have undergone continuous change since Unification owing to the impact of many of the trends listed above. It is for that reason that the focus of this chapter is on how the Canadian Forces (CF) changes in an increasingly complex and dynamic security environment. The chapter will commence with some very basic, yet fundamental, aspects of managing change. This will be followed by issues that are specific to change management in the public sector and in particular DND and the CF. Next, a review of the four most prominent change initiatives since 1970 -- Unification, the Management Review Group (MRG), the Management Command and Control Re-engineering Team (MCCRT) and CF Transformation -- will be undertaken in an attempt to highlight that instituting change in large organizations portends prospects of both promise and peril.

What is Change Management?

Change can affect five aspects of an organization: culture, structure, technology, physical setting, and people. Change management can be defined as the broad processes for managing organizational change. Change management encompasses planning, oversight or governance, project management, testing, and implementation.[1] Change management is a growing discipline.[2] In January 2007 a quick search on the Chapter-Indigo website indicated more than 1700 books on the topic and when the same search was executed on "Google", more than 500 million "hits" registered. Somewhat less superficial, business schools have incorporated a greater focus on the management of change at both the undergraduate and graduate levels in universities. As such, when an organization decides to undergo change, it is faced with a plethora of references and resources and choosing which method or model to follow can in itself be a daunting task.

It is well known that no one change approach fits all organizations[3] and "...no single change model should be departmentally cast in stone and deemed to be the correct one for use in defence."[4] With this in mind, the CF has deemed 16 "change elements" which must be addressed in any change initiative: vision, leadership, policy, priority setting and business planning, standards and performance measurement, risk management, evaluation and audit, accountability and reporting, recognition and incentives, effective communications, knowledge management, continuous improvement, financial resources, management of people, functional direction and project management.[5] Regardless of the model or process[6] used, consideration of these 16 "change elements" should increase the likelihood of success with a change initiative.

But what drives change? Change within an organization is generally incremental and seldom in large organization-wide steps. As change always creates a certain degree of stress, there is a general acceptance to a philosophy of logical incrementalism. Organizations that master this technique are often those that can withstand the stress and strain of larger organizational change initiatives. Nonetheless, change is the result of one of four circumstances listed in Table 9.1 below:

Table 9.1: Types of Organizational Change

Types of Change	Conditions	Actions
Imperative Change	Real crisis or some abrupt change to environment drives change	Demands immediate comprehensive action
		Ability to move quickly often determines success or failure
Contrived Crisis	Organization creates own crisis in attempt to create sense of urgency	Very risky
		Same actions as imperative change
Responsive Change	Sufficient time to respond to required changes	Actions and required time are clearly stated
Foreseeable Change	Changes are forecasted	Actions and required time remain uncertain
		Often difficult to generate interest and action

Source: Adapted from Paul W. Beamish and C. Patrick Woodcock, Strategic Management: Text, Readings and Cases, 4th Edition (Toronto: Irwin, 1996): 125-6.

In addition, there are generally three phases to managing change - preparation, managing and reinforcement phases - which can be articulated as follows:

- Phase 1: Awareness and Capability Planning. Widespread awareness within the organization is necessary to implement successful change. However, even this may not be enough. A shared view of the direction and the capability within the organization must exist if change is to be successful.

- Phase 2: Commitment and Adoption. One person, particularly in large organizations, seldom enacts change. Negotiations and coalition building and as necessary, coercion or personnel changes are tools used to get the commitment and adoption required for successful change. An escalating sense of irrevocability usually characterizes this phase.

- Phase 3: Reinforcement and Recycling. Follow-up effort and reinforcement are typically required once change has been enacted. Equally important as the other phases, efforts to reinforce change and to keep pace with changes in the environment are necessary to ensure overall success.[7]

Change can be viewed as both a condition and a process. As a condition, it describes what is happening to our environment; it is external. As a process, change describes the leadership and managerial actions taken to transform our organizations; it is internal. Change as a condition is part of the reality we must accept; change as a process is ours to influence.[8]

Generally speaking, the process of organizational change has traditionally been viewed as an episodic activity -- there was a beginning, middle and an end. Further, some view organizational change as balancing a system of interacting variables -- people, tasks, technology, structure and strategy. Each of these views change as a disturbance to the status quo requires proper management to establish equilibrium through a series of defined steps.[9] This episodic approach to change (developed in the 1950s and 1960s) was the dominant paradigm during the Cold War where conditions were more predictable and stable. However, this condition fails to reflect the current environment thereby rendering the episodic approach inadequate.

Change in today's environment is quite another matter. Change is now viewed as an ongoing activity. Change is considered a natural state where stability and predictability do not exist. Disruptions to the status quo are not episodic or predictable but rather constant often bordering on chaos. The environment is dynamic where rules are made up as the game progresses; in effect, the conditions have changed thereby necessitating a change in process. In recognition of this condition, the CF employs a continuous improvement process -- ongoing evaluation and change of processes, products, programs and services to make them work better -- to meet the challenges and demands of today and tomorrow.[10]

CHANGE RESISTANCE AND FAILURE

Research has suggested that although most mangers understand the necessity to change it is often the case that those same mangers fail to understand how to bring it about. As noted earlier, there exists a plethora of change management literature in general and most commence with reasons why change initiatives fail. John Kotter, perhaps one of the most respected writers on change, offers a list of why change initiatives fail: allowance of too much complacency, failing to create a sufficiently powerful guiding coalition, underestimating the power of vision, under-communicating the power of vision, permitting obstacles to block the vision, failing to create short-term wins, declaring victory too soon, and neglecting to anchor changes firmly in the organizational culture.[11]

Others claim that change initiatives may fail due to "the fallacy of programmatic change"[12] where the greatest obstacle to revitalization is the idea that change comes about through companywide change programs. Whatever the rational for change failure most authors offer a prescriptive list of steps to undertake change which resemble each other in many ways as can be seen in Table 9.2:

Table 9.2: Steps in Organizational Change

Kotter	Beer, Eisenstat, Spector
Increase Urgency	Mobilize Commitment
Build Guiding Team	Develop a Shared Vision
Get the Vision Right	Foster Consensus
Communicate for Buy-in	Spread Revitalization
Empower Action	Institutional Revitalization
Create Short-term Wins	Monitor and Adjust Strategies
Don't Let Up	
Make Change Stick	

Source: John Kotter, Leading Change (Boston: Harvard Business School Press, 1996) and Michael Beer, Russell A. Eisenstat, and Bert Spector, "Why Change Programs Don't Produce Change," Harvard Business Review, November –December 1990: 158-166

It is worth mentioning that while both of these lists seem similar and intuitive, the execution of these steps has been problematic. Many, but not all, of the problems associated with change in DND and the CF stem from the unfettered application of these private sector change methods to the public sector. This issue will be addressed separately later in this paper.

It is well documented that organizations are resistant to change either individually or collectively. However, this resistance offers both promise (promotion of stability and predictability) and peril (hindrance of adaptation and progress). Resistance can manifest itself in two principle ways: overt and immediate – easier to deal with; or implicit and deferred – harder to deal with. Change resistance comes in two forms – individual with the following concerns: security, economic factors, fear of unknown, selective information processing and cynicism; and organizational with the following concerns: structural inertia, limited focus of change, group inertia, threat to expertise, threat to established power relationships and threats to established resource allocations. Overcoming resistance to change is a key aspect of any change initiative.

Change Fatigue. There has been much discussion within DND and the CF on the issue of change fatigue. Change fatigue -- personnel get tired of new initiatives and the way they are implemented -- is generally regarded as a principle factor underpinning many failed change projects or at the very least, it has been responsible for disappointing results. Several business management gurus have taken up the call in an attempt to resolve this problem and some tangible results have been achieved. However, in acknowledging globalization as a key driver for contemporary and future society and the pace of technological change today, organizations will be subject to faster change as the trends listed above come to fruition. As British Prime Minister Benjamin Disraeli rightly commented, particularly in today's global environment, change is inevitable, change is constant. Within DND and the CF, failure is not an option for to fail would have a serious impact on Canada as a state and actor within the international community. As such, dealing effectively with change must become imbedded within our culture; the emerging global environment demands it. As noted by Robbins and Langton "[i]f an organization is to survive, it must respond to changes in its environment."[13]

Change resistance and fatigue are generally predictable as organizations attempt to balance the demands of today with the accelerating and more complex demands of to-morrow. The first step in overcoming these hurdles is for management to be cognizant of the issue. As change management is ultimately about people and changing ingrained and valued behaviours, acknowledging that change will take time is important. Tactics that have been offered to overcome resistance and fatigue include: communication and education, participation, facilitation and support, negotiation, manipulation and coop-eration and even direct coercion of resisters.[14] However, and perhaps most significant, change management leadership characterized by senior leader involvement, senior leader advocacy through informal channels, and senior leader employment of formal mechanisms must be firmly in place to enact successful change thereby overcoming resistance and fatigue issues.[15]

Issues in Change Management in DND

Before looking specifically at past change management initiatives, it is worthwhile to review two theoretical aspects that require careful consideration prior to undergoing any change initiative – differences between the private and public sector and differing views of efficiencies and effectiveness between the two sectors. The failure to recog-nize these fundamental differences can often lead to less than favourable results with a change initiative that, from a statistical standpoint, already has a high prospect of failure.[16]

Private Sector versus Public Sector. The most obvious and fundamental differ-ence between private and public sector "business" is that of the profit motive. Private sector managers answer to the "bottom line" whereas public sector managers answer to everyone and no one. The private sector obtains their money from customers whereas the public sector obains its money from taxpayers. Customers can opt out of a commer-cial contract; citizens cannot opt out of the social contract with the state. The private sector is driven by competition whereas the public sector is run by monopolies. Risk is viewed very differently in that in the private sector, making mistakes is acceptable, to a point, as long as you operate at a profit. In the public sector, you can have 99 suc-cesses and nobody notices, [but] make one mistake and your're dead.[17] The private sector moves very fast and with secrecy while the public sector must remain open and democratic and thus moves much slower which creates inefficiencies. In other words, "government" [public sector] and "management" [private sector] are not interchange-able concepts.[18] Additionally, few would want the public sector to be run as the private sector; however, many would like to reduce the level of bureaucracy in the public sec-tor.

Although one could easily argue that the private sector and public sector are after the same results -- worthy goals, well-designed rational processes, strict accountability and effective leadership -- there are profound differences in their purposes, their cultures and the contexts within which they conjure up quite different obstacles. As such, successful change in the public sector is not so much about identifying solutions but rather, working around unique obstacles, which are in part identified above. Therefore, successful change in the public sector must consider the following obstacles listed in Table 9.3 below.

Table 9.3: Change in the Private and Public Sectors

Public Sector	Private Sector
Leaders tend not to be chosen for their ability to institute reform but rather they are chosen for their command of policy, technical expertise and political connections.	Leaders can be chosen based on their ability to lead reform or respond to large scale change efforts.
Generally speaking, tenure in one particular leadership position tends to be shorter rather than longer and as such reforms tend to focus on those that can be achieved quickly.	Change requires a sufficient period of time. Achieving short term wins quickly is important but building on momentum and not declaring victory too soon is imperative.
Rules governing the public sector tend to be less flexible and inhibit initiative. The penalties for failure are almost always greater than the rewards for exceptional performance.	Private sector can and does move fast allowing for greater flexibility and initiative. More so than the public sector, mistakes are tolerated as long as you operate at a profit.
Almost all public sector work must be transparent.	Private sector works in secrecy.

Source: Table adapted from Frank Ostroff, "Change Management in Government", Harvard Business Review, May 2006, 141-147; John P. Kotter, "Leading Change: Why Transformation Efforts Fail", Harvard Business Review, March-April 1995, 59-67; and John Micklethwait and Adrian Wooldridge, *The Witch Doctors, The Witch Doctors: Making Sense of the Management Gurus*,(New York: Random House, Inc., 1997).

These facts of public life may never go away and often have far reaching impact on change initiatives within the public sector. However, there have also been those who have been able to overcome these hurdles and lay the groundwork for change so clearly and systematically that progress continues even when the leadership changes.

Private Sector Management Theory in the Public Service. In the 1990's, it was difficult to walk the halls without hearing catch phrases such as "outsourcing non-core functions", "management by objectives", or "aligning core processes." Although the management theory industry was thriving in the private sector, there was little development in the public sector. Peter Drucker has been arguing for half a century that the place where management theory is most needed is in the public sector.[19] The public sector's thirst for private sector management theory can be explained by three factors:

• **A crisis in faith**. The end of the Cold War and the emergence of globalization resulted in the need for greater transparency and accountability within the public sector and particularly in DND. No longer could DND make the claim that security was paramount and thus, redundancy and low account-ability, for the good of wartime effectiveness, were questioned.[20] Additionally, globalization began to challenge the effectiveness of government institutions as they began to be perceived as fat, bloated, inefficient, uncreative, and too powerful.[21]

- **An obsession to "do more with less"**. With the threat of global conflict diminished, most liberal Western democracies decreased defence spending in the 1990s and Canada was no exception having decreased defence spend-ing by 25% in real terms. Doing more with less meant managing the affairs of the state more efficiently, exacting a greater return on the public dollar. Many governments were quick to note that this was a fundamental practice in the private sector and as such, a new enthusiasm grew for private sector management theory within the public sector. The political leadership virtu-ally everywhere in the Western world, even in countries with left-of-centre parties in power, concluded that management practices in the public sector "should either emulate the private sector or simply privatize the function."[22]

- **A desire to remain current**. The push to have public administrators emulate private sector managers and run government operations as though they were private concerns led to a desire to adopt the private sector management theo-ries apace with private sector businesses. As a result, deregulation, streamlin-ing, empowerment and customer focus were all catchwords as the new era of public management approached.[23] Programs such as Defence 2000[24] and New Public Management[25] in the 1990s were as much about moving with the times as they are about management in the public sector

The use of private sector management theory in the public sector is not the "silver bul-let" governments had hoped for but it is incontestable that some aspects of the public sector management are done better today than yesterday. It is recognized today that while the private sector is at the forefront of management theory, wholesale application is a recipe for failure. While private sector "fads" may take up to five years before they appear in the public sector, judicious application is required for successful implemen-tation in the public sector due to those reasons highlighted in the previous section. This is even more critical when dealing with change management theory, as the pros-pects for success are already low.

Efficiency to Effectiveness. There is a well-known adage that to understand where you are going, you must understand where you have been. This adage has never been more prevalent within a Canadian context than within DND and the CF. Our unique blend of politicians, public servants and military officers has led to a certain amount of administrative confusion and conflict that has been well documented throughout his-tory. The central business of DND is the provision of a potential capability versus the normal goods and services that are the usual end products of a private sector business. The development of this potential capability is different in peacetime than in wartime creating a dichotomy between efficiency and effectiveness.

The Canadian defence establishment, as all large organizations, is concerned about efficiency as well as effectiveness. However, due to the particular nature of DND and the CF, these definitions are often used interchangeably without due regard to their meaning and application to the defence establishment. In the broadest economic sense, an organization is *effective* when it successfully delivers its goods and/or services to its clientele. It is *efficient* when it can do so at the lowest cost. More specifically, Douglas Bland states, "[e]fficiency in economic terms has to do with determining a perfect balance, usually expressed in money costs, between input and output: just enough, no more, no less".[26] Bland further states that efficiency in terms of military theory has to do with winning battles with the least cost in blood and treasure which is quite another matter when compared to the economic definition of efficiency. The real issue at hand is that *effectiveness* in a military context implies inefficiency in an economic sense. Edward Luttwak makes this point where he argues:

> The great irony is that the defence establishment is under constant pressure to maximize efficiency, and that its leaders believe in that goal when they ought to be striving for military effectiveness-a condition usually associated with the deliberate acceptance of inefficiency.[27]

Although the premise extolled by Luttwak is simple to understand, the concept of military effectiveness is difficult to measure as it is usually expressed in terms of potential rather than a tangible good or service. Brigadier General E. Leslie made precisely this point in his article entitled *Too Much Management, Too Little Command.*

> On the cost efficiency question, the military faces human and technical problems not met in the commercial world, not the least of which is that war, the only truly valid test of military cost/effectiveness, is infinitely variable in most aspects and fortunately, but a rare occurrence.[28]

In addition, besides the differences noted above, DND and the CF also have unique characteristics that separate them from other federal ministries: size, cost, dual authority, cost of obsolescence, as explained in the McGill Reports.[29] This concept is not lost in the eyes of citizens and the government during times of conflict and/or emergencies; however, in times of relative peace Canada's focus turns towards economic imperatives. Unrest or conflicts from around the world are delivered to us through the media instantaneously and responses are demanded within a corresponding time frame. As a result, military effectiveness and the associated inefficiencies must be maintained if we wish to respond to unrest or conflicts in a timely and effective manner. Napoleon's maxim, "God favors big battalions," is still very relevant today, although the way in which we define "big" is very different. Four historical change efforts serve to illustrate this point.

Change Management in DND and the CF

HELLYER'S REORGANIZATION

Paul Hellyer (MND 1963-67) made the most significant changes to defence administration in recent history. Although he is best known for Bills C-90 (single CDS, es-

tablished separate Canadian Forces Headquarters (CFHQ) and integration of the CF)
and C-243 (reorganization of the CF), he is also known for the active role (leadership)
he took in the administration of DND. Essentially, Hellyer put defence administration
into the hands of three men, the MND, DM, and the CDS. He had good reason, for
DND was not in good order during the early 1960s. Inattention to detail by military
authorities compounded by Government dithering resulted in enough confusion to
provide justification for reformers' zeal.[30] This aspect, coupled with his negative personal experiences with the Air Force and the Army, internalized his drive to lead one
of the most significant change initiatives in the history of DND and the CF; namely,
integration and unification.

Hellyer's vision was for flexible forces capable of meeting the demands of modern
warfare much swifter than ever before in history.[31] He believed that unification would
move the CF away from its service-oriented planning to more unified, mission-ori-
ented planning. Hellyer remarked that history had proven that the tendency was in
the direction of integration, particularly in the fields where it was essential to conserve
scarce professional and technical resources.[32] Thus integration was seen as a necessary
step towards unification. Unification was to be based on operational imperatives and
administrative efficiency was seen as a supplemental goal, not the driving force.

Hellyer discovered that Cabinet did not support his unification policy based on
operational imperatives until it was too late. Being the aggressive and self-confident
(economist) minister that he was, he reoriented his arguments for unification from
operational imperatives to narrower economic and administrative imperatives.[33] As a
result Hellyer had to impose his unification policy onto the CF even though there was
support for some of his reforms in Ottawa; most notable was the general acceptance of
the single CDS. Hellyer became scorned for his imposition of unification and the concept soon collapsed despite the fact that the CF is a single service by law today. It has
been said that had he settled for integration versus unification, he would be regarded
in a different light today.

From a change management perspective, it was clearly evident that Helleyer had
the leadership -- characterized as "gritty determination" -- required to see this change
initiative through to fruition. He also built his case for a sense of urgency around the
natural evolution of the CF towards unified missions, versus service related missions,
rising defence costs and a likely decline in defence funding. There is general agreement
that he even had the vision correct -- flexible forces capable of meeting the demands of
modern warfare much swifter than ever before in history; an operational focus; however, he failed to achieve buy-in or win-over stakeholders from Cabinet. As such, unification was "pushed" through from an administrative focus, thereby loosing further
support from key stakeholders and senior CF leadership. Although the CF remains a
unified organization today, one might easily debate that this was a successful change
initiative. However, it can also be argued that the cost of this change initiative was far
too high -- destroyed Canadian traditions, harmed military morale and decapitated
operational arms of the services.[34] The point to be made is no one man can enact successful change within large organizations and the unique obstacles prevalent within
the public sector, for example, particularly defence, monopolistic in nature, requires
transparency, and must be carefully negotiated.[35]

MACDONALD'S MANAGEMENT REVIEW GROUP (MRG)

The MRG was born out of the administrative nature of the 1971 Defence White paper delivered by the MND Donald Macdonald thrusting the CF into "a long dark night of the spirit."[36] Despite the change initiates immediately preceding the MRG – principally integration and unification -- "...there were still problems in the Department of National Defence management".[37] Macdonald's main idea was that efficiency in management could overcome resource inadequacies and make the "sharp end sharper."[38] Besides Macdonald's reluctance to routinely manage his department or defence policy, he interpreted questions on policy from the senior military leadership -- they were never consulted during the development of the 1970 white paper on defence -- as obstinate rebellion.[39] Further, it is important to note that most of the MRG were businessmen with very little expertise in matters of defence. In fact, it was a firmly held belief by the members of the MRG that the correction of "management deficiencies" would "in turn correspondingly improve the departmental end product, ...the operational readiness and effectiveness of the Canadian Forces."[40] From this statement it can be deduced that the MRG believed that operational readiness and effectiveness of the CF was contingent upon the singular issue of management efficiency. This statement, of course, is not surprising when you consider that the members of the MRG -- external and non-stakeholders -- did not mention warfare once in their report.

One of the boldest recommendations of the MRG was the amalgamation of the Canadian Forces Headquarters (CFHQ) and the civilian Defence Headquarters. In essence, policy makers and executors were brought together as a "defence team" and the effects on organization, command and control and management were significant. This led to the much-debated "civilianization"[41] of NDHQ and was perceived as the major factor influencing accountability and responsibility within NDHQ at the time. Prior to 1972, it was clear the CDS had responsibility for the command and administration of the CF and the DM approached his own organization and administration utilizing public sector management principles. Risks or differences between these two separate entities were resolved by political means. Arguably, even today in some areas it remains difficult for most to determine exactly where DND ends and where the CF begins.

As a result of the MRG, the defence problem became a single managerial problem as managerial skills were promoted in order to achieve efficiencies, which were to result in greater operational effectiveness. Although it is a well-known fact that DND and CFHQ pre-1972 were as beleaguered by internal problems similar to those experienced today, it was clear that the CFHQ was responsible for the implementation of policy, not its formulation or departmental administration. The MRG report's failure to pass parliamentary scrutiny, particularly in the area of control of the CF being delegated to the DM but also due to its focus on peacetime activities, led to its demise and the report was "buried" until it became declassified in 1984.

As a change initiative, Macdonald refused to "lead" change but more importantly, he failed to build the correct guiding team by choosing businessmen with little or no experience in defence matters. This leadership failure was exacerbated by the tension created by Macdonald between senior military leadership and himself concerning issues of defence policy. The peacetime efficiency focus of the MRG was considered a significant failure as they only dealt with half of the problem. It was already well documented within the Glassco Report in 1962 that DND and the CF were unique even within the public sector and as such, this uniqueness does not lend itself easily to peacetime efficient norms. The axiom of "will it work in war" must be addressed at every turn in order to ensure the effectiveness of the armed forces. The drive and focus of any change initiative must therefore be on the whole problem; the creation of an organization that functions efficiently during peacetime and effectively during wartime.[42]

Further, there was clear failure to establish buy-in from key stakeholders as the immediate burial of the report until the mid-1980s aptly demonstrates. Further still, the recommendation that the DM be responsible for the routine direction and management of DND was bold and contentious, one which stakeholders were not ready to accept or acknowledge. Despite the opposition to the report, some ideas were advanced secretly and this was most evident with the creation of NDHQ as a single entity. This was probably the best example of how "not" to undertake organizational change for under this new arrangement, operational issues withered, civil servants advanced in power and influence, and command authority and responsibility in the CF atrophied.[43] The end result of the MRG was a decrease in operational effectiveness of the armed forces, ironically the one aspect of defence the MRG praised in 1972.[44]

DND and the CF have undergone continual restructuring and reorganization since 1968. Both Unification and the MRG -- arguably the two most important change initiatives since the end of the WWII -- were failures or marginally successful. However, the 1990s proved to be a greater challenge to DND and the CF as they attempted to come to terms with both external (end of Cold War, globalization) and internal (federal deficit, perceived mismanagement and waste) influences. The next portion of the paper will address the two most important change initiatives since the end of the Cold War – MCCRT and CF Transformation -- as DND and the CF, headed towards a crisis.

COLLENETTE'S MANAGEMENT COMMAND AND CONTROL RE-ENGINEERING TEAM (MCCRT)

The end of Cold War brought promise of a "new world order" marked by western democratic nations decreasing their defence spending in search of the elusive "peace dividend." It is within this context that in 1993, a Liberal government was elected on a platform to reduce federal spending while preserving key social programs.[45] At the same time, the defence budget was viewed as expansive mostly due to "administrative overlap and increased bureaucratization"[46] and thus became a target for cost-cutting measures. This was translated to DND and the CF by way of the 1994 and 1995 Budget Impact Statements as well as a new White Paper in 1994. DND implemented this direction, in part, by way of the MCCR initiative which commenced in January 1995 in order to reduce resources consumed by headquarters, infrastructure and wasteful business practices to ensure the preservation of combat capability. Re-engineering[47] was chosen as the method to enact this mandate and was heralded as the path to successful change within DND and the CF.

By the mid-1990s DND and the CF had a well-established historical precedence of attempting to increase the tooth-to-tail ratio through administrative reform. In the 1990s, the target for change was the command and control (C2) structure, in particular the restructure of National Defence Headquarters (NDHQ), which was considered to be consuming too large a portion of defence resources. Specifically, a new C2 structure was to be put in place based on sound military C2 principles and it was to respond to the need to increase the proportion of operational personnel – thus increasing the "tooth-to-tail" ratio. Additionally, by 1999 DND and the CF were to reduce by at least one-third the personnel and resources committed to headquarter's functions.[48] The structure designed to undertake this change initiative was the Management Command and Control Re-engineering Team (MCCRT) which was stood up in January 1995 with the following three mandates: to recommend by the end of 1995 a new headquarters' organization for DND and the CF; to co-ordinate re-engineering efforts across the department – through National Defence Headquarters (NDHQ), through Command and subordinate headquarters, to the base/unit level; and to identify resource management and support services that can be re-engineered to reduce costly overhead.[49]

Components of re-engineering in management theory include the elimination of wasteful and non-productive work, replacing the traditionally hierarchical authoritative structure permeating most organizations with a flatter structure in which employees are "empowered" to make decisions, and a high reliance on information technology. In essence, the "re-engineered" corporation runs more smoothly, has a higher level of productivity, and employs fewer people than its less competitive counterparts.[50] An organization re-engineers to create competitive advantage[51] and in the process, downsizing and alternate service delivery become byproducts of the re-engineering process as the organization strives to become more efficient. In the words of Hammer and Champy, "re-engineering means doing more with less."[52] In the face of the Federal budget released in 1995 that called for a 25% (approximately 3 billion dollars) reduction in "real" terms for DND, re-engineering was seen as the path to Nirvana.

MCCRT established four core processes for defence -- strategic direction, force generation, force employment and common support services. In accordance with re-engineering theory, these four core processes would conceivably form the basis of the new NDHQ organizational structure. There is little doubt that if developed, this would have led to a radical redesign of DND and the CF as espoused by re-engineering theory. However, this was inconceivable, as public sector management theory is much more pragmatic and risk averse which prevents such radical change. Further, there was institutional hesitation to radically redesign NDHQ based purely on organizational re-engineering[53] in noting "...to change the top level structure has to be based on something more than re-engineering theory, or concerns about optics or even internal politics, before we abandon a model that has done the job over the past three decades".[54] As a result, the four processes were mapped onto the old structure thereby ensuring the maintenance of status quo.

From both a change management and re-engineering methodology perspective, leadership is vitally important. Despite this imperative, the MCCRT underwent three "handoffs" in two years and interestingly, the Chief of Defence Staff (CDS) did not play a role. The issue at hand did not question the capability of the leaders responsible for the MCCRT, but rather the rate of "handoff" between the senior leaders. One might immediately question whether each of these leaders had the same vision of the change initiative. Although we know that leadership in the public sector can overcome this characteristic, we also know that there was little, if any, agreement on the vision of the MCCRT further complicating this issue.

> There was a strong view that we did not have an agreed strategic vision or focus for change. Change has been more incremental in nature. Some had an underlying concern that we didn't know what business we were in (warfighting, peacekeeping, humanitarian assistance), leading to further uncertainty. Most believed that we could not afford to keep doing everything.[55]

It is also known that not all departments adopted the re-engineering methodology (due to resistance to change, change fatigue, etc.) and there was uncertainty as to whether the core processes identified by MCCRT actually reflected the outputs of NDHQ.

Although there was evidence of short-term wins at the tactical and operational levels, and although the intentions of the Change Team responsible for the restructure were noble, it appears that they did not have the time to complete their work and the need to downsize, once again, became the overriding reality as noted by Lieutenant-General (Ret'd) Raymond Crabbe and Vice Admiral (Ret'd) Lynn Mason.

> Despite the best intentions to apply pure and objective re-organizational methodology, the need to cut headquarters and personnel became the overriding reality. A complete clean-sheet review, conducted in accordance with the scope of the Charter, would have taken too long and the resulting implementation would have been too disruptive.[56]

In addition to re-engineering, the reduction of resources consumed by strategic and operational headquarters throughout the CF, with a view to directing those resources to operational capability was a major goal of MCCRT. The 1994 White Paper assigned a reduction of at least 33% in headquarters personnel and resources.[57] It has been stated previously that this reduction target frequently obscured the re-engineering aspect of MCCRT and prevented any real progress. The Review clearly states that these reductions created the sense of urgency needed to motivate managers to seriously examine what was being done and how it should change. However, as seen above, the drive to downsize did not afford the Change Teams the necessary time to complete their work or if it was complete, it was simply ignored. This is borne out by the fact that virtually all those interviewed believed that the MCCRT initiative was focused primarily on reductions and not re-engineering.

DND and the CF downsized and re-engineered concurrently and throughout the life of the MCCRT and to this day there remains debate as to the real objective of the initiative, downsizing or re-engineering.[58] Further, even today, NDHQ does not have a corporate view of the impact or effectiveness of reorganization undertaken by MCCRT.[59] Although there were some successes with this change initiative -- adoption of more robust business planning norms and a conflict resolution capability --, it fell well short of its stated vision and was considered by some as a "grand ruse". The competing management approaches of downsizing and re-engineering being undertaken simultaneously created a tremendous burden on those responsible for the change initiative and those responsible for the day-to-day functioning of the CF. This ultimately led to disappointing results mostly attributable to a lack of adherence to the tactics of change outlined earlier in this chapter.

HILLIER'S TRANSFORMATION

The appointment of General Rick Hillier as the CDS and the promulgation of a new defence policy statement (DPS) in 2005 heralded a new change initiative for DND and the CF. The International Policy Statement (IPS) of which the DPS was a component, provided a CF vision aimed at "fundamentally reorienting and restructuring the functions and the command and control of the CF to better meet the emerging security demands at home and abroad."[60]

General Hillier clearly articulated his vision in the DPS and personally crafted many parts of the policy statement. This is clearly a departure from past policy papers -- perhaps the first – where a CDS had taken a lead role in the articulation of defence policy through a white paper. Indeed, in some instances, as with the 1972 Defence White Paper, then MND Macdonald did not even consult the defence staff. Immediately following the promulgation of the DPS, Hillier released a Canadian Forces wide statement announcing his change initiative – CF Transformation. To guide his transformation initiative Hillier articulated six principles:

- Canadian Forces Identity
- Command Centric Imperative
- Authorities, Responsibilities and Accountabilities
- Operational Focus
- Mission Command
- An Integrated Regular, Reserve and Civilian CF

In becoming more effective, relevant and responsive,[61] it is clear that Hillier's focus for CF Transformation is "excellence in operations" both domestic and international. This is further supported in his Concept of Operations (CONOP) for CF Strategic Command where he speaks solely to the "command of operations" and does not address functional or corporate responsibilities". The Deputy Minister appointed a Chief of Institutional Alignment to resolve the changes needed in corporate responsibilities. The Transformation Steering Group, headed by VCDS LGen Walter Natynczuk, addressed the corporate and functional responsibilities as well as the operational changes required to accomplish the CDS's vision.

Increasing the effectiveness of the CF was primarily achieved through an "operational-level" restructure. As noted by Stone and Gosselin,

> ...General Hillier's CF transformation of the CF command structure is be-
> ginning at the 'middle' of the command structure, at the operational level.
> It is not aimed at restructuring NDHQ, but is focused upon the most im-
> portant point of change for this transformation. "Operational effectiveness,
> and in particular operational command, is at the heart of the transformation
> agenda."[62]

The Hillier transformation saw the disintegration of the DCDS Group (Strategic Joint Staff and Joint Operations Group) and the creation of a more operationally focused command structure. This included the creation of new operationally focused command headquarters that are affectionately known as the "dot coms": Canada Command (Canada COM), Canadian Expeditionary Command (CEFCOM), Canadian Special Operations Forces Command (CANSOFCOM) and Canadian Operational Support Command (CANOSCOM). Equally significant is the fact that these new structures were established outside NDHQ. However, there remained a requirement to establish a Strategic Joint Staff (SJS) intended to be "modest in size and agile by nature" to provide the CDS with "timely and effective military analysis and decision support" and provide the CDS with the means to "effect strategic command."[63] While these new structures were not to generate increased growth in headquarters personnel the CDS SITREP 4 identifies 700 new positions generated by CF Transformation of which only about half have been rationalized.[64]

It is interesting to note that the creation of the operational-level headquarters or the "dot coms" is precisely counter to the restructuring under the MCCRT mentioned above where the direction from the 1994 Defence White Paper was "...one layer of headquarters will be eliminated"[65] and that layer was identified as the operational level.

> The objectives of MCCRT were to reorganize NDHQ along more of a process
> basis (as opposed to a functional basis), close the command HQs, stand up
> the Environmental Chief of Staffs (ECS) as part of NDHQ, and reduce the
> number of operational level HQs from 14 to 10.[66]

In terms of personnel, MCCRT was aimed at reducing headquarters personnel by 33 %; however, "[o]ne of the goals of senior management was to attempt to stretch the reductions of headquarters up to 50%."[67] With the elimination of the command headquarters (operational level) the DCDS Group and the Joint Staff then assumed greater responsibility for domestic and international operations in a centralized fashion within the confines of NDHQ. In essence then, in terms of operational-level headquarters and the creation of the "dot coms", an argument can be made that the CF has gone full circle within a decade despite the fact that the new command structure has a different mandate than the mandate of the service headquarters of a decade previous. From a change management perspective, it can also be argued that change for the wrong reasons (i.e. efficiency over effectiveness) will soon lose traction as the core business of a large organization reasserts itself, in this case, warfighting.

The change initiatives outlined above (Unification, MRG and MCCRT) highlight the use of management reform to make "the sharp end sharper" or increase operational effectiveness. This is not the case with CF Transformation. Hillier's focus is on operations with no mention of achieving greater managerial efficiencies designed to fund greater operational effectiveness. Additionally, the DPS does not mention controlling costs; improvement of management methods, or creating efficiencies, unlike the 1994 Defence White Paper which used an entire chapter to outline how the new defence policy would be "managed."[68] The commitment of increased defence spending by first the Liberal government followed by the Conservative government certainly assisted Hillier in realizing his CF vision set out in the DPS. The increase of defence spending linked to CF Transformation not only signaled a difference from the previous change initiatives listed above, but also, and perhaps more importantly, signaled the "top cover" or "stakeholder buy-in" Hillier had established for CF Transformation.

From a theoretical change management perspective General Hillier has most clearly demonstrated strong leadership in articulating his "vision to mission". Backed by extensive operational experiences, Hillier has been described as "…a very down to earth guy. He has got a certain way of speaking to the common soldier that people just love. And for sure, when he came here he really electrified the place and there is a lot of good feeling, a lot of people looking forward to hearing him speak."[69] From both external and internal appearances, there is little question that Hillier is "leading" CF Transformation, a key aspect of any change initiative.

Hillier also established a well-respected guiding team -- CF Transformation Team (CFTT) -- headed by the equally effective LGen Walter Natynczuk now the Vice Chief of Defence Staff. Despite Hillier's impressive drive and commitment to change, no one man can exact large organizational change alone and it is well documented that "…a sufficiently powerful guiding coalition can make apparent progress for a while… [b]ut sooner or later countervailing forces will undermine their initiative."[70] As such, a strong leader and guiding team are necessary to overcome change resistance and keep the change initiative moving forward.

Complacency is the enemy of change. Anecdotal evidence suggests that to effect sustainable change, a leader must move small and fast. Small in the sense of achieving short term "wins" and fast is generally accepted to mean 6-8 months in a large organization. Hillier and the CFTT effectively created a sense of urgency as best evidenced by the quick "stand –up" of CANCOM, the first of the new operational level headquarters, a mere four months after official declaration of CF Transformation in Apr 2005.[71] Hiller's aggressive campaign briefings where the analogy of 'fighting snakes' was juxtaposed to the 'fighting the bear' during the Cold War made sense to soldiers, sailors and airmen -- both Regular Force and Reserves -- and created a "buzz" within the CF. Further stakeholder buy-in was achieved through an aggressive communication strategy and the establishment of the Deputy Minister as the Champion of Defence Institutional Alignment. Further, Hillier did not wait for the development of a master plan to move forward with transformation in stating that "…I'm actually pretty comfortable if we can lay it out 75 to 85% in detail, we can sort out the rest of it on the move."[72] As a result, in researching the documentation on CF Transformation, one is faced with a number of reports, briefing slides and minutes which contain the genesis and evolution of CF Transformation. There is indeed a risk associated with this methodology, one Hillier fully accepts. However, at the same time, would Hillier have been able to move as expeditiously as he has by creating a comprehensive action plan? This aggressive approach -- creating a sense of urgency and implementing at 75% versus 100% — is well articulated within many texts on how to enact change in the form of increasing urgency and not letting up.

While it may be too early to accurately determine the successor failure of CF Transformation, cracks are starting to appear in the armour. Colonel Mike Cessford, a key player throughout the CF Transformation process, suggests that that there are now more headquarters than needed to exercise command over a force that can only deploy 26,000[73] and the focus on staffing of the new operational-level headquarters has been too disruptive to the CF. It has also been suggested the rationale for the Strategic Joint Staff was indeed correct but the SJS has been subsumed by the day-to-day bureaucratic focus of NDHQ limiting their impact. The principle of mission command -- the leadership philosophy in the CF – remains an elusive goal that is often perceived as being at odds with the principle of command centricity. There is concern over the fact that the intended role of the Environmental Chiefs under CF Transformation has not been actioned thereby further obfuscating the principle of command centricity noted above. In the long term, maintaining the momentum of CF Transformation is also a concern as it is well documented that change initiatives that do not become anchored in the social norms and shared values of the organization often fail. As a result, the book is not closed on CF Transformation and much work needs to be done. Nevertheless, these cracks should not come as a surprise to those who undertake change management in large organizations. Second and third order effects of change, although difficult to accurately define in the early stages, will most certainly arise and the true strength of the change management team, their vision, commitment and leadership will be measured by how well they respond and make change stick.

Conclusion

The global environment continues to change at an increasingly faster rate driven primarily by globalization and technological advances. While these forces of change may affect the private sector first and to a larger degree, the public sector does not remain untouched. This is perhaps why the public sector often looks to the private sector for guidance in matters of management, including change management. Unfortunately in the case of DND and the CF, results of applying private sector management techniques have been less than impressive over several decades.

Unification, MRG and MCCRT attempted to apply private sector techniques and principles with hopes of achieving greater operational effectiveness though administrative efficiency. While administrative efficiency is always commendable in any organization, each change initiative was accompanied with a decrease in defence spending. Further, each change initiative met with some degree of success; however, on the whole, it is safe to say that either the cost was too high or the results were considered a disappointment falling well short of the anticipated outcome.

However, CF Transformation is different. While it may too early to declare victory or defeat significant differences from other change initiatives exist which may portend a more favorable outcome. CF Transformation was coupled with an increase in defence spending signaling plenty of political support allowing for a focus on operational effectiveness and not the administrative efficiencies required to attain it. Perhaps more significantly, there is clear and unfaltering leadership form the CDS General Hillier who has had a key role in many aspects of transformation as well as garnering support from DND. However, there are aspects that may impact on the final outcome; such as, the anchoring of the changes within DND and the CF, the creation of the "dot coms" and the growth in headquarters staff. While both promise and peril have characterized previous change initiatives in DND and CF, CF Transformation -- from vision to mission -- offers a different change management approach when compared to Unification, MRG or MCCRT perhaps signalling the best prospect for long overdue success.

Endnotes

1. www.ffiec.gov/ffiecinfobase/booklets/operations/22.html.

2. By, Rune Todnem, "What is Change Management?", *Journal of Change Management* 5, no. 4 (December 2005), 370.

3. Hughes, Mark, "The Tools and Techniques of Change Management", Journal of Change Management 7, no. 1 (March 2007), 39.

4. National Defence, "What is Change?", viewed 11 Jan 2006, < http://otg-vcd-webs017.ottawa-hull.mil.ca/moreChange_e.asp>.

5. National Defence, "What is Change?", viewed 11 Jan 2006, < http://otg-vcd-webs017.ottawa-hull.mil.ca/>.

6. For a description of two popular change models see Kotter, John and Cohen, Dan S., *The Heart of Change* (Boston: Harvard Business School, 2002) and Lewin, Kurt, *Field Theory in Social Science* (New York: Harper & Row, 1951).

7. Beamish and Woodcock, *Strategic Management: Text, Readings and Cases*, 123-124.

8. Sullivan, Gordon R. and Harper, Michael V., *Hope is not a Method* (New York: Broadway Books, 1996), 155.

9. Robbins, Stephen P. and Langton, Nancy, *Organizational Behaviour: Concepts, Controversies, Applications*, Canadian Edition (Scarborough: Prentice Hall Canada, Inc., 1999), 652.

10. Continuous improvement, viewed 11 Jan 2006, <http://www3.gov.ab.ca/env/air/Info/definitions.html>.

11. Kotter, John, *Leading Change* (Boston: Harvard Business School Press, 1996).

12. Beer, Michael, Eisenstat, Russell A., and Spector, Bert, "Why Change Programs Don't Produce Change," *Harvard Business Review* (November –December 1990), 158-166.

13. Robbins and Langton, 651.

14. *Ibid.*, 666-667.

15. Cowley, Bill, ""Why Change Succeeds:" An Organizational Self-Assessment," *Organizational Development Journal* 25, no. 1 (Spring 2007), 28.

16. By, Rune Todnem, "Ready or Not…", *Journal of Change Management.* 7, no. 1 (March 2007), 3.

17. Osborne, David and Gaebler, Ted, *Reinventing Government: How the Entrepreneurial Spirit is Transforming the Public Sector* (Toronto: Penguin Books Canada, Ltd., 1993), .21.

18. Micklethwait, John and Wooldridge, Adrian, *The Witch Doctors, The Witch Doctors: Making Sense of the Management Gurus*, (New York: Random House, Inc., 1997), 306.

19. *Ibid.*, 291.

20. Bland, Douglas L., ed., *Issues in Defence Management* (Kingston: School of Policy Studies, Queen's University, 1998), 37.

21. Savoie, Donald J., *Globalization and Governance* (Ottawa: Minister of Supply and Services Canada, Canadian Center for Management Development, 1993), 1.

22. *Ibid.*, 12.

23. *Ibid.*, 13.

24. "The Department of National Defence and the Canadian Forces will, in particular, continue to improve resource management through initiatives such as Defence 2000 to ensure the best possible use of resources at all levels of the organization. This management policy emphasizes the delegation of decision-making authority, the empowerment of personnel, the elimination of 'red tape' and overlapping functions, and the promotion of innovation was an initiative aimed to increase efficiency within DND by adopting modern management concepts and business practices of the 1990s." Canada, Department of National Defence, *1994 Defence White Paper.* (Ottawa: Canada Communications Group, 1994), Public Works and Government Services Canada 1994 can be viewed at <http://www.forces.gc.ca/site/Minister/reports/94wpaper/seven_e.asp>. More information on Defence 2000 can be found at <http://www.vcds.forces.gc.ca/dgsc/d2000nws/intro_e.asp>.

25. Savoie, Donald J., "What is wrong with the new public management?" *Canadian Public Administration*, Volume 38 Number 1, (Spring 1995), pp 112-121. General overview of NPM - Sandford Borins, "New Public Management: North American Style" in McLaughlin, Osborne, and Ferlie, eds., *The New Public Management: Current Trends and Future Prospects* (London: Routledge, 2002).

26. Bland, Douglas, *The Administration of Defence Policy in Canada 1947 to 1985* (Kingston: Ronald P. Frye & Company, 1987), 202.

27. Luttwak, E.N., "The Price of Efficiency," *Military Logistics Forum* (July/August 1984), 203.

28. Leslie, Brigadier General E., "Too Much Management, Too Little Command," *Canadian Defence Quarterly* (Winter 1972): 32.

29. McGill Reports – The Royal Commission on Government Organization (RCGO) – known as the Glassco Commission – organized several project teams to complete work on DND specific issues. Air Vice Marshal F.S. McGill was requested to head Project 16 in order "to assess the administrative system of the unique characterization of the operation of DND and on the basis of this assessment to coordinate the conduct within the Department of all [Glassco related] functional investigation." The reports highlight difficulties in how to develop a system of defence both "efficient in peace and applicable without change to the conditions of war" and "the chronic conflict in civil-military relations between the minister with authority and the military with technical expertise." Douglas L. Bland, ed, Canada's National Defence Volume 2…, 21-26.

30. Bland, Douglas L., ed, *Canada's National Defence Volume 2…*, 36.

31. Hellyer, Paul, Minister of National Defence, "Address on The Canadian Forces Reorganization Act 7 December 1966" in *Canada's National Defence Volume 2: Defence Organization*, ed by Douglas L. Bland, (Kingston: School of Policy Studies, Queen's University, 1998), 135.

32. Bland, Douglas L., ed, *Canada's National Defence Volume 2…*, 94.

33. *Ibid.*, 96.

34. *Ibid.*, 95.

35. In September of 1960, J. Grant Glassco was appointed as the head of the Royal Commission on Government Organization (The Glassco Commission) to inquire into and report upon the organization and methods of operation of the departments and agencies of the Government of Canada and to recommend the changes therein which they consider would best promote efficiency, economy, and improved services in the dispatch of public business. The Department of National Defence was singled out for a number of reasons but most important to this study was its need to harmonize an administrative system that had to function in peacetime but be prepared for war. *Report 20: Department of National Defence* was the title of the report delivered by the Glassco Commission. For a detailed account of the conduct of business within defence see the Glassco Report: *The Royal Commission on Government Organization. Volume 4 Special Areas of Administration* (Ottawa: Queen's Printer, 1962-63).

36. Granatstein, J.L. and Bothwell, R., *Pirouette: Pierre Trudeau and Canadian Foreign Policy* (Toronto: University of Toronto Press, 1990), 235.

37. Critchley, W. Harriet, "Civilianization and The Canadian Military," in *Canada's Defence -Perspectives on Policy in the Twentieth Century*, ed by Hunt, B.D. and Haycock, R.G. (Toronto: Copp Clarke Pitman Ltd., 1993), 234.

38. Bland, Douglas, *The Administration of Defence Policy in Canada 1947 to 1985…*, 62.

39. Bland, *Canada's National Defence: Volume 2*, 160.

40. *Ibid.*, 66.

41. Civilianization can be used to describe three different phenomena: civilian control over a nation's military organization, the development of a nine-to-five mentality within a defence organization, or the marked increase in public servants employed within DND who are occupying military jobs or are making military decisions. Within NDHQ, it was believed that the third had been instituted within NDHQ and was a result of unification. Critchely, Harriet W., "Civilianization and The Canadian Military," in *Canada's Defence - Perspectives on Policy in the Twentieth Century*, ed Hunt, D.B. and Haycock, R.G. (Copp Clarke Pitman, Ltd., 1993), p 227.

42. The peacetime efficiency-wartime effectiveness debate was a central issue for defence reformers during the 1970's. Those who demanded peacetime efficiency often found that the forces had little depth and few policies suitable to see them through to warfare. On the other hand, those who demand wartime effectiveness often find themselves isolated from government.

43. Bland, *Canada's National Defence: Volume 2*, 164.

44. *Ibid.*

45. Detomasi, David, "Re-engineering the Canadian Department of National Defence: Management and Command in the 1990s," Defense Analysis 13, no. 3 (December 1996): 329.

46. *Ibid.*, 330.

47. Re-engineering can be defined in layman's terms as follows: when someone asks us for a quick definition of business re-engineering, we say that it means "starting over." It doesn't mean tinkering with what already exists or making incremental changes that leave basic structure intact. It isn't about making patchwork fixes – jury-rigging existing systems so that they work better. It does mean abandoning long-established procedures and looking afresh at the work required to create a company's product or service and deliver value to the customer. It means asking this question: "If I were re-creating this company today, given what I know and given current technology what would it look like?" Re-engineering a company means tossing aside old systems and starting over. It involves going back to the beginning and inventing a better way of doing work. See Hammer, Michael and Champy, James, *Reengineering the Corporation: A Manifesto for Business Revolution* (New York: Harper Business, 1993): 31.

48. Department of National Defence, *1994 Defence White Paper* (Ottawa: Canada Communications Group, 1994), 40-41.

49. Management, Command and Control Reengineering, *Fact Sheet*, November 1995, 1.

50. Detomasi, "Re-engineering the Canadian Department of National Defence . . .", 331.

51. Competitive Advantage – The success or failure of any firm depends on competitive advantage – delivering the product at a lower cost or offering unique benefits to the buyer that justify a premium price. Porter, Micheal E., *Competitive Advantage: Creating and Sustaining Superior Advantage* (New York: The Free Press, 1985).

52. Hammer, Michael and Champy, James, *Reengineering the Corporation:...*, 48.

53. Management Command and Control Re-engineering Team, *Background information for senior CF/DND mangers on re-engineering and change: questions and answers* (Ottawa: DND Canada, 1996), 14/32.

54. *Ibid.*

55. Department of National Defence, "NDHQ 99: Review of Restructuring and Re-engineering," Vol 1: Background and Review Framework, Annex A: Level 1 Feedback (Chief of Review Services: File 7050-10(CRS), 2001), 1/3.

56. Mason, Lynn Gordon and Crabbe, Raymond, *A Centralized Operational Level Headquarters* (unpublished Report for the Department of National Defence, December 2000), 10.

57. Department of National Defence, "NDHQ 99: Review of Restructuring and Re-engineering," Vol 3: Results in Brief, Annex B: HQ Resource Reduction (Chief of Review Services: File 7050-10(CRS), 2001), 1/3.

58. Department of National Defence, "NDHQ 99 : Review of Restructuring and Re-engineering," Vol 2:..., 4/20.

59. Department of National Defence, "NDHQ 99: Review of Restructuring and Re-engineering," Vol 3: Results in Brief, Annex A:..., 2/3.

60. Gosselin, Brigadier General David and Stone, Doctor Craig, "Canadian Forces Transformation", *Canadian Military Journal* 6 no. 4. (Winter 2005-2006): 5-15.

61. For a complete description see Government of Canada, "Defence," *International Policy Statement* (Ottawa: Department of National Defence, 2005): 10-11.

62. Stone and Gosselin: 11.

63. CDS Transformation SITREP 3 Dec 05.

64. Interview18 Jan 2007, Cessford, Colonel Michael - COS CFTT and Deputy Leader Cat 4 – Institutional Alignment.

65. Department of National Defence, *1994 Defence White Paper*, 41.

66. Rostek, Michael A., "Peacetime Efficiency to Wartime Effectiveness: Defence Management in the 1990s", Diss. Royal Military College, 2001, 104.

67. Garnett, Vice-Admiral (Ret'd), "The Evolution of the Canadian Approach to Joint and Combined Operations at the Strategic and Operational Level", *Canadian Military Journal*. 3, no. 4 (Winter 2002): 3-8.

68. Department of National Defence, *1994 Defence White Paper*, 40.

69. CTV News http://www.ctv.ca/servlet/ArticleNews/story/CTVNews/20061224/ hillier_kandahar_061224/.

70. Kotter, John, *Leading Change*, (Boston, Harvard Business Press, 1996): 6.

71. It should be noted that the Chief of Defence Staff Action Teams (CATs: Command and Control, Force Generation, Operational Capabilities and Institutional Alignment) were studying transformation initiatives since their creation in Feb 2005.

72. General Hillier's remarks to the press on 15 July 2005. DND, Assistant Deputy Minister of Public Affairs, media transcript 05071501.

73. Bland, Douglas and Manson, Paul, "Transforming DND administration next challenge for Graham", *The Hill Times*, September 26, 2005.

Appendix 1

The following chart summarizes the structure of the Defence PAA:

Department of National Defence - Program Activity Architecture (PAA)

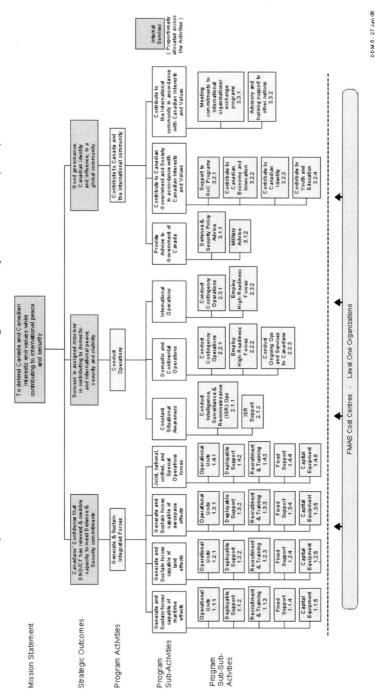

DDM 5 - 27 Jan 06

Appendix 2

ACTUAL DEFENCE EXPENDITURES 1951 TO 2006

Fiscal Year	Personnel	Operations and Maintenance	Capital	Statutory Grants and Contributions	Total
1951-52	299,184	421,781	557,555	136,954	1,415,474
1952-53	378,863	497,140	982,600	23,815	1,882,418
1953-54	468,117	514,713	1,031,604	23,804	2,038,239
1954-55	523,125	458,780	686,185	272,083	1,940,173
1955-56	554,252	435,729	722,073	187,511	1,899,565
1956-57	621,354	464,479	684,081	148,492	1,918,407
1957-58	685,890	457,751	523,391	133,705	1,800,738
1958-59	699,052	430,743	502,482	88,037	1,720,313
1959-60	706,186	415,072	373,893	34,645	1,529,796
1960-61	724,661	405,828	363,411	27,991	1,521,891
1961-62	795,597	408,515	401,530	27,687	1,633,330
1962-63	808,269	415,403	321,289	44,188	1,589,150
1963-64	918,208	447,809	294,601	48,718	1,709,336
1964-65	833,820	428,626	256,829	53,736	1,573,012
1965-66	859,284	429,738	232,145	60,089	1,581,256
1966-67	959,268	442,846	257,261	42,874	1,702,249
1967-68	1,046,567	449,203	299,277	46,265	1,841,311
1968-69	1,106,403	443,053	289,775	35,767	1,874,999
1969-70	1,158,992	440,187	262,669	30,461	1,892,309
1970-71	1,226,510	451,382	211,590	39,895	1,929,377
1971-72	1,291,999	497,324	221,010	38,817	2,049,150
1972-73	1,335,073	519,453	167,526	115,958	2,138,010
1973-74	1,524,524	581,353	229,489	46,334	2,381,700
1974-75	1,725,337	681,139	248,742	44,007	2,699,225
1975-76	1,937,045	828,894	329,620	75,350	3,170,909
1976-77	2,106,706	917,492	447,437	84,591	3,556,226
1977-78	2,259,185	1,081,198	528,348	107,424	3,976,155
1978-79	2,318,515	1,202,377	657,282	148,412	4,326,586
1979-80	2,363,115	1,223,767	810,103	203,380	4,600,365
1980-81	2,586,703	1,481,215	930,613	313,519	5,312,050
1981-82	3,037,557	1,812,615	1,139,401	341,101	6,330,674
1982-83	3,405,907	2,060,076	1,466,365	363,979	7,296,327
1983-84	3,710,528	2,296,729	1,894,320	382,288	8,283,865
1984-85	3,929,076	2,409,010	2,468,806	375,225	9,182,117
1985-86	4,148,323	2,652,423	2,212,348	444,752	9,457,846
1986-87	4,466,622	2,755,425	2,430,144	534,782	10,186,973
1987-88	4,671,195	2,982,575	2,759,520	563,555	10,976,845
1988-89	4,933,952	3,242,953	2,614,775	664,418	11,456,098

1989-90	5,243,311	3,538,432	2,508,570	630,898	11,921,211
1990-91	5,723,114	3,690,333	2,523,117	684,709	12,621,273
1991-92	5,764,956	3,495,579	2,544,143	258,435	12,063,113
1992-93	5,834,695	3,566,067	2,600,580	278,557	12,279,899
1993-94	5,737,680	3,584,839	2,570,640	433,172	12,326,331
1994-95	6,036,261	3,336,858	2,534,257	246,656	12,154,032
1995-96	5,440,689	3,525,006	2,528,393	247,472	11,741,560
1996-97	4,826,592	3,562,181	2,246,676	339,533	10,974,982
1997-98	4,783,059	3,513,029	1,808,403	449,343	10,553,834
1998-99	4,777,047	3,620,063	1,566,379	656,078	10,619,567
1999-00	5,264,484	3,409,659	2,705,524	526,072	11,905,739
2000-01	5,449,257	3,440,980	2,604,628	381,455	11,876,320
2001-02	5,709,535	3,936,279	2,561,427	459,347	12,666,588
2002-03	6,129,703	4,215,022	2,188,899	365,927	12,899,551
2003-04	6,483,501	4,590,918	2,097,512	447,139	13,619,070
2004-05	6,905,787	4,582,830	2,463,365	392,673	14,344,655
2005-06	7,202,857	5,014,723	2,536,420	404,728	15,158,728

Appendix 3

DEPARTMENT OF NATIONAL DEFENCE GOVERNANCE AND COMMITTEE STRUCTURE

DEFENCE MANAGEMENT COMMITTEE (DMC)

DMC and/or DEC will provide DM/CDS with decision support/advice with respect to issues of strategic importance relating to: advice to the MND; development of departmental Defence Policy; delivery of defence program/plan including strategic direction and strategic resource allocation; and the overall effective management of the department. Membership includes all L1s.

Primary Focus Areas

DMC will focus discussion on the wider strategic-level issues of the Department with the following primary focus areas:

Defence Policy. DMC/DEC will assist the DM/CDS in providing advice to the Government of Canada regarding defence policy;

Strategic Direction. DMC/DEC will assist the DM/CDS in the development and execution of the strategic direction to the Department;

Departmental Institutional Issues. DMC/DEC will assist the DM/CDS in the management of pan-departmental, institutional issues; and

Performance Management Oversight. DMC/DEC will assist the DM in establishing performance goals that would be used to monitor and assess the department's ability to deliver the Defence Program and prove oversight of the Departmental performance management program. DMC/DEC shall ensure performance reflects directed strategic outcomes.

DEFENCE EXECUTIVE COMMITTEE (DEC)

DEC provides DM and CDS with decision support and advice on emerging issues of strategic importance. Membership is a sub-set of DMC.

AUDIT AND EVALUATION COMMITTEE (AEC)

AEC reinforces the independence, effectiveness and accountability of the department's internal audit (Chief of Review Services) and evaluation functions. Members are selected L1s.

ADMs' Council

ADMs' Council provides the DM with decision support and advice with respect to departmental and pan governmental issues of strategic importance. Members are the department's ADMs.

Civilian Human Resources Committee

CHRC provides the DM with a policy-making and decision-making body for civilian human resources issues. Members are L1s.

Commanders' Council (CC)

Commanders' Council consists of all direct reports to the CDS, who examine CF issues concerning the force generation-force employment interface and issues of strategic operational importance. Members are Operational Level Commanders and the Environmental Chiefs of Staff.

Armed Forces Council (AFC)

Armed Forces Council is the CDS' venue to discuss CF strategic institutional issues. Members are the Environmental Chiefs of Staff and the Director of Staff, Strategic Joint Staff.

Proposed Mandate of AFC and CC

To provide CDS with decision support/advice with respect to subjects concerning the force generator/force employer interface and issues of strategic importance related to the overall administration and management of the Canadian Forces.

Primary Focus Areas

Although depicted together to highlight the interrelationship that exists, Armed Forces Council (AFC) and the Commanders' Council (CC) have two distinct "raisons d'être". AFC does not include membership of the operational commanders and exists to deal with CF institutional issues including personnel policy. CC on the other hand is intended to provide the forum in which the CDS can meet with all of his direct reports to discuss issues that affect both the primary Force Generators (FG) and the primary Force Employers (FE). It is envisaged that AFC and CC meetings will alternate to capture the full range of issues facing the CF at the strategic level. Individual AFC or CC meetings will address the following themes:

Commanders' Council

Quarterly Strategic Outlook: Issues relating to the military component of Defence Engagement Strategy including Theatre Engagement Plans (Op Level Comds) and supporting plans by DG IS Pol, ECSs, CMP.

Force Generation/Force Employment Interface. Alignment and synchronization of Force Employers' requirements with the Force Generators capacity to deliver. Issues relating to operational capability shortfalls, action on lessons learned, establishment of readiness levels and development of the CF Integrated Training Plan.

ARMED FORCES COUNCIL

CF Personnel Policy: A forum for the discussion of military personnel policy issues that will assist the CDS with guiding the development of the CF personnel and approving CF-specific personnel policy.

CF Policy Implementation: Provide decision support/advice to CDS on non-operational policy implementation issues peculiar to the CF.

DEFENCE PLANNING BOARD (DPB)

Defence Planning Board (DPB) provides the VCDS with decision support and advice regarding oversight and development of the Defence Plan. Members are L1s.

Mandate

To provide VCDS with decision support/advice with respect to the development of a coherent and implementable defence plan and the implementation of the Defence Program.

Primary Focus Areas

The Defence Planning Board (DPB) is the key forum to assist the VCDS in the provision of oversight to defence capability management and the Defence Program as follows:

Provide decision support and advice required to translate strategic guidance and direction into a viable defence program;

Assist the VCDS in the establishment of achievable capability development/sustainment goals that will be tasked to Force Generators and Functional Authorities to deliver the desired strategic outcomes through the business planning process;

Assist the VCDS in the assignment of resource allocations for the Defence Program; and

Assist the VCDS in the provision of oversight of the capability development planning process.

DEFENCE MANAGEMENT OVERSIGHT COMMITTEE (DMOC)

Defence Management Oversight Committee (DMOC) assists the VCDS with resolving emerging cross-functional issues and challenges of a transactional nature. Members are deputy-level representatives from L1 organizations.

Mandate

To assist the VCDS with resolving emerging cross-functional issues and challenges.

Primary Focus Area

Defence Management Oversight Committee (DMOC) will provide a venue to assist the

VCDS with the resolution and coordination of emerging multi-faceted and/or complex issues that require horizontal examination. The Team is convened as required when VCDS considers horizontal collaboration is essential to resolve emerging issues.

Capability Development Board (CDB)

CDB supports CFD in formulating decisions, direction, guidance and recommendations pertaining to force development. Membership includes force development representatives from across NDHQ and the operational commands.

Mandate

To assist the CFD with the development of coherent Defence Capability Plan recommendations.

Primary Focus Areas

Capability Development Board (CDB) will assist CFD with the integration of defence capability development from identification of the initial requirement through to capability divestment, with the following key focus areas:

> Defence Capability Planning;
>
> Capability Development Oversight; and
>
> Guidance to Capability Management Teams.

Programme Management Board (PMB)

PMB provides C Prog with decision support and advice with respect to implementing the Defence Programme. Members are deputy-level representatives from L1 organizations

Mandate

To assist the C Prog with the implementation of the approved Defence Program.

Primary Focus Areas

The primary focus of PMB rests with assisting C Prog in the implementation and management of the approved Defence Program as follows:

Management of approved resource allocations (Horizon 1);

Management of unprogrammed resource requirements and mitigation of unforecasted pressures on the Defence Program; and

Implementation of a performance management system to meet strategic goals and objectives.

Appendix 4

INTEGRATED RISK MANAGEMENT IN THE DEPARTMENT OF NATIONAL DEFENCE

Good risk management achieves a balance between exploiting potential opportunities for gain while minimizing losses. It is an integral part of good management practice and an essential element of good corporate governance. Organizations that manage risk well are more likely to achieve their objectives and do so more effectively and efficiently.

Integrated Risk Management (IRM) has a well developed, proven methodology that is used from the strategic level through to individual projects. This policy is supported by IRM Guidelines, which outline the methodology and provides a suite of tools for the consistent application of risk management.

Operational Risk Profile

Areas where there is potential risk are categorized, or broken down into common domains (eg. HR, environment, operational, transformation etc) so that like or related risks can be grouped together, and so that a common frame of reference for these areas of risks can be used across the department.

Risk areas are identified through environmental scans and the direct input of the leadership. Individual risks are identified and assessed for each of these areas and a "risk profile" of the department is made. Once validated and approved by the CDS/DM, the risks identified in the Corporate Risk Profile must be managed and should be revised annually or when significant changes to the environment occur.

Establishing an Integrated Risk Management Function

Although risk management is practiced widely throughout Defence, better integration of risk management horizontally and vertically is required. The VCDS is responsible for providing management direction on risk management, and communicating it through the department through the issuance of policies and guidelines. Risk is identified, assessed and managed throughout the course of other business processes as shown in Figure A4-1 below.

Figure A4-1: Risk Management

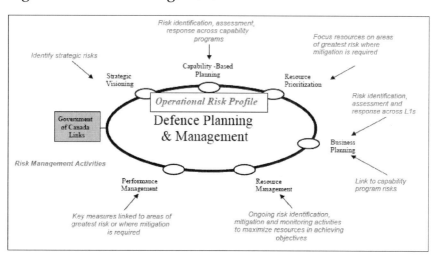

Risk Management Process

There are four key steps to the Risk Management process: identify; assess/prioritize; respond; and monitor and evaluate. Each of these steps will be discussed in more detail.

STEP 1 – RISK IDENTIFICATION

The first step in managing risk is to identify specific events (risks), which, if they materialize, may prevent, degrade, delay or enhance the achievement of the organization's objectives. The following steps are recommended:

a. Identify the primary mission/objective that may be at risk and the time frame being considered;

b. Decide on necessary people, expertise, tools and techniques (e.g., scenarios, brainstorming, checklists, criteria to be used) to complete the risk assessment;

c. Consider possible causes and scenarios to explain why/how risks might occur;

d. Define the problems or opportunities, scope, context (social, cultural, scientific evidence, etc.) and associated risk issues;

e. Perform a stakeholder analysis (determining risk tolerances, stakeholder position, attitudes); and

f. Identify the risk owner and the degree of control that exists over the risk.

Although there are some options to consider for use in the risk identification process, a risk identification workshop is a viable approach. It should include key members of the organization and appropriate stakeholders. The objective of the workshop is to increase the overall understanding of risk management by identifying and analyzing the specific risks that may affect the organization. Using the "brainstorming" technique, the participants should identify the risks that they believe may affect the organization. During the risk identification process, both short and long term risks should be determined.

The risk identification is complete when a comprehensive list of risk areas has been defined. In addition, the risk identification steps should be revisited on a periodic basis to ensure that the actual list of risks remains complete and valid.

STEP 2 - RISK ASSESSMENT AND PRIORITIZATION

The assessment of the key risk areas identified is the next step and the aim of this analysis is to identify the most serious risks. In some cases, each individual risk may not be significant but a logical combination of similar risks grouped together may change the overall risk ranking. As part of the analysis, the existing controls (processes or practices) that minimize negative risks or enhance positive risks need to be considered. In effect, the question: What are we doing now to mitigate this risk? should be answered.

Subsequently, each risk area is analyzed to determine the likelihood (probability) of the risk occurring and impact (or consequences) if it does. The following tables provide guidance on the thresholds that may be used to determine the likelihood and impact of the identified risk areas.

QUALITATIVE MEASURES OF LIKELIHOOD

Each risk is assigned a Likelihood rating, ranging from Rare to Almost Certain as shown in Table A4-1 below.

Table A4-1: Risk Likelihood Definitions

Likelihood	Definition
5 Almost Certain	Expected to occur in most circumstances
4 Likely	Will probably occur in most circumstances
3 Possible	Could occur at some time
2 Unlikely	Not expected to occur
1 Rare	Occurs in exceptional circumstances only

QUALITATIVE MEASURES OF IMPACT

Each risk is assigned an Impact rating, ranging from Insignificant to Severe. Table A4-2 provides guidance on some criteria that may assist organizations in assessing the impact of risks in various categories (e.g. mission success, environment and reputation).

Table A4-2: Risk Impact

Impact	Mission Success	Environment	Reputation
5 Severe Would stop achievement of functional goals/ objectives	Fail to achieve mission objectives	Very serious, long-term environmental impairment of ecosystem functions	Significant loss of client group trust. Public outcry for removal of Minister and key officials
4 Major Would threaten functional objectives	Some mission objectives at risk, overall marginal effective-ness	Serious, long-term environmental impairment of ecosystem functions	Serious public or media outcry (international coverage) Severe criticism by review agencies
3 Moderate Necessitates significant adjustment to overall function	Mission achieved with day-to-day crisis issues. Supporting tasks at risk	Serious medium term environmental effects	Adverse national media/public/NGO attention Criticism by OAG, TBS. Some loss of client group trust
2 Minor Would threaten an element of the function	Most objectives met	Moderate, short-term effects but not affecting ecosystem functions	Attention from media and/or local community. Criticism by NGOs
1 Insignificant Lower consequences/ impact	Mission achieved with minor shortfalls	Minor effects on biological or physical environment	Some unfavorable media attention. Setback in building of client trust

Source:

The combination of Likelihood and Impact for each risk would produce an overall Risk Level from Low to Very High, defined in Table A4-3 as follows:

Table A4-3: Risk Level

Risk Level	Definition
Very High	Upward reporting and detailed action plan required
High	Detailed action plan required
Significant	Needs senior management attention
Medium	Specify management responsibility
Low	Manage by routine procedures

Risk Map

When displaying impact, likelihood and risk level, a risk map like that shown in Table A4-4 is a useful tool. The prioritization or ranking of the risks is based on the analysis that was completed to determine the likelihood and impact of the identified risks. The risks are mapped into the following grid to determine the overall threat to the accomplishment of objectives.

Table A4-4: Risk Map

I M P A C T		Rare 1	Unlikely 2	Possible 3	Likely 4	Almost Certain 5
	Severe 5	Significant	High	High	Very High	Very High
	Major 4	Medium	Significant	High	High	Very High
	Moderate 3	Low	Medium	Significant	Significant	High
	Minor 2	Low	Low	Medium	Medium	Significant
	Insignificant 1	Low	Low	Low	Medium	Medium
				Likelihood		

This mapping of risks assists decision-making as it identifies those risks that need to be managed actively based on their threat to accomplishment of the mission. From this mapping, the leadership explicitly define their tolerance, that is, establish the risks that will be pro-actively managed. This analysis contributes to the making of decisions on whether the risks need to be treated and, if so, the most effective treatment strategy.

Step 3 - Risk Responses

Risk response planning involves developing a plan for each risk to either reduce the likelihood of occurrence or to minimize or eliminate an impact of a risk should that risk occur. As there may be several risks that could affect the organization, the leadership must decide on a threshold for risk response planning. This threshold may be determined in one of two ways. First, the leadership may determine a threat level above which a response for specific risks will be developed. Alternatively, they may assess the maximum number of risks that they believe that they can effectively plan for and manage on a day-to-day basis (i.e. 10 of the 25 identified). The threshold options and actual threshold to be used should be defined as soon as possible.

There are four generic risk response strategies as follows:

- **Avoid** – the planned activity, task or project is cancelled thereby eliminating the likelihood that the risk will occur;

- **Transfer** – the risk associated with an activity, task or project is transferred horizontally or escalated to an appropriate level within the organization. Transfer may also include to a third party (often through insurance).

- **Accept** – An acceptance or "do nothing" approach may be employed when the effort to mitigate or eliminate the risk is not justified. In this case the strategy is to either develop a contingency plan to execute when the event happens or to do nothing until the risk occurs and then react to deal with its impact; and

- **Mitigate** – Action taken prior to the risk event occurring to reduce the likelihood that the risk will occur or reduce the impact should the risk occur or both. Mitigation is similar to risk avoidance however the action taken has only had a limited affect – it has not eliminated the risk.

The selection of the best risk response will depend on a number of factors:

a.   Are the risks within tolerable limits?

b.   If not, can you do anything to better manage the risks?

c.   If the risks are within your control, what mitigation activities can you implement, at what cost?

d.   If the risks are not within your control, can they be escalated or simply accepted? Alternatively, should you develop a workaround strategy?

The risk response or contingency plan is created in advance of the risk event occurring – ideally in a low stress environment. The risk owner(s) should develop plans for all risks above the risk threshold. The "brainstorming" technique is an effective method to develop these plans. Once the plans are completed, the leadership should review them. The following activities may be considered in determining the risk response:

a.   Setting Desired Results - Defining objectives and expected outcomes for ranked risks, short/long term;

b.   Developing Options - Identifying and analyzing options, that is ways to minimize threats and maximize opportunities. Risk treatment options should consider the values and perceptions of the stakeholders and the most appropriate way of communicating with them;

c.   Selecting an Option – Selecting the best option must take into account the expected residual risk once the option has been implemented. One consideration is the assessment of the costs of implementing the options against the benefits gained by it; and

d. Planning and Implementing the chosen response - Developing and imple-
    menting a plan should include:

(1) Proposed actions and resulting resource requirements;

(2) Responsibilities, that is who is accountable for the plan and bringing
     risk within acceptable levels;

(3) Timing or milestones; and

(4) Reporting and monitoring requirements including performance
     measurement.

Step 4 - Monitoring and Evaluation

Risk monitoring and evaluation is a continuous loop of risk identification and analysis;
effective execution of risk response / contingency plans as necessary; and the evaluation of the effectiveness of these plans in reducing the likelihood of a risk occurrence
and its impact should it occur. Managing risk is not an exact science. Nevertheless,
lessons can and should be learned from the development and implementation of risk
responses. Some questions that need to be addressed are:

a. Were the responses effective?

b. Were the responses timely?

c. Were the risk and the response(s) chosen accurately assessed from a cost
    and performance perspective?

The steps and guidelines outlined above detail the fundamentals of how risk management is accomplished in the department. Here is an example of a risk assessment
using these tools, in this case a draft risk profile for the stand-up of the Strategic Joint
Staff.

Risk Analysis Example – Strategic Joint Staff (SJS) Stand-up

This risk analysis was completed by the initial cadre of the Strategic Joint Staff. The
analysis identified risks associated with the SJS capacity to attain operational readiness
by the mandated date and to continue operation beyond that date. The risks identified
were plotted in a standard five by five matrix as shown in Table A4-5 below.

Table A4-5: Risk Analysis Example

Impact	Rare 1	Unlikely 2	Possible 3	Likely 4	Almost Certain 5
Severe 5	Significant	High	High	Very High	Very High
Major 4	Medium	Significant	High	High	High
Moderate 3	Low	Medium 1, 2, 6	Significant 10	Significant 4, 5, 7, 8, 9	Significant
Minor 2	Low	Low 3, 12	Medium	Medium 11, 13	Medium
Insignificant 1	Low	Low	Low	Medium	Medium

Likelihood

SJS Risk Log

The following risk log summarizes notable risks associated with the stand-up of the SJS. The numbers in the Table A4-5 above correspond to the ID number in the Table A4-6 below.

Table A4-6: SJS Risk Log Example

I D #	Risk Area	Description/Statement	Risk owner	Existing measures	Mitigation
1	Primary Function 1	Translate CDS intent/policy into strategic direction. All cells of the SJS would carry out this task.	CDS	Strat/Ops Wargame	Assign higher manning priority
2	Primary Function 2	Issue guidance and orders on behalf of CDS. All cells of the SJS would carry out this task.	CDS	Strat/Ops Wargame	Assign higher manning priority
3	Primary Function 3	Maintain strategic SA for CDS. Primarily carried out by the Ops cell.	CDS	Coordination with NDCC/CDI	None
4	Primary Function 4	Undertake strategic planning for future commitments. Primarily carried out by the Plans cell.	CDS	Liaison with J3 Intl/Cntl	Assign higher manning priority.Effective training program executed prior to 01 Feb 06
5	Primary Function 5	Maintain liaison with Government, National and International Agencies, and Allies. This task is currently carried out by ADM (Pol). SJS will have to assume an increasing liaison role.	CDS	Coordination with ADM Pol	Once key pers are selected, wargame scenarios with ADM (Pol) and OGDs
6	Primary Function 6	Coordinate staff efforts with National/ Departmental Staff. All cells of the SJS would carry out this task.	CDS	Matrix approach will allow good interconnectivi ty	Establish and exercise strategic battle rhythm
7	Leadership – decision-making	The timeline to create and stand-up the SJS is limited by and dependant upon rapid decision-making. The	CDS	Nomination of GO/FO within the next few weeks	Increase size of planning team Focus effort on Ops cell and accept risk

I D #	Risk Area	Description/Statement	Risk owner	Existing measures	Mitigation
		separation of the strategic and operational functions will require development of new procedures (CONOPS, SOPs) some of which may not be in place by 01 Feb 06.			on Plans & Requirement cells
8	Personnel availability	A full complement of qualified, experienced personnel may not be available for posting into the HQ to allow appropriate orientation, training and certification.	CDS	Process controlled through CFTT	Assign higher priority to SJS. Focus efforts on Ops cell
9	Infrastructure	The SJS Operations and Plans Cells will operate from spaces currently occupied by COS J3. Lack of space in Star Top building may prevent COS J3 from moving into its new location by 1 Feb 06, which would in turn delay the physical establishment of SJS.	CFTT	Plans being developed by CFSU(O)	Requires contingency plan to address need for "swing space" Higher priority assigned to SJS floor space requirements
10	Communication	Related to the previous point. SJS requires an extensive suite of classified systems (TITAN, SIGNET) to communicate with its main point of contact. These systems are already in place in COS J3 area but can hardly be moved for security raisons.	CFTT	None	Requires contingency plan, likely to include exigency for shared space with current COS J3 staff